The Democratic Tradition
Four German Constitutions

D1825818

The Democratic Tradition
Four German Constitutions

Edited by
Elmar M. Hucko

BERG

Oxford / New York / Munich

Distributed exclusively in the US and Canada by
St. Martin's Press, New York

Published in 1987 by
Berg Publishers Limited
– Editorial Offices –
77 Morrell Avenue, Oxford OX4 1NQ
165 Taber Avenue, Providence R.I., 02906, USA
Westermühlstraße 26, 8000 Münchens, FRG

Originally published as *Von der Paulskirche zum Museum
Koenig. Vier deutsche Verfassungen*. English edition by
permission of the German publishers, Bundesanzeiger Verlagsges.mbH,
Cologne. © Bundesanzeiger verlagsges.mbH 1984
English translations of the Preface, the Introduction and the
1849 Constitution © Berg Publishers 1987

Reprinted 1989

British Library Cataloguing in Publication Data

[Von der Paulskirche zum Museum Koenig.
English] The democratic tradition:
four German constitutions.
1. Germany—Constitution
I. Hucko, Elmar M.
344.302′23   JN3215

ISBN 0-907582-60-5

Library of Congress Cataloging-in-Publication Data

Von der Paulskirche zum Museum Koenig. English.
The democratic tradition.

Translation of: Von der Paulskirche zum Museum Koenig.
Bibliography: p.
Includes index.
I. Germany—Constitutional history.   2. Germany
(West)—Constitutional history.   I. Hucko, Elmar M.,
1939–   .   II. Title.
KK4455.V6613   1987   342.43′023   86–32711
ISBN 0-907582-60-5   344.30223

Printed in Great Britain by SRP Ltd, Exeter

Contents

Illustrations

Preface

Constitutions are fascinating documents, not only for the lawyer but also for the historian and for anyone interested in politics. This may not be immediately plausible to those who tend to associate constitutions with a jumble of clauses whose convoluted legal jargon becomes comprehensible only if read very slowly and at least twice. However, constitutions can also be approached in a different and most rewarding way; they can be seen as the most basic document by which a particular society has agreed to operate. To be sure, what is on paper often diverges markedly from daily political practice and there are quite a few authoritarian systems around the world which cynically use democratically-worded constitutions as mere window-dressing. By and large, though, the parliamentary democracies of Western Europe and North America, in so far as they have written constitutions, present a different case. In these countries constitutional documents provide a gauge for the nature of politics and hence help us to gain an understanding of contemporary reality.

But there is also the historical perspective to be considered. Constitutions were, after all, created at a particular historical moment and hence raise many intriguing questions about the why and how of their creation. Nearly all constitutions have emerged from a revolutionary situation; they are new departures and hence reflect the values and political ideals which guided that fresh start. They provide a flashlight insight into the ideologies of the age and are thus of considerable interest to the student of political thought. But behind these ideas were the real individuals who advocated them in the constitutional assemblies and behind them, in turn, were ranged specific political and social groups for whom the deputies acted as spokesmen. Moreover, as any one group is unlikely to have total control of their society and its politics, compromises become necessary between different factions in the assembly and these compromises will also be reflected in the constitutional document. A careful reading and analysis will therefore yield important insights into the balance of socio-economic forces and the political power structure of the country which is in the process of giving itself a constitution. In this sense such documents are of the greatest interest to the political scientist and social historian.

1

It was these general considerations which guided the publication of this book. Germany experienced major upheavals in the nineteenth and twentieth centuries. The fact that between 1849 and 1949 no less than four constitutions were given to the Germans is a telling reflection of the country's tumultuous recent history. It hints at the revolutionary character of the German development, even if not all of the four constitutions reprinted below were products of a 'revolution from below'. The 1871 document might more accurately be seen as the result of a 'revolution from above', prepared and staged by the Prussian *Junker* and politician Otto von Bismarck, whereas the 1949 Basic Law has been termed by Alfons Steiniger as an outgrowth of a 'revolution from the outside', triggered by the Western Allies after the Second World War. So these problems may also be found in the documentary past.

However, the editor felt, rightly, that the reader should not simply be left to read the documents, as it were, 'cold'. Being a lawyer who is now a higher civil servant in the Ministry of Justice in Bonn, Dr Hucko was in an excellent position to explain the structure of the four constitutions and to bring out the logical links between the various sections. However, he also always saw himself as a social and political historian who tried to put the four constitutions into their respective historical contexts. I think he has succeeded particularly well in reconstructing these contexts. The drama of the situation of 1848–9, 1870–1, 1918–19 and 1948–9 is very tangible. The people he portrays and whose passionate speeches he cites really come alive with all their human strengths and weaknesses. And Dr Hucko shows how the seeds of doom and ultimate collapse were sown with three of these German constitutions. My suggestion, therefore, is not to skip his introduction. It is only through reading it that the significance of the four documents becomes not only intelligible, but their detailed study more enjoyable and rewarding.

Volker R. Berghahn
Warwick
October 1986

Introduction

The 1849 Constitution

In 1848 it looked as if the time had definitely come for a change of the order which the Congress of Vienna had established in 1815 and which could only be maintained for so long under the pressure of the Restoration. The Austrian Chancellor Metternich had been the symbol and the embodiment of this old order. His system of reactionary politics and traditionalism was no longer able to offer contemporaries anything beyond law and order. Over the years this system had become an anachronism.

However, what did the *Zeitgeist* consist of in whose omnipotence the burghers of Germany set so much store and hope? What were the causes of the 1848 Revolution? Or, to put it more precisely, of the revolutions; after all, there were many separate uprisings in Vienna, Berlin, Cologne, Breslau, Konigsberg, Dresden, Darmstadt, Mannheim, Heidelberg, Stuttgart. In short, the revolutions affected the Hanseatic cities in the north and spread all the way to the Swiss border to Lörrach where, as late as the autumn of 1848, an attempt was made to proclaim the creation of a German republic.

There were several and quite divergent causes which contributed to the general revolutionary mood and movement. Some were based on material considerations; others were motivated by ideas.

To begin with, there was that spirit of criticism, of opposition and rebelliousness which the eighteenth-century Enlightenment had awakened and which the French Revolution had unleashed so excessively that its German supporters had temporarily become frightened by their own courage. The 1848 Liberals were the epigones of the revolutionaries of 1789 to the extent that they were opposed to absolutism and to social hierarchies dependent on birth. They were in favour of monarchism, but it had to be legitimised and restricted by a Constitution drawn up in mutual agreement with the political forces of the age. These were the dominant demands of the time. In this respect the ideas of the French Revolution provided the models. Thus there was the demand for human and citizens' rights which was now raised all

3

Procession to Hambach Schloss near Neustadt a.H., 27 May 1832

over Germany. People wanted freedom for the individual and the guarantee of property rights, freedom of speech and of the press, of assembly and of association; they demanded equality before the law, equal taxation, equal voting rights and access to public office on the basis of merit. These demands were some of the motives to inspire the 1848 Revolution. However, in themselves they would probably not have sufficed to unleash such a powerful movement in so many different places throughout Germany. What provided the 1848 Liberals with their mass impact were two further factors: the movement for national unity which fired the imagination of many Germans and the general dissatisfaction with existing conditions in the face of an economic crisis which had been taking its toll since 1846.

Since the early nineteenth century, the people of Europe had begun to discover anew their national identity and to cherish it with warm enthusiasm. The victories of the French *Grande Nation* had demonstrated impressively to Europe to what heights such a nation was capable of rising. The Germans had also learned, from their defeats by Napoleon's armies, how little they were able to achieve if they were disunited and did not involve themselves in public affairs. Many had been disappointed that their subsequent

Barricades in Berlin, during the evening of 18 March 1848

victory over Napoleon had not been followed by the unification of the German states. But the patriotic sentiments which the united liberation from foreign domination had generated survived this set-back and stood opposed to the decisions of the Congress of Vienna, by which Germany was kept divided into thirty-nine states. The idea of the nation brought conservatives and progressive democrats together. While some people bemoaned the waning of the good old days of the Holy Roman Empire under the leadership of the Emperor, which had been dissolved in 1806, others has begun to dream about a democratic unitary state.

What contributed to the success of these high-flown ideals in bringing the crowds out into the streets was a dissatisfaction which had its roots in material conditions; this dissatisfaction was waiting to find an outlet in a protest movement. The economic crisis had started with bad harvests in 1846. Food had become scarce and expensive. The poorer strata of society — the workers and peasants — suffered from starvation and misery. A general economic crisis had come on the heels of the food shortages. Demand had slumped in textiles and the construction industry at a time when, on the eve of the Industrial Revolution in Germany, supply was expanding. The crisis manifested itself in bankruptcies, declining wages, unemployment, corruption and speculation. Output in manufacturing engineering in Berlin fell by 42 per cent. Borsig had to dismiss 400 of its 1200 workers. On 13 March 1848 Berlin workers, meeting in the Tiergarten park, ratified a petition which demanded that the King of Prussia do something to combat unemployment.

To be sure, '1848' was not a social revolution, but an uprising by the propertied and academic bourgeoisie. The *Communist Manifesto*, published by Karl Marx and Friedrich Engels and proclaiming the slogan 'Working men of all countries unite!', was ahead of its time by as much as the Metternich System was lagging behind it. However, the social crisis had caused many workers in the towns and cities to join the demonstrations, and it had united them with students and middle-class burghers on the barricades.

A whiff of Romanticism was also pervading the 1848 Revolution. This Revolution was a manifestation of a striving for an ideal. It opened up the political stage for emotional speeches full of pathos in which the lyrics of the Romantic period can be discerned. At Dresden such totally different characters as the anarchist Michael Bakunin and the composer Richard Wagner stood side by side on the barricades. The 1848 Revolution was a popular festival of Romanticism.

The historians have advanced very good reasons for explaining why the Revolution failed and, indeed, why it was condemned to failure from the start.

Certainly the early successes were unexpected and can only be explained by the fact that the monarchs and their governments were paralysed by the sight of the insurgents; nor were they brutal enough to call out the army to restore law and order without regard for human lives.

Nevertheless, its great initial successes notwithstanding, the Revolution was bound to fail. There was no single centre of action but a whole variety of them. They were uncoordinated and lacked the leadership of a charismatic personality. There was no consensus among the revolutionaries about their programme and their aims. Nor in their majority were they actual revolutionaries, but 'merely' reformers. Finally, despite the initial successes, the balance of power was unchanged. Ultimately, the new ideas were unable to defeat the old bayonets. The path towards the creation of a German national state was blocked by insurmountable internal and foreign policy obstacles and it required the tactical skills of a

Members of the Vorparlament entering the Frankfurt Paulskirche

Bismarck to overcome them.

There have been few revolutions in the history of the German people, and none of the peasant revolts was particularly successful either. But does this mean that they were senseless and superfluous? As with so many other uprisings in German history, the crucial point would seem to be that they occurred in the first place, not that they were successful as a bloody drama or driven to their extreme with incalculable consequences. This would appear to be as true of the 1848 Revolution as it applies to the July 1944 uprising against Hitler. As far as their historical significance is concerned, 'failed' revolutions can at times be just as successful as those which actually succeeded. The 1848 Revolution could not establish unity and legality and freedom but the call for these principles could be heard widely and loudly. When the Constitution of the German Reich was published in the *Reichs-Gesetz-Blatt* on 28 March 1849, it proclaimed to everybody and for all time what kind of constitutional system the German people wished to live under.

On 18 May 1848 the newly-elected deputies of the German

National Assembly filed into the Paulskirche at Frankfurt. The city where the emperors had once been crowned was flooded by a sea of black-red-golden flags. The population was jubilant. Where up to now the Diet of the German Confederation had embodied the restorative forces in society, elected representatives from all parts of Germany were now supposed to create a democratic Germany.

The country's best and brightest were among them: Ludwig Uhland, Ernst Moritz Arndt, *Turnvater* Jahn, Robert Blum, Jakob Grimm, to mention merely the most prominent names. It was a parliament of notables. Neither before nor thereafter was there ever a parliament of so many highly educated men: 319 lawyers and civil servants, 104 academics, thirty-eight merchants and industrialists, one farmer and not a single worker. The tone was set by the lawyers, professors and the *haute bourgeoisie*. Parties had not yet come into existence, but there were club-like parliamentary parties who took their name from their hotel. Thus the middle-of-the-road Liberals met at the Casino, and Württemberger Hof. The Left gathered at the Deutscher Hof and the Donnerberg and the liberal Conservatives met at the Steinernes Haus and the Café Milani. The political centre commanded a broad majority.

A great deal of idealism and optimism was assembled at Frankfurt. There was a belief in the good-naturedness of human beings, a belief which extended also to the monarchs who, after all, had already made so many concessions. After the bloody clashes of the March days, there was a desire for reconciliation, for combining the old and the new. Friendliness, tolerance and legality were to be the imperatives. Above all, the members of the Frankfurt Parliament wanted to talk freely and at length, which they had been prevented from doing for so long. Most of them thought it right and proper and saw it as a path towards the commonweal, if they presented their perfectly agreeable theories in well-measured prose. They had yet to learn about practical politics, if they were hoping to move something. Heinrich von Gagarn, a Hessian and an advocate of the golden mean, was elected president of the Assembly. Like many of his political friends, he feared anarchy more than he did the resurgent power of the princes.

It was in the spirit of the Frankfurt Parliament that the assembled began their constitutional deliberations with a debate on the basic rights of the German people. The securing of the hard-won civil liberties was to be the cornerstone of the new German Reich that was to be built. The National Assembly began this particular debate on 3 July 1848. The first reading of the basic rights section

Heinrich von Gagern, as president of the Constituent National Assembly

of the constitution lasted until 12 October. Not until 19 October did the full Parliament resume its discussion of the organisation of the Reich. By this time the fortunes of the Revolution had begun to turn and the forces of reaction had begun to recover.

Today the National Assembly is generally reproached for committing a great tactical error by leading off with a debate on basic rights and by spending so much time with it. This criticism is no doubt correct if general principles of political tactics are applied. If, on the other hand, one follows the overwhelming majority of historians in believing that, for a variety of reasons, this Revolution could not achieve its aims in any case, it may, with the benefit of hindsight, be thought logical and well that the deputies, with the keen support of the public, talked about the liberties of the Germans for over three months.

The fruits of this discussion were published in the *Reichs-Gesetz-Blatt* on 28 December 1848. This 'Law Relating to the Basic Rights of the German People' was the actual climax of the 1848 Revolution.

Following the debate of basic rights, the activities of the National Assembly became increasingly routine. Very little was left of the enthusiastic *élan* of the spring days. To organise the new

Germany proved most difficult even on paper. The progressive consolidation of the old feudal forces increasingly shunted the parliamentarians of the *Paulskirche* into the sidings. An attempt was made to create a provisional central authority and this led to the somewhat pathetic result that the aged Archduke Johann of Austria was elected Regent (*Reichsverweser*). He was popular because he had married a postmaster's daughter and thus appeared to be the embodiment of the reconciliation between the nobility and the bourgeoisie. As his 'central authority' was not endowed with any real power, he was soon ridiculed as 'Johann without Land'.

As early as September 1848 the National Assembly had to call on the help of Prussian and Austrian troops for protection against the irate masses who protested against its attitude towards the Schleswig-Holstein question. On 9 November 1848 the Austrian government unceremoniously sent Robert Blum, who had travelled to Vienna to offer his support to the revolutionaries there, before the firing squad.

The well-known argument over whether Austria should be included in a unified Germany was decided finally on 28 March 1849 when Frederick William IV, the King of Prussia, was elected hereditary Kaiser. But Frederick William never intended to accept the crown offered to him by the *Paulskirche* deputies. Clearly, subjects without power could not possibly bestow crowns!

The position of the National Assembly thenceforth became increasingly untenable. More and more deputies simply left. On 1 May 1849 Ludwig Uhland complained in a letter: 'The sinking ship, as they see it, is now being abandoned by quite a few rats'. By 30 May there were a mere 130 deputies in the *Paulskirche*. They decided to move to Stuttgart. But the rump parliament did not fare much better there either. On 18 June soldiers demolished the furniture of the *Fritzsche Reithaus*, the last meeting place of the remaining 138 deputies, and chased them away. The final end of the 1848 Revolution had come. What remained of it was the constitutional document of 28 March 1849, which was never implemented but nevertheless served as a model and yardstick of the quest for a democratic Germany for the next one hundred years.

According to this Constitution, a German Reich was to be established on the territory of what had been the German Confederation. The new state was to be a federated constitutional monarchy. The individual states were to retain their independence in so far as it was not limited by the Reich constitution. According to

Art. 5 the states were to have 'all the privileges and rights of states where these are not explicitly extended to the Reich authority'. This prioritisation and presumption of competence in favour of the individual states is an essential element of federalism which is characteristic of all four constitutions published in this volume. It has proven its worth as an element of decentralisation, of efficiency in the sense that it is closely linked to issues and the immediate concerns of the citizen. It has also promoted competition between the different regions and a division of power. Centralist national states like France have meanwhile recognised the disadvantages of their system and begun to regionalise state power.

According to the 1849 Constitution the position of emperor and head of state was to be bestowed on one of the ruling German princes and to be hereditary. This principle of personal union emulated the former position of the Habsburgs who had been emperors of the Reich and rulers of the Habsburg lands until Francis II had stepped down from his position as emperor on 6 August 1806. The founding of the later Bismarckian Reich was anticipated here in the sense that the National Assembly chose the Prussian King as emperor.

The new head of state was to have the title 'Kaiser of the Germans', indicating his legitimation by the people. The '*Roi des français*' of the July Monarchy and the '*Roi des Belges*' of the Belgian monarchy of 1830 served as models. If the Prussian king was to be called 'German Emperor' under the Bismarckian Constitution of 1871 this was in conscious dissociation from the 1849 title of 'Emperor of the Germans'. It is no less significant that King William I of Prussia did not like this title either and would have much preferred to be called 'Emperor of Germany'.

The emperor was to reside in the same city as the Reich government (Art. 71), which was to be Frankfurt rather than Berlin. Although the Hohenzollerns were to be the bearers of the Imperial crown, the Reich was not to fall under Prussian hegemony.

Given the revolutionary origins of the 1849 Constitution, the position and powers of the emperor are suprisingly generous. Thus the emperor has the right to nominate and to dismiss governmental ministers (Art. 73); he is the Reich's representative under international law (Art. 76); he disposes over the armed forces (Art. 83); he is expected to secure the peace of the Reich (Art. 82); he opens and dissolves the Reichstag and he also has the power to dissolve the *Volkshaus*, the second chamber of the Reichstag

(Art. 79); the emperor initiates laws and he is able, through his government, to veto all Reichstag resolutions and to suspend them for no less than three ordinary parliamentary sessions (Art. 101).

How was it possible that a freely elected parliament would agree to endow the monarch with all these powers? Indeed, if the proposals of the Casino faction and the right-wing had been followed, the emperor would even have been given an absolute right of veto against all Reichstag resolutions. It was by only 267 to 202 votes that this idea, which would have meant the still-birth of the parliamentary principle, was thrown out. At the other end of the political spectrum, the Left had spoken in favour of obliging the Reich government to implement Reichstag decisions. They also aspired to a participatory role for Parliament in matters of war and peace. But they had failed to assert their views. In looking for the roots of the majority attitude towards these essential questions of power, we encounter once again the Romantic mood of the Frankfurt Assembly, which inclined towards upholding illusory positions. The majority of deputies did not see the concentration of powers in the hands of the monarch as a vote against parliamentary rights. They took a very optimistic view of future executives. Thus deputy Professor Dr Christoph Dahlmann, a philologist, declared as late as 11 December 1848: 'The events of this year have laid the foundations for the victory of constitutionalism in our German fatherland. Henceforth governments, that is to say cabinets, will emerge from the majorities in the chambers'. And deputy Professor Dr Karl Theodor Welcker, a lawyer, added that it was sufficient for the Reichstag to have the power 'to chase ministers off their chairs by means of a vote of no-confidence [and] by means of refusing to approve tax proposals'. Of course, after the recent setbacks in Vienna and Berlin such optimism was quite unfounded. Nor did the Constitution contain clauses relating to such powers of the Reichstag. Ministers, it is true, were supposed to be responsible (Art. 73), but nothing was to be found in the constitutional document about the circumstances and consequences of a vote of no-confidence; and the idea of bringing about the downfall of a minister by refusing to vote taxes was perhaps conceived rather too much in the ivory tower.

The underlying patriotic mood of the 1848 Revolution was ultimately the decisive factor which motivated the majority of the deputies to endow the monarch with extensive powers. In representing German interests abroad the emperor was to be able to appear on the international stage with prestige and authority.

Among his princely peers the new imperial office was to look desirable by virtue of the honour and influence which it bestowed upon its occupant. If the emperor was no more than the executor of Reichstag decisions, the assumption was that 'the German princes would not be willing to take on such an inferior office'.

Moreover, six months after democracy had been established, fear of the masses had already become greater on the Right of the National Assembly than mistrust of the old authorities. As Welcker proclaimed: 'Let us organise a strong executive; then we shall be safe'. And Dahlmann praised the idea of an absolute veto for the executive as 'the law of salvaging action (*rettende Tat*)'. Was the King of Prussia completely wrong when he saw the National Assembly as a gathering of subjects?

The Reichstag was made up of two chambers, the *Staatenhaus* and the above-mentioned *Volkshaus* (Art. 85). A motion by the Left that the future Parliament consist of only one chamber had been rejected by 331 votes to 95 during the debate on this section of the Constitution.

A two-chamber system also existed in the United States of America, at this time the land of hope for almost all democrats in Europe. Although the proposed federal structure of Germany was similar to that of the US, there was no precedent in modern constitutional history for a union of monarchical states within a democratic federal state. Articles 86 to 92 of the Constitution tried to take account of this peculiarity.

Several proposals had been put forward. There was the concept of a senate to which all states, large and small, would send an equal number of representatives. Another solution was to establish an upper chamber which was not based on the federal principle and would be elected on the basis of a limited suffrage or of estates. Finally, there were proposals to have a state-based chamber whose distribution of seats would be dependent on the size of the population in each federal state. The solution that was found represented the golden mean — a compromise between a number of counter-vailing forces. Thus the idea of a united Reich is reflected in a ceiling imposed on the number of deputies from the two major powers in Central Europe. If their representation had been proportional to their populations, they would have held about one-third of the seats each. Under the proposed Constitution, Prussia was to hold forty and Austria thirty-eight seats out of a total of 192. As the individual states retained their separate identity, it was logical that they also retained the right to nominate half of the members of the *Staatenhaus*. As to the principle of a popular assembly (Art. 186) which was also to apply to all individual states, the National Assembly took the view that the other half of the *Staatenhaus* membership should be elected by the popular diets of those individual states.

The *Volkshaus* as the second chamber was to be made up of the deputies of the German nation as a whole (Art. 95). It was to be the hub of the new democratic state. Deputies were to be elected for four years in the first instance. Thereafter a three-year term of office was envisaged. The details of the election procedure were to be left to an electoral law (Art. 94) to be ratified at a later date.

The Articles relating to the *Volkshaus* are few and brief. But this should not distract us from the fact that the *Paulskirche* deputies agonised a great deal over the shape of these clauses. Nor do they say much about the heated debates that accompanied their ratification. Originally it had been envisaged to include the principles of the voting rights in the Constitution. After all, it should be a matter of course for a democratic constitution to spell out these principles, and the three subsequent constitutions of 1871, 1919 and 1949 did so. However, differences of opinion occurred in the Constitutional Committee over the question of the equal vote. It was therefore agreed to exclude this problem from the document and merely to refer to a special electoral law. However, the Committee then began to draft such an electoral law on its own accord and came forward with the following formula: 'All honourable Germans who have completed their twenty-fifth year of age are eligible to vote. All servants, day-labourers, journeymen and factory workers are excluded from the right to vote. The vote is direct, but public'.

Under this proposal a good half of the German male population — the vote for women was barely contemplated — would have been deprived of a voting right which they had already exercised when the National Assembly was elected. Moreover, voters would not have been able to cast their vote in secret and freely, but in public.

What was it that was going on in the minds of the majority of the Committee? Had the National Assembly not ratified a catalogue of basic rights several months earlier? And had this catalogue not contained a straight-forward clause: 'All status privileges are abolished. The Germans are equal before the law'?

It therefore required some courage for the Committee to put forward and to justify its new proposals. This the members did not lack, and with proven eloquence they enlightened the *Paulskirche* plenum as to why no more than one in two male Germans should have the right to vote.

Deputy Professor Georg Waitz, a historian, argued that voting rights were not at all part of general basic rights. The 'best of the whole' was to determine who was capable of exercising this privilege. He saw no injustice in refusing to grant the masses, who were so frequently aimless, volatile and the uncritical victims of agitation and demagogy, an influence on political decision-making. Only after the fourth estate had become part of bourgeois society, thanks to social reforms, would it be possible to extend political rights to its members.

Hermann von Beckrath, banker and Reich Finance Minister, thought the task was to make certain that decision-making did not fall into the hands of the 'numerical' nation. As Friedrich Daniel Bassermann, a book-trader and State Secretary in the Reich Ministry of the Interior put it, 'the reasonable popular will' was to dominate.

Other deputies belonging to the Third Estate expressed the same idea in different words: the suffrage was to be formulated in such a way 'that the owners would feel secure with their property'; the task was to protect property against an attack by the proletarians who 'abandon themselves to socialist doctrines advocating crude, animal-like and ephemeral indulgence'. Heinrich von Gagern, a land-owner and head of the Reich government, put these attitudes in a nutshell when he said: 'The trend of this age is to secure for the middle classes an overwhelming influence in the state'. Professor Robert von Mohl, another deputy and first Reich Justice Minister, made a similar comment in his textbook on Württemberg public law. These middle classes, he wrote, combined the total material and intellectual power of the nation.

Within a few months the deputies of the Casino had developed such an inflated image of themselves that one is reminded of George Orwell's *Animal Farm*; if their notion of equality is to be captured in a sentence: 'All animals are equal, but some animals are more equal than others', was also their view of the situation. Democracy as a dictatorship by one class — this was an idea realised, albeit on reverse terms, in the twentieth century in East Germany, but conceived and proposed in the Frankfurt Assembly a century earlier. It was only thanks to an accident resulting from an over-cunning manoeuvring on the part of a few right-wing Liberals that an unequal suffrage clause failed to get included in the

Constitution.

The Centre Left and the various factions of the Left rejected all these proposals of the Casino faction during the suffrage debate in the Assembly and demanded the introduction of a universal, equal, direct and secret ballot. They argued that it was misguided to open up a rift between half the (male) population and the rest of state and society, nor, according to deputy August Hermann Ziegert, a lawyer and higher civil servant, was it right to expose the labouring classes to the political hegemony of a monied aristocracy which instead of protecting them would exploit them. The critics also refuted the generalised notion that two-thirds of the population were politically immature and condemned the attempt by the Constitutional Committee to divide the nation into an illiterate mob ('*plebs*') on the one hand, and the 'true' and 'rational' people, on the other.

Even Friedrich Ludwig Jahn, the *Turnvater* who belonged rather more to the right wing in the Assembly, got himself into a rage when hearing such arguments and tried to explain to his friends in the Casino faction that the lower strata represented the real strength of the nation and the source of its constant regeneration. 'The people', he said, 'whom you propose to exclude are the true generators of German national life!' And Professor Karl Vogt, a scientist from Hesse, added that the Casino faction demonstrated what was behind the chit-chat about majority rule; what it ultimately had in mind was the rule of an 'extract of the minority'.

These criticisms did not go unnoticed in the National Assembly. When a vote was taken on 20 February 1849 the elitist draft of the Constitutional Committee was thrown out by a large majority, even though it probably reflected the image which many *Paulskirche* deputies had of themselves. Nor did a number of motions aiming to restrict the suffrage by various other means find a majority. The last of these amendments, however, which proposed to tie the suffrage to either the ownership of land, to an independent household, to communal citizen's rights or to employment by the state, barely and unexpectedly missed a majority. There were rumours that a number of right-wingers from South Germany and Austria had voted in favour of an equal suffrage in order to make the Constitution look so democratic that the King of Prussia would find it impossible to become emperor of a new Reich.

Whatever the motives of some deputies may have been, it is majorities that count in a parliamentary assembly. The men of the *Paulskirche* ultimately ratified a law relating to the elections to the

Volkshaus which implemented the principle of a universal, equal, direct and secret ballot. Seen in historical perspective this was probably the most important decision which the Assembly had to take. The inclusion of a restricted suffrage would not have given any kudos to the constitutional document; nor would it have lasted. Indeed, the 1848 Revolution would have degenerated into a bad joke.

The debate on basic rights and their incorporation into the Constitution remains, and especially from a present-day perspective, the outstanding achievement of the Frankfurt Assembly. In the whole of Germany liberty raised its voice clearly and rapturously here. Hitherto Germany had been prevented from linking up with the bourgeois emancipatory movement which swept through almost all Western nations; now she was able to follow the advance guard of democracy and especially in America and France which had provided the models.

Accordingly Section IV of the 1849 Constitution, relating to basic rights and reprinted below, was a clear statement and does not require any further elaboration. However, many of the arguments put forward in support of these rights are so powerful and far-sighted and still, in many cases, retain all of their present-day significance, that a few of them shall be presented here.

Thus Art. 139 abolishes the death penalty, except where it is mandatory under martial law or in the case of mutiny covered by maritime law. It was to be another century before this great idea came to be realised.

The Constitutional Committee had taken the view that the abolition of the death penalty and of corporal punishment should not be included in the catalogue of basic rights. It was to be left to the penal codes of the individual states to deal with this question. One of those to argue against this in the Assembly was Friedrich Ernst Scheller, President of the High Court at Frankfurt an der Oder in Silesia. 'Corporal punishment and death penalty', he insisted,

concern [the question of] dignity and human life. If both [penalties] are to be abolished, there is no more suitable place to say so than in the section dealing with basic rights. The basic rights [proposals] that have been put before us merely concern property and some other inferior personal matters. Dignity and human life, however, which are on the agenda at this point, are the highest goods of man. If we do not wish to rank them lower [than the other rights] we shall have to say something about them in this Section.

The substance of the argument culminated in Scheller's statement: 'No man has the right to take away by force even so much as one minute of another man's existence, a minute which that person might use to prepare himself for the Other World and become more worthy for living in it'.

Ernst Moritz Arndt, the poet from Bonn, put the following point: 'The system of deterrence seems beneath dignity to me because it does not even work with your own children; the system of rehabilitation is very powerful if only we could do more to improve [people]!' Speaking about the death penalty for political crimes, Arndt concluded: 'I would have been sent to the gallows or to the guillotine, if my old King had not been a better man than those who would have liked to get rid of me'.

Deputy Franz Wigard, a professor from Dresden, argued that one might have inserted the following sentence into the catalogue of basic rights: 'The life, the liberty and the dignity of all Germans are inviolable'. Wigard summed up his speech against the death penalty with the words: 'Let us usher in, through our resolution, a new era in criminal law: an age of humanity, an age of genuine Christian love!' The verbatim minutes record a 'bravo' at the end of this speech.

The basic rights catalogue also contains Art. 144 which guarantees freedom of worship and of conscience. This explicitly includes the right not to have to reveal one's religious faith. The alliance of church and state which had grown up over a thousand years could not withstand the onslaught of the rational criticism of the liberal age. To the majority of deputies the religious issue appeared to be so crucial for the liberties of the individual that they wanted it to be included in the catalogue of basic rights. They wanted church and state to be independent of each other. At the same time, the churches were to be subject to the law of the land. No provision was made for them to have the status of institutions under public law.

Deputy Theodor Paur, a doctor of philosophy and school teacher, probably reflected the majority opinion of the Assembly when he argued that the churches could not be free to intervene into the state sphere and in particular into education. Teachers had to be unhampered in their task of developing the minds of young people. Paur added that it was the duty of the state to protect all religious convictions as long as they did not interfere with the state's actions and concluded that:

The church must be free and must always remain free inasmuch as it works within itself for the spiritual life of its members. However, wherever religious activity penetrates the state sphere and tries to assume a public role, the political state has the right to preserve its position in so far as it is called upon, in its public function, to regulate and to protect the liberties of all its citizens.

Moreover there was Art. 153, which stipulates that education, except for religious education, was to be taken out of the hand of the churches and to be placed under state supervision. In 1848, given the existing system, this had been a particularly revolutionary idea which Deputy Ernst Ludwig August Reinhard depicted as follows:

[There is], for example, a German state called Bavaria where a poor primary school teacher has no other indigenous rights than those of a burial. During the Abel Ministry decrees were issued which made the teacher dependent on the Church. Suspensions from duty did not occur via the judiciary and on the basis of justice and the due process of law, but by simple administrative fiat. . . .

He went on to say that the majority of German primary school teachers were demoralised and dejected paupers. If, on the other hand, schools became state institutions with teachers who were equal citizens and servants of the state, all would be different. Reinhard asked for support of those motions which tried to establish these principles.

Denominational schools were a particular irritant to many deputies. Peter Dewes spoke for this faction when he thought that the separation of church and state would open up the possibility of secular institutions: 'All I am saying is: possibility; for I know very well that our clerics will do everything to maintain this division and the denominational divide as sharply as possible. And yet slowly the various denominations will come together in one school and under one teacher; only in this way will intolerance and denominational strife disappear . . . and at last become a matter for ridicule'.

Faced with the strength of majority opinion, Wilhelm von Ketteler fought from a hopeless position, when he told the Assembly:

You have no right to demand that a father should have his children educated according to your educational system. Gentlemen, that is the most violent course of action to which you might be inclined. I propose that the atheist be allowed to educate his children without religious instruction; however, the most loyal Catholic must be permitted to educate his children in the Catholic faith.

Since outside the Assembly the idea of democracy had not yet taken a firm hold in the minds of the majority of the population, the democrats of the *Paulskirche* fought all the more emphatically for a renewal of the school system. As Reinhard put it, without improvement of popular education the whole democratic edifice would be a castle built on sand.

By the late 1840s, the Social Question had begun to pose itself in the most blatant terms, and the deputies in the Frankfurt Assembly were quite conscious of it. Nevertheless the catalogue of basic rights does not contain a reference to the effect that property carried with it social obligations; nor is there any kind of social programme to be introduced by the new federal state. The social deprivation of the mass of the population was a problem for the Frankfurt Parliament, but it was not one affecting these assembled representatives of the upper classes. It was to take another seventy years for the Social Question to be given the rank of a problem to be dealt with in a Constitutional document: the Weimar Constitution.

This did not mean that no words were lost over this issue. There was a minority at Frankfurt which felt obliged to take action, demanding in a number of motions the 'right to work'. Thus Bernhard Eisenstuck, a factory owner from Chemnitz, proclaimed: 'I am in favour of the right to work for the simple reason that one cannot possibly be opposed to it. All men have a right to work. It is a natural right, and a natural right which conforms to the needs of the individual is firmly fixed; it is immovable; it cannot be quantified or modified by man-made laws. I also favour giving a guarantee of a job'.

Eisenstuck was supported by deputy Friedrich Jacob Schütz, a lawyer from Mainz:

> The right to work has frequently been denigrated and attacked. Yesterday it was said from this rostrum that the right to work was nothing but a device to support sloth. Gentlemen, I do not pretend that the right to work is the means by which all misery can be made to disappear in our fatherland. I am incapable of holding such a view. What I see in the right to work and what I hope to achieve by incorporating this Article into the constitution is [to trigger] the start of a new epoch. [I see] the possibility that the state, which was a military, clerical or merely a

monarchical state before and is a state of money now, would at last become what human society should be, that is, a society of workers; a society which offers all men the opportunity of gaining a benefit commensurate to his job by applying his intellectual and physical skills.

Finally special attention must be drawn to Art. 125 which provided for the institution of a Reich Court. It was not to be what the later Reich Court evolved into — a supreme court of appeal in civil and criminal matters. Rather it was to be a Reich Constitutional Court with all-embracing powers. According to Art. 126g individual German citizens were to be able to turn to this court to complain about violations of rights which had been granted to them in the Constitution. That concept of a Constitutional Complaint which is now available under the Basic Law of the Federal Republic was already incorporated into the 1849 Constitution of a century earlier.

None of these rights came into force because circumstances were against their practical implementation. The response to the question as to whether it could have become a viable constitution must remain ambiguous. To be sure, basic rights and legal protection had been given a model framework whose regulations pointed into the future. For this reason, these sections of the 1849 Constitution were essentially revived a century later. On the other hand, the organisational norms of the Constitution relating to the executive and the legislative organs would probably have not been sufficient to put democratic participation and liberty in Germany on a permanent footing. There was too much trust and too little control. The House of Hohenzollern could have ruled with this Constitution very comfortably. In the long run the Emperor and his government would not have been any less powerful than William I was under the Constitution of 1871. In fact, he might well have had even greater power in view of the fact that the peculiar composition and lack of directive powers of the *Staatenhaus* would not have provided an effective counterweight by the federal states to the powers at the centre. Nor would so much unchecked power have been beneficial to the basic rights of the German people. After all, basic rights, even those which have been enshrined in a constitutional document, require open breathing spaces where political life can organise and express itself. Above all, these must be defended and fought for day after day.

The Reich Constitution of 1871

The failure of the 1848 Revolution had long-term repercussions. The demand for national unity continued to be heard. There were the passions with which the revolutionaries had fought for this objective and which were kept alive thereafter. But increasingly rational arguments were also put forward against particularism and fragmentation. The political revolution was followed by the industrial revolution which was more successful by far. The decades after 1850 are characterised by a rapid acceleration of technological progress and growing economic concentration. Germany became an industrial country and its capitalist economy began to flourish. Willy-nilly, political change had to come in the wake of economic change, if the economy was to survive in the face of competition from unified national states like France and Britain.

Prussia had recognised these realities quite early on and, through the creation of the *Zollverein* (Customs Union) of 1834, had made herself the guardian of the interests of the industrial and commercial bourgeoisie in Central Europe. Thenceforth there existed an association of states within the larger German Confederation. It was a union which excluded Austria and offered a common customs area to the rest of the Central European states. However, by the 1850s this was no longer sufficient; industry and commerce demanded complete political unity as well.

Prussia, as the hegemonic power of the *Zollverein*, felt called upon to take the lead in this movement for unification. The Prussian King had refused to accept the imperial crown from the hands of the parliamentarians at Frankfurt. Nevertheless he felt flattered that the German bourgeoisie had confirmed him as a candidate for the post in front of the world. The legacy of the *Kleindeutsche* solution (i.e. one excluding Austria), which the Frankfurt Parliament had opted for, remained a factor in the course of events leading up to the founding of the Empire of 1871.

The legacy of 1848 could also be seen to be alive in the fact that almost all German states retained their constitutions. Even Prussia kept the one which the monarch had imposed after the failure of the 1848 Revolution, although the suffrage was severely restricted. The Prussian ballot was public and voters were divided into three classes which seriously disadvantaged the lower-income groups. Nevertheless, the principle that the people should participate in decision-making through elected parliaments became firmly established in Germany. Power struggles, it is true, occurred between the monarchical governments and their assemblies and time and again the former tried to reduce or circumvent the influence of the latter. The principle of popular representation, however, became generally accepted; monarchism remained constitutional. Whoever was keeping up with the political thinking of the age was convinced that a future unified German state would be a constitutional monarchy. Bismarck was not least among those who were clear from the start that a reordering of the political framework in Central Europe without parliamentary institutions and without a constitutional document would be anachronistic and hence be impermanent. The Revolution of 1848 had left its mark in this respect.

However, during the years of reaction in the 1850s, the German bourgeoisie no longer felt called upon to complete the unification process under its own revolutionary steam. The defeat of 1849 and the policies of repression which followed had a sobering effect. The political movements which re-emerged around the late 1850s were much less impatient and pushing. The parliamentary assemblies, and the Prussian Diet in particular, were made up of mostly well-to-do notables, whose democratic radicalism was strictly limited. There were also many tame associations which organised their fêtes and rallies under the benevolent eyes of the authorities and used these occasions to demand national unity. The commercial and industrial bourgeoisie was so absorbed by making money in the boom years of the 1850s and 1860s that little time was left for engaging in politics. Revolutionary ideas were increasingly treated with disdain, especially once the incipient working-class movement began to adopt such ideas and claimed for itself the democratic legacy of the left-liberal fighters on the barricades of March 1848 and 1849. In the 1860s a long-drawn-out struggle broke out between the Prussian King and the Diet over the appropriation of the military budget, known as the Constitutional Conflict. But even these dramatic events did not induce the bourgeoisie to try to mobilise the masses. They simply 'sat out' this conflict.

The experience of powerlessness at Frankfurt increasingly led the leading middle-class groups to look towards Prussian power and to invest their hopes for national unity in the policies of a strong man. Otto von Bismarck appeared to be such a leader. However, it would be too simple and even misleading to characterise him just as such a strong man. No doubt his personality left a deep mark on the age and the effects of his policies can be felt to this day. But he was not a Teutonic knight who realised the aim of national unity by sheer force of will against all odds. On the contrary, Bismarck's many-faceted personality was dominated by other traits whose combination explains his strength: he possessed a good analytical mind and a go-getting cleverness; he was a realist unencumbered by ideological or idealistic proclivities; he displayed flexibility and an ability to compromise where possible; but he could be brutal, if necessary; he was a loyal servant of the King, but without lacking a well-developed self-confidence; he was circumspect in his dealings with Parliament to the point of giving the impression that he sought its partnership; he spoke several languages and knew his way around the world; he was sufficiently principled and possessed both political ambition and a healthy acquisitive instinct. Had Bismarck lived a century later, he might have felt the call to become president of one of the multinationals. He certainly had all the skills required for such a position. However, in his time it seemed more appropriate for a man of his background to feel called upon to become minister-president of Prussia. It was in this office that he put into practice the widespread desire in Germany for national unity.

Bismarck thought it inevitable that two wars would have to be waged along the path towards unity. The first conflict with Austria was to decide the question of hegemony in Central Europe. The second war 'against a neighbour who has been an aggressor for centuries' was to be about the final inclusion of the south German states in a united Germany. Both wars were started on some minor pretext and amounted to a continuation of Bismarck's policies 'by other means'. Unity was the joint achievement of Bismarck and Helmuth von Moltke, the Chief of the Prussian General Staff. At the end of this process stood the conclusion of treaties with the south German princes and the proclamation of William I of Prussia as Kaiser of the German Empire at Versailles on 18 January 1871.

The selection of Versailles and the annexations of Alsace and Lorraine were to prove to be fatal mistakes which burdened the new Empire from the start. The Reich which had been created through wars already bore within itself the seeds of its later destruction. Bismarck and his contemporaries in Germany did not see it this way in 1871. As Bismarck put it in a decree: 'The only correct policy is in these circumstances to incapacitate at least somewhat an enemy whom we cannot hope to convert into a genuine friend'.

The proclamation by the Kaiser at Versailles, 18 January 1871

Speaking in the parliament of the North German Federation which Bismarck had founded in 1867 after his victory over Austria, August Bebel, a left-winger and later leader of the Social Democrats, took a different view:

> Gentlemen, the latest King's Speech reveals that we are far from assuming that, following the recent conclusion of peace, it will be possible to maintain the peace with France for any length of time; it [also] reveals that France, filled with a sense of revenge, will do everything to resume the fight; that she will try her best to regain what she has now lost, if not under her own steam certainly in alliance with other powers. Well, if this is the prospect, wisdom counsels that we must not hurt our opponents unnecessarily and incite them to take revenge.

However, the mood in Germany was different. The verbatim minutes of Bebel's speech record 'great commotion, laughter' at the end.

In the formal sense, the founding of the German Empire occurred on 18 January 1871, the day on which it was proclaimed. In fact, however, the proclamation merely finalised what had been started in 1866 and 1867 when the German Confederation was dissolved and Prussia annexed Hanover, Kurhessen, Schleswig-

Holstein, Nassau and Frankfurt; when the North German Federation was established and protective military agreements were signed with the German states south of the River Main. Accordingly, the Constitution of the German Empire of 1871 is no more than a slightly modified version of the Constitution of the North German Federation of 1867. This complex document was largely conceived by Bismarck and deliberately tailored in such a way as to facilitate the accession of the South German states at a later date. In view of this far-reaching identity of the two documents any comments upon them pertain to both constitutions.

Even by its origins the Bismarckian Constitution of 1871 is a complicated blend of divergent elements. Within a typology of constitutions it must be given a unique place in constitutional history. During the drafting stage princes and city-states were involved. They all combined to form a federal state based on formal treaties and to agree on a joint constitution. As a next step the population participated, at first through the diets of the individual states and the North German Federation. Then there was the proclamation of Kaiser and Reich. Finally the Kaiser nominated the Federal Council (*Bundesrat*) and called for elections to the new national Parliament, the Reichstag. Once elections had been held on 3 March 1871, this *Kleindeutsche* Parliament discussed the Constitution in its capacity as a national representative body and ultimately voted for it. The last step was taken when the Kaiser promulgated this Constitution for the German people with the words: 'We, William, German Kaiser by the Grace of God [and] King of Prussia, . . . decree herewith the following in the name of the German Empire [and] after obtaining the consent of the Bundesrat and the Reichstag: . .'.

Yet however many bodies had been involved in the ratification process, the final result had been clear from the start. As has already been mentioned, the Constitution which was officially published on 20 April 1871 deviated little from that of the North German Federation of 17 April 1867. It provides an example of a German-type constitutional monarchy. This type is rooted in the so-called monarchical principle as defined, for instance, in the Bavarian Constitution of 1818: 'The King is the head of state: [he] combines in his hand all rights of the state's authority and exercises them within the clauses which have been laid down in the current constitutional document'.

The point is that this type of constitutional monarchy does not emerge from a democratic revolution. Nor is the constitution ratified by the people as the constituent authority and freely agreed between the popular representatives and the crown, as envisaged by the Frankfurt Assembly. Rather it is the monarch as the bearer of all power who deigns to allow the people to share in the exercise of state power and to grant this privilege in the shape of a constitutional document.

The introductory clause 'We, William, German Emperor by the Grace of God' signals who gives this constitution. There is one peculiarity, however, in comparison with earlier practice: the other German princes granted their assent beforehand and the Kaiser therefore spoke also in their name. Hence, in 1871 the German people confronted a college of princes all of whom, as crowned heads, condescended to grant this Constitution. If the opening formula referred to both Bundesrat and Reichstag the emphasis was on the consent of the former, comprising as it does the sovereign princes and city-states who are taken seriously as partners to the agreement. In the eyes of the founders of the new national state the involvement of the Reichstag in the process was less important. One of the deputies, Dr Waldeck, had analysed this situation as early as 9 March 1867 during the general debate on the Constitution of the North German Federation:

> Well, Gentlemen, we shall not produce anything well-rounded and fairly good through our vote; it will only be what is feasible, [and] with this we shall of course have to be content. I had occasion the other day to remark that we are not a constituent assembly. All we can do is to reject [the entire document]. If we accept it or [merely] introduce amendments to it, we shall be nothing but consultants. We have no power over the governments, neither over our Prussian [ministry] nor over the governments of other states. We are in no position to exert pressure upon them to abandon rights beyond those which they have already given up in the negotiations which have taken place so far.

We know that even at this earlier stage, in 1867, Bismarck was determined to dissolve Parliament should the deputies put forward amendments that were unacceptable; following the example of the imposed Prussian Constitution of 1850 he planned to promulgate his draft irrevocably. In short, the constitution was not an agreement between free parties. On the other hand, Bismarck was sufficiently interested in preserving the semblance of a mutually agreed compact to be prepared for paying a certain price for it. Here the deputies of the North German Federation had limited opportunities which they did exploit. The later Reich Constitution was to benefit from this.

Among the amendments which the North German Parliament was able to build into the draft constitution that had been put to it, the one concerning its budgetary rights turned out to be the most decisive. The draft proposed that only Federal expenditure would be subject to parliamentary scrutiny, with the budgetary period covering three years. Moreover, the army and navy budgets were to be removed from parliamentary debate. The deputies succeeded in establishing the principle that all revenue and all expenditure would be fixed annually through a finance bill. With respect to the armed forces a compromise was found which provided that, following a four-year transitional period, Parliament would also dispose over rights of legislation and control in this area. These concessions amounted to a considerable success, given that they were obtained from a position of virtual powerlessness.

The North German Parliament became a popular assembly which had to be taken seriously only after it had asserted itself in the budgetary domain. After all, the real power position which the legislature holds over the executive lies in its control of public revenue and expenditure. It was against the background of these earlier compromises that the discussion of the 1871 Constitution in the spring of that year could confine itself to a routine revision of the 1867 text. The main battle had already been fought and won four years earlier.

There were quite a few deputies in the 1871 Reichstag who had been members of the Frankfurt Parliament in 1848/9. Thus Eduard Simson was elected first president. Simson had been Gagern's successor in the presidency of the National Assembly. He had also been leader of the delegation sent from Frankfurt to Berlin to offer the Imperial crown to the King of Prussia. In 1867 he had been elected president of the North German Parliament and in this capacity had headed another Kaiser delegation. This time his task was to ask King William I that he complete the process of German unification by accepting the Imperial crown. Simson was a lawyer and later returned to this profession as president of the new Reich Court.

The new German Empire was made up of twenty-five states which are listed in Art. 1. Prussia remained the hegemonic power thanks to the size of its territory and its population, to its military and economic strength and to the leading role it had played in the process of unification. These realities are also reflected in the

Eduard Simson

Reich Constitution. Although Bismarck's policy towards the member states was deft and considerate enough not to highlight Prussia's position too much, Prussian hegemony was also safeguarded in the Constitution.

According to Art. 6, Prussia had seventeen out of fifty-eight votes in the Bundesrat, i.e. less than one-third. But Art. 5, Section 2, Art. 37 and Art. 78 introduced special voting arrangements which made certain that no decision could be taken against Prussia in matters relating to the armed forces and to customs and taxes. Nor could the Bundesrat change the Constitution against Prussia's will.

Art. 11 firmly bound the office of Kaiser to that of the Prussian crown. This again emphasised Prussia's elevated position, even if the powers of the Kaiser were restricted by the participatory rights of Bundesrat and Reichstag. For example, according to Art.

Otto von Bismarck in 1847

11, Section 2, the Kaiser could declare war only with the consent of the Federal Council. The Frankfurt Parliament had been prepared to let him have the exclusive right of decision-making in this sphere! The armed forces of the Reich were subordinate to the Emperor. Under Art. 63 and 64 soldiers were expected to take an oath obliging them to obey the Kaiser unconditionally.

In practice there was another mechanism which secured Prussian hegemony but which was not mentioned in the constitutional document: the offices of Prussian minister-president and of Reich Chancellor were combined in a personal union and hence in the hands of that great Prussian, Otto von Bismarck. As a result Prussia penetrated the Reich administratively and this was of the greatest importance as far as constitutional practice was concerned. On the other hand, whereas Prussian hegemony was strengthened by this bureaucratic interpenetration at the beginning, in the long term the Prussian civil service was forced to think and act more and more from a Reich perspective. A generation later Prussia was beginning to be absorbed by the Reich. In 1871 Bismarck saw himself as Prussian minister-president who happened to be the Reich's top administrator at the same time. When he was dismissed in 1890, he left as a Reich Chancellor who happened to be co-administering the office of Prussian minister-president.

The Kaiser's office is not given a particularly strong emphasis in the Constitution. The first constitutional organ to be mentioned is the Bundesrat (Art. 6). It is supposed to represent the contracting federal states as the embodiment of national sovereignty. It is thus the supreme organ of the Constitution and the Kaiser is intended to act as the Reich sovereign. He is the King of Prussia who, as president of the Federation, also bears the title of Kaiser (Art. 11). According to this interpretation, the Kaiser would have been no more than an executive secretary of the Reich and it would have been quite appropriate therefore to introduce his office after the Federal Council. However, constitutional reality looked differently. This was due not only to the hegemonic position of Prussia, but also, and probably even more so, to the dynamic of the idea of the Reich which was carried forward with much patriotic fervour. Increasingly the nation came to see the Kaiser as its actual sovereign.

Being the supreme commander of the armed forces in the Reich, the Kaiser moreover controlled, largely without checks and balances, the ultimate power-factor within the state. There was no primacy of the civilian authority over the military. The War Ministry, the General Staff and the Military Cabinet (in charge of Army personnel matters) were Prussian offices and hence not subordinate to the Reich Chancellery. This meant that the military also remained outside the sphere of parliamentary control. Thus the Kaiser virtually remained an absolutist monarch in the military field. The Army was a state within the state, with dangerous consequences which could be felt well into the twentieth century.

William I became Kaiser at an advanced age and was hence inclined to give Bismarck a free rein and to confine himself to representative tasks. But his grandson William II who ascended to the throne in 1888, only a few months after the death of William I and the subsequent untimely death of his father Frederick, was more conscious of his power and wanted to rule personally. What he may have had in mind was the role of the President of the United States whose constitutional position — except for its finite term of office — was stronger than that of the German Kaiser. However, the responsibility which this carried with it inescapably caught up with William II in 1918 and cost him his throne. The history of European monarchism demonstrates that in the bourgeois age only those monarchical systems had a chance of survival which were prepared to share their power generously and in good time.

Bismarck had envisaged that the Bundesrat would act as the joint ministry of all federal states. Apart from being involved in Reich legislation (Art. 5) and constitutional jurisdiction (Art. 76 and 77), the Bundesrat was also intended to be the executive of the Reich. This explains why one looks in vain for articles in the Constitution which relate to something like a Reich government. However, in practice the Bundesrat never came to occupy the role which it had been given under the Constitution. The business of government was left to its president Bismarck whom the Kaiser had appointed. The Bundesrat restricted itself to being a federal chamber in conjunction with the popular assembly through which bills were being introduced into the legislative process. Beyond this the power to issue decrees in accordance with Art. 7 assumed a certain significance. The Bundesrat's involvement in the shaping of constitutional law was very limited and was never used in practice.

Although the first and most important organ of the Constitution, the Bundesrat used its powers only in a very measured way. It remained inconspicuous as far as its non-public duties were concerned and did not leave a clear mark on the popular mind. It was not that Bismarck as Reich Chancellor tried to outmanoeuvre the Federal Council. On the contrary, he was always most accommodating with the ministerial plenipotentiaries from the Federal states in order to encourage and strengthen a positive disposition towards the Reich. If the work of the Bundesrat was unspectacular this was due partly to the fact that Bismarck's circumspect promotion of good relations prevented differences of opinion from arising. Above all there was the fact that the unitary force of democratic nationalism became the dominant trend turning the Kaiser and the Reichstag into the most popular organs of the German Empire.

The Reichstag was the democratic counterpart of the Kaiser and the unitary counterweight of the Federal Council. It embodied, like the office of the Kaiser, the novelty of the events of 1871; it embodied the nation.

The first sitting of the Reichstag, 21 March 1871

The Reichstag was elected on the basis of the universal, equal, direct and secret ballot along the lines of the 1849 suffrage clause. There were single-candidate constituencies, and candidates were elected on the basis of an absolute majority. Thus, while Prussia retained its three-class voting system, the equal ballot was introduced in the Reich. However, this was not a victory which the parliamentary assembly had achieved on its own accord. On the contrary, the suffrage debate in the North German Parliament in 1867 took a similarly peculiar course to that of the Frankfurt Assembly. Bismarck had constituted the 1867 Parliament on the basis of equal suffrage because he considered the Prussian three-class voting system badly flawed. Of course, what motivated him was not an impeccable democratic credo, but a power-political calculation in support of the crown. Bismarck was convinced that the poorer classes were loyal subjects of the King and that the monarchy was not threatened from this direction. This had been his experience in March 1848 when it proved almost impossible to restrain the peasants around his Schönhausen estate from taking up arms and coming to the rescue of the beleaguered King at Berlin. In 1866 Bismarck put the problem as follows in one of his decrees:

> In a country with monarchist traditions and a loyal mentality the universal suffrage, by removing the influence of the liberal bourgeoisie, will

result in monarchical elections, just as anarchism is the outcome of elections in countries where the masses harbour revolutionary sentiments. However, in Prussia nine-tenths of the people are loyal to the King; it is only through the artificial mechanism of a [restricted] suffrage that they are being prevented from expressing their opinions.

The Conservatives and National Liberals, on the other hand, vigorously criticised the idea of an equal suffrage. This, they polemicised, was the first step towards a democratic dictatorship. Bismarck refused to budge. He countered that 'no other state had dreamed up a more illogical and miserable electoral law than the Prussian one'. The outcome of this debate was a most peculiar one: a representative of the Prussian monarchy ultimately bullied a democratically elected parliament into accepting a democratic suffrage.

However, Bismarck failed in 1867 in his attempt to prevent civil servants from putting themselves up as candidates. What he was hoping to avoid was a practice which was much lamented in the diets of the German states, i.e. that the government was subject to control and criticism from its own public servants. A successful move of this kind would have hit the North German parliament all too hard. No less than 190 out of a total of 297 deputies were civil servants, who were naturally loath to give up their seats.

Although Bismarck failed to get his way on this point, he remained immovable in his rejection of the idea of emoluments and expenses for deputies (Art. 32). He wanted to prevent the rise of professional full-time politicians. Deputies were to be personalities who pursued a normal professional life and did not form a caste above the ordinary citizen. Despite opposition from the deputies this remained the rule until 1906 when the Constitution was changed. However, Bismarck's refusal to make payments did not prevent the emergence of a new type of professional politician. And those deputies who did not have a private income to maintain themselves, soon received financial support from the parties which they had helped to create. According to Art. 29 members of the Reichstag were to be representatives of the country as a whole and could not be tied by an imperative mandate. But how could they be expected to do this if they were not paid for their parliamentary work?

Up to 1918 women were unable to vote and also could not stand for election. In this respect the German Empire was as backward as other liberal-democratic states of the time — they, too, did not widen the suffrage until the twentieth century, with Australia being the first in line in 1902.

In the 1871 elections the turn-out was still as low as 50.7 per cent. But it rose continuously thereafter, reaching a peak at 84.5 per cent in 1912. These figures may be taken as indications of the growing politicisation of the population.

Reichstag legislative activity was of the greatest significance for giving substance to the idea of national unity. Consider the laws relating to the judiciary, which have shaped jurisdiction to this day and which created the Reich Court at Leipzig. Or consider the Penal Code, the Commercial Code or, finally the *Bürgerliches Gesetzbuch* (Civil Code) of 1900, to name but a few important pieces of legislation.

As mentioned above, Bismarck wanted to avoid the establishment of a central government. The Federal Council was to be the executive arm of the Reich. But the North German Parliament subsequently succeeded in making the Chancellor a minister responsible under the Constitution, and this principle was incorporated into the 1871 document. The Reich Chancellor was a responsible minister in his own right. He was selected and appointed by the Kaiser and was hence largely independent of the Reichstag. He could not be toppled by Parliament. But being a responsible minister under the Constitution provided the Chancellor with a certain degree of independence from the Kaiser. In the Reichstag chamber he could invoke his dependence on the monarch, while he could point to his constitutional responsibility *vis-à-vis* the Reichstag when it came to resisting pressure from the Kaiser.

There was no Reich Cabinet composed of several ministers; there was only the Chancellor. All Reich Offices, the equivalents of specialised ministries; emerged successively as off-shoots of the Chancellor's Office. The heads of these departments were state secretaries who were subject to the Chancellor's directives.

Unlike the other three constitutional documents reprinted below, Bismarck's Constitution does not contain a catalogue of basic rights. Hermann Wagener, a Conservative deputy and Counsellor in the Prussian Ministry of State, could barely conceal his delight with this omission when he spoke during the general debate in the North German Parliament:

> Where one is used to find basic rights, clauses on railways and telecommunications can now be found; and where otherwise one looked for human rights, we can now look up references to cheap transport of coal

and cereals to be used as relief in case of an impending national calamity. That's all very mundane and very sober. But, Gentlemen, it is just because it is so mundane and sober that we hold high hopes that this sober prose will at last become reality. At last, Gentlemen, we are relieved of the fixation on theory and empty phrases; at last we have been moved onto a ground where facts and realities count.

It is difficult to demonstrate more drastically than through this statement just how much the spirit of the age had changed since 1848. The Romantic Age of Revolutions had come to an end. The epoch of the men of action had begun.

This was also one of the reasons why the Reich Constitution, unlike the constitutions of the German states, did not grant basic rights. There was, on the one hand, the pragmatic realism of Bismarck, who gave a higher priority to political organisation than to the formulation of a value system. His abstinence was also due, however, to the fact that he always bore in mind the rights and sensibilities of the individual states. The implicit argument ran as follows: basic rights are designed to protect the citizen against the interventions of state authority. However, at the time of the founding of the Empire, the power of such interventions had been left to the individual states. Basic rights as instruments to counter interventions therefore logically seemed to be part of the state constitution. To incorporate basic rights into the Reich Constitution might have been interpreted as an attack on the autonomy of the individual states.

These arguments may still have been defensible at the time of the founding of the German Empire. Soon, however, the Reich began to take over more and more tasks and powers of intervention, and there was hence an increasing justification for criticising the omission of a catalogue of basic rights from the Constitution. To be sure, such basic rights do not have to take the form of written norms. England, where the idea of basic rights originated, but which does not have a written constitution, would in that case not have any. As time went by, the Reich therefore also created a number of norms relating to basic rights by simple legislation. The protection of property, freedom of trade, freedom of movement, of association and of religion may be mentioned here. There was also the ban on the retrospective application of criminal codes, the privacy of letters, press freedom, the independence of the courts and the freedom of assembly. Thus the bulk of the classic basic rights found its way into ordinary Reich codes. Although these codes were not protected in the same way as they would have been in a catalogue of basic rights in the Constitution, they were nevertheless important for legal practice. It must also be remembered that under Art. 78 of the 1871 Constitution simple majorities were sufficient for constitutional amendments. In the Bundesrat by contrast at least forty-five out of fifty-eight votes were required for such amendments.

There are two famous instances when Bismarck interfered with basic rights in a major way: the *Kulturkampf* (his struggle against political Catholicism) and the proscription of the Socialists. Both measures took the form of legislation. This implies that as early as the 1870s the Reich government, though nominated by the monarch, was dependent on the support of the majority in Parliament and of public opinion, if basic rights were to be set aside. But these cases also represented early examples of legalised injustice, as the eminent lawyer Gustav Radbruch later put it.

Power was distributed in many different ways in Imperial Germany. With the passage of time, gains were made by the military and the bureaucracy, on the one hand, and by the assemblies, on the other. These assemblies and the Reichstag in particular participated in decision-making and this also implied an increased role for the political parties. Even 'enemies of the state', as the Social Democrats tended to be viewed, were not totally excluded from wielding influence. The SPD increasingly worried those in positions of power as it began to win more and more seats. In 1871, the Social Democrats had two deputies in the Reichstag; by 1912 they had become the largest party in the national assembly. This growth was helpful when it came to identifying social injustices and occasionally it even forced the government and the other parties into action. Thus Germany's examplary social insurance system is more a product of Bismarck's fear of the socialists than of pure Christian love.

As long as external peace prevailed, the majority of people were happy with the monarchy. The ruling princes and the aristocracy, it is true, had not lost their former positions of power and influence completely. The military remained an unchecked state within the state. The bureaucracy grew and augmented its influence. But the bourgeoisie gained satisfaction through economic success and a share in power which was reflected in its position in the legislative process. A feeling of exuberant patriotism veiled existing inadequacies and above all the authoritarian character of the German Empire. The monarchy tried persistently to stem the tide of a

modern political development which other Western nations experienced. And last but not least there was the unresolved Social
Question.

By the turn of the century things had gone so far that the
bourgeoisie, successful and proud of the nation's achievements as
it was, had begun to feel ashamed of the Revolution which its
forebears had staged in 1848. Good Germans did not make revolutions. In 1897 the son of Robert Blum, who after all had died
before the firing squad in Vienna in November 1848, published a
comprehensive analysis of the 1848 Revolution. In it he depicted
the events of March 1848 in Berlin as an irresponsible act by
French, Polish, Communist and Jewish agitators who had come to
Berlin in order to stir up trouble. The wire-pullers of the Berlin
events, he wrote, had been the 'scum' of the Revolution, 'in which
solid and enthusiastic workers, students and burghers thought to
sacrifice their blood for the highest ideals of humanity'.

It was only in July and August 1914, when the First World War
broke out, that it became clear where the decisive power of
decision-making lay in Germany. The state of war was proclaimed
in accordance with Art. 68 of the Constitution. Thenceforth
executive power was in the hands of the regional military commanders who were subordinate to the Kaiser. The military took the
view that all political decisions had an impact on the conduct of the
war and accordingly they persuaded the Kaiser to assert the primacy of military considerations over those of politics. Later actual
power fell into the hands of the Army High Command under Field
Marshal Paul von Hindenburg and his Quartermaster-General Erich
Ludendorff. For a long time the middle classes continued to adhere
to the national consensus of 1914 and, expecting final victory over
all of Germany's enemies, repressed all the disconcerting aspects
of the Hindenburg–Ludendorff dictatorship. It was only when they
were faced with defeat and hence with the natural collapse of their
power position that the military transformed Germany into a parliamentary monarchy through a 'revolution from above'. But this
move came too late and was motivated primarily by Ludendorff's
desire to put the responsibility for the catastrophe on the shoulders
of the democrats.

The nationalist idea had paved the way for the creation of the
German Empire. The exaltation of this idea after the turn of the
century turned out to be the grave-digger of that Empire.

The Weimar Constitution

The 1918 Revolution began in September of that year with a 'revolution from above' which had been unleashed by the Army High Command. Once it became clear that defeat was unavoidable, Ludendorff sought salvation in pressing for an immediate armistice. Obtaining an armistice seemed possible only if the request came from a government which had a parliamentary–democratic legitimation. The US President Woodrow Wilson, in particular, did not think much of entering into negotiations with a Germany which was ruled by a military dictatorship. Finally Ludendorff also thought it appropriate that not the Army, but its opponents in the Reichstag — Social Democrats, Left Liberals and Catholics — should shoulder the humiliating task of suing for peace and asking for lenient treatment by the Allies.

It was through these manoeuvres that Germany was given a government based on the support of a centre-left majority in the Reichstag and led by Prince Max von Baden, a liberal. But the constitutional change came too late to stave off a 'revolution from below'. Faced with mass demonstrations and revolutionary upheavals, Prince Max in turn handed over to Friedrich Ebert, the chairman of the Majority Socialists, on 9 November 1918. It may have been a constitutional impossibility for the Reich Chancellor to nominate his own successor; but things were in a general state of confusion in Berlin during those November days. Thus the abdication of the Kaiser was proclaimed without William II actually having abdicated. It was therefore fitting that Germany should have, on this fateful day, a Social Democratic Reich Chancellor who believed in a parliamentary monarchy and who issued a public statement urging the population to stop milling through the streets and to re-establish law and order.

In the meantime the revolutionary tide had swept through Germany. First there had been a meeting by sailors on the German battle-fleet at Wilhelmshaven who refused to leave port for a final do-or-die battle with the British Royal Navy. When the ships were sent to Kiel, the sailors went ashore and unleashed mass demonstrations in the city. The revolt turned into a Revolution which quickly spread to other parts of Germany.

Between 4 November and 10 November the western parts of the country were taken by the tide and the former military authorities were toppled. The soldiers and workers who were the mainstay of this revolution were above all anti-militarist, but were content with tearing their officers' insignia from their lapels and with establishing workers' and soldiers' councils to replace the regional military commanders. These councils tried to keep the local administration going and to restore order. There was hence little bloodshed. The Revolution was passionate, but relatively good-natured; its protagonists freed political prisoners and were surprised at their swift initial success.

Thus on 9 November 1918 the dynamism of the 'revolution from below' caught up with, and overtook, the earlier 'revolution from above'. Ebert, the SPD Chairman, stood at the hub of both revolutions. From 2 p.m. on 9 November he occupied the position of Reich Chancellor. At the same time he saw himself confronted with the task of assuming the leadership of the Revolutionaries who had taken to the streets and who, in their heart of hearts, saw themselves as Majority Socialists. It was a difficult choice for Ebert. A skilled craftsman and master saddler, he was a man who loved order, discipline and peace; he hated revolution like sin. It was by these principles that he had worked in his professional life; it was also in this sense that he perceived his chairmanship of the SPD. He and his Party, he believed, had already reached their goal with the implementation of the October reforms. The old demands had been fulfilled: Germany had a government which was responsible to the Reichstag and the Prussian three-class voting system had been abolished. On 9 November he himself had been made Reich Chancellor! What more could he wish for? He had never had any fundamental objections to a monarchical constitution. On the contrary, he was a conservative reformist at heart. On 9 November Prince Max had proclaimed the abdication of the Kaiser without being authorised to do so. In the afternoon of that day, Ebert urged him to remain as Regent in Berlin. Prince Max refused.

Meanwhile hundreds of thousands of demonstrators were converging on the Reichstag building in which Ebert and Philipp Scheidemann, the deputy leader of the SPD, had gathered. The demonstrators shouted: 'Down with the war! Down with the

(opposite)
Philipp Scheidemann proclaiming the Republic
from a window of the Reichstag building on 9 November 1918

Emperor! Hurrah for the Republic!' The masses, most of whom were supporters and voters of the SPD, expected, not without some justification, that Ebert would address them. But Ebert declined, whereupon his deputy did what at this point was the inevitable: spontaneously, he opened one of the windows of the Reichstag building and said to a jubilant crowd: 'Long live the German Republic!'

Reluctantly Ebert now assumed the leadership of the Revolution in his capacity as SPD Chairman. He had not desired this Revolution and would have liked, above all, to end it. But first Reich Chancellor Ebert became the People's Deputy Ebert who, together with Hugo Haase, the leader of the Independent Socialists, assumed the chairmanship of the 'Council of People's Deputies'. This Council was subsequently recognised as the central authority of the Reich by the Workers' and Soldiers' Councils which had emerged in Berlin and other parts of the country. On 12 November the Council of People's Deputies published a proclamation 'to the German People' which, in brief form, contained a number of civil liberties and social rights. Moreover it spoke of a Constituent Assembly shortly to be elected.

There was something peculiar about this German revolution. A revolutionary, pacifist and republican mass movement had, within four days, gained power throughout the country; at the same time it had given a leadership mandate to a man who hated the Revolution and who was on good terms with the representatives of the Imperial Army, bureaucracy and judiciary. Ebert became a revolutionary leader because he preferred law and order and wanted to prevent worse from happening. He was haunted by the course of the 1917 Russian Revolution, which had ended in the victory of the Bolsheviks. The representatives of the monarchical state among the traditional elites, whom he saved from total downfall, never showed any gratitude for this. As soon as the immediate danger receded, they propagated the legend of the 'stab in the back' and turned Ebert and his fellow Social Democrats into 'November criminals' who were accused of having unleashed the Revolution. Ultimately, by continuing to spread such malicious rumours and by casting doubt on his honour they contributed to his early death in 1925.

The decision concerning the political and constitutional future of Germany was made during 16 to 19 December 1918, when the Councils from all over Germany held a congress at Berlin. It was at this congress that two divergent concepts of political organisation

Friedrich Ebert

clashed. Was Germany to be run on the basis of a republic of councils or a parliamentary democracy?

The Majority Socialists took the view that the Councils had fulfilled their task of securing law and order during the revolutionary phase. They were now to give way to a National Assembly so that a new Reich Constitution could be drawn up in accordance with the free will of the entire nation. As to socialist ideas, only as many were to be realised as a popular majority was prepared to carry through. A socialist programme which had been forced through against the will of the majority would lack a firm basis for the future.

The groups to the left of the SPD countered this position by proposing the establishment of a system of Councils. Thus the Independent Socialist Ernst Daumig put the following motion: (1) The meeting of delegates declares that the council system is to be maintained at all costs as the basis of the constitution of the Socialist Republic; this is to take the form that the councils hold the highest legislative and executive power. (2) The meeting of delegates mandates a commission to work out, without delay, a generally applicable electoral system for the election of the councils of workers, soldiers and peasants in Germany. (3) On the basis of this electoral law, elections are to be held for a national congress of workers' and soldiers' councils, which will decide on the future constitution. (4) As long as no final constitution of the Socialist Republic has been decided upon, a Central Council of fifty-three members, to be chosen from all parts of Germany, will be the highest controlling body of the Council of People's Deputies and of the Reich Offices.

On 19 December the congress, which was dominated by the SPD by something like a 60 per cent majority, approved a Social Democratic motion to hold elections for a National Assembly on 19 January 1919. Ultimately the great majority of delegates — 344:98 votes — opted against the introduction of a council system.

Elections for the National Assembly duly took place on 19 January. The electoral law provided for a universal, equal, secret and direct ballot for all men and women aged twenty and above. For the first time a new system of proportional representation was in operation which resulted in the following percentages:

SPD	37.9
Catholic Centre	19.7
Left Liberals (DDP)	18.6
Nationalists (DNVP)	10.3
Indep. Socialists	7.6
People's Party (DVP)	4.1
Others	1.6

This meant that the population voted by a clear majority against a socialist republic. Had there not been a female suffrage, the SPD could have gained the absolute majority. But the majority of women showed no gratitude to the SPD for having been enfranchised by the Social Democrats. Nevertheless, the SPD was pleased with the result. There was no question of a socialist republic being established in conjunction with the Independent Socialists with whom the Social Democrats were now at loggerheads. For the SPD the most desirable solution was a return to a coalition with the Centre Party and the Left Liberals, such as had already existed in October 1918 before the outbreak of the Revolution. An alliance of this kind also harmonised with Ebert's feelings. It provided a broad parliamentary majority for the fresh democratic start and it pointed in the direction of compromise and consensus politics when it came to drafting a new Reich Constitution.

The National Assembly gathered for the first time at Weimar on 6 February 1919. The quiet town in Thuringia had been chosen in order to escape the upheavals and the pressures of the Revolution which had vexed Berlin. The choice was also an expression of a desire to revive the memory of the country's cultural heritage. Weimar had been the town of Wieland, Goethe, Herder and Schiller; it was a symbol of intellectual freedom, German humanism and national unity on the basis of culture and morality. It was the town in which Goethe had written his *Faustus* and Schiller had composed his drama *Wilhelm Tell*. It was on such intellectual foundations that the new democratic republic was to be built, rather than in the tradition of the spirit of Potsdam and the Prussian monarchy.

The new Weimar theatre building which had been opened in 1908 in the same place as the *Altes Komödienhaus* (of which Goethe had been the director until 1825) was chosen as the venue. It was renamed *Deutsches Nationaltheater* and now became the stage of the fresh beginning in German parliamentarism.

As People's Deputy, Ebert was the first to speak during the opening session, welcoming the assembled. He extended a particularly cordial welcome to the 'women who appear in the Reich Parliament for the first time on an equal footing'. There were quite a few women, among them Dr Gertrud Bäumer, Marie Juchacz and Helene Weber. Ebert also made clear from the start that 'the Provisional Government owes its mandate to the Revolution; it will [now] put its back into the hands of the National Assembly'.

There followed the Assembly's senior president, the 77-year-old Deputy Pfannkuch who stated: 'The German people is its own master now and holds its own supreme authority. It will now have to pass the great test as to whether it is mature [enough] for a life in liberty or whether it will once more fall under a brutal regime of violence [run] by a minority'. Given that a brutal dictatorship followed some fourteen years later, these words read today like the warnings by the chorus of a Greek tragedy.

Dr Eduard David, a Social Democrat, was elected the first president of the National Assembly. As he became a minister in the new Reich government a few days later, the Centre Party deputy Constantin Fehrenbach was chosen to replace him.

Emulating the ritual adopted by the Frankfurt Parliament in 1848, the Weimar Assembly first instituted a Provisional Reich Authority by passing a law to this effect on 10 February. This emergency constitution referred back to the reforms of October 1918, except that the Kaiser's position, now that a republic had come into existence, was taken by Ebert who was elected Reich President by the Assembly. Government business was looked after by a cabinet which was nominated by the Reich President but was responsible to the National Assembly. From the constitutional point of view the Revolution had thus come to an end. The remnants of the revolutionary movement in Berlin and other cities which decided to resort to violent protests against this outcome were systematically squashed in a bloody civil war which ended in May 1919. This war was waged on behalf of the government by newly-established volunteer units, the Free Corps, whose members were loyal to the monarchist officers in charge of these campaigns.

As a rule the resolutions of parliamentary assemblies tend to be the work either of one person or of a small circle of people who draw up the decisions and secure the necessary majorities in the debating chamber. In this sense, the Weimar Constitution is largely the work of Hugo Preuß, the author of the first draft. Who was he and how did he come to hold such a crucial position at this time?

Born in Berlin on 28 October 1860, Preuß was the son of a merchant and a convinced left-liberal democrat. He was a lawyer by training and also gained his *Habilitation*, a qualification to lecture at a university. But his academic success was not such that he influenced the constitutional theory of the Wilhelmine period. He taught at the Berlin Business School and was never offered a university chair. His publications, often in newspapers and journals,

(Hugo Preuß)

were outside the mainstream of the legal thinking of his time. His work was not marked by a wrestling with philosophical concepts; nor did he describe the status quo in order to secure its substance in perpetuity. Hugo Preuß wrote academic articles which were characterised by political commitment, elegance and the capacity to captivate. Courageously, he moved against the dominant opinions of his age. Next to famous constitutional lawyers of the stature of Paul Leband and Georg Jellinek, Preuß's position might be compared with that of Heinrich Heine among the classic authors of German literature.

His message was invariably that of democracy for which he put up a brave defence. Thus in 1888 he wrote an article commemorating the centenary of the French Revolution and propagandising its intellectual roots: 'A new world view replaces the old; the citizen was aroused in the (former) subject; homo sapiens who thought for himself emerged from his [earlier existence as] a weak-minded object of an almighty state authority'.

Preuß took Karl von Stein as his model and inspiration, that great Prussian reformer during the period of the Napoleonic occupation. He believed that Stein's *Städteordnung* of 1808 which aimed, in essence, at reviving local government in Prussia, represented one of the great democratic departures in Prussian history and hence a treasured legacy. 'Educating the people in the ideas of freedom and self-reliance', he wrote, 'after it has been drilled for centuries and with all available means to accept bondage and dependence, was the task which [Stein's] reforms had set themselves.' Preuß was also strongly influenced by Otto von Gierke's theory of communal cooperatives which he applied to constitutional thought. The city as an entity in public law, he argued, ought to be integrated into the regional authority above it in such a way that it becomes a part of the higher entity without losing its character as a legal entity in its own right'. Today such arguments may seem self-evident; but they were pioneering at a time when the absolute monarch still appeared as the all-powerful counterpart of citizens and city administrations.

What Preuß thought to be the timelessly valid aspect of Stein's reforms was that the city constitution should become the core of a modern self-administering national constitution. Moreover he saw it as the object of Stein's work to bring about 'the political education of the unpolitical population'. Preuß's ideas culminated in the aim of replacing the 'authoritarian state' by a 'people's state'.

What moved Ebert to appoint this liberal democrat state secretary in the midst of a revolutionary upheaval and to ask him to draft a new constitution? After all, in the past Preuß had his tussles with the Social Democrats just as he had quarrelled with the representatives of monarchical authoritarianism. Thus in an article published in 1891 he had called the SPD 'the most dangerous enemy of parliamentarism'. Such earlier views notwithstanding, Ebert saw in Preuß the kind of man he needed in November 1918. He was a constitutional expert and politician; he had shown courage towards opponents from all sides; he represented the political middle ground, but had always fought on the side of the ruled, rather than the rulers. Finally, in 1917 Preuß had worked privately on a draft designed to transform the Bismarckian Constitution into a parliamentary one capable of coping with the changed circumstances of the age. This draft merely had to be pulled out of his pocket. Also, Preuß may have recommended himself to a likeminded Ebert when, in an article in the liberal *Berliner Tageblatt* of 14 November 1918, he criticised the council system as an 'authoritarian state in reverse'.

It is against this background that Preuß became State Secretary for Home Affairs in November 1918 and Reich Minister of the Interior in February 1919. He did not stay for long. The Scheideman Cabinet, of which he was a member, resigned after four months, because the Left Liberals (DDP) refused to support the signing of the Versailles Treaty. When the DDP rejoined the government coalition after a proper delay, times had changed. In the face of ambitious party politicians there was no room left in the Cabinet for a non-partisan expert like Preuß.

The Weimar Constitution was the product of a successful revolution. Undoubtedly, the destruction of the monarchy and the establishment of a democratic republic was a revolutionary achievement. Beyond this, however, there was nothing in the new Constitutional document which did not link up with former institutional arrangements and tendencies and which could not have been achieved in an evolutionary fashion. Thus the National Assembly wished to have next to the Reichstag an institution which was endowed with real powers. This indicates that people wanted to create a certain analogy to the old monarchical head of state. It may not even be too far-fetched to engage in the following speculation: if the Kaiser and his advisers had read the signs of the age correctly before September 1918 and had allowed a man like Hugo Preuß to realise his proposals for a modern monarchical constitution, the Hohenzollerns would probably still hold their

Imperial position, just as the Belgian or British ruling houses do to this day.

The guiding principles of the new constitution were as follows:

(1) At a time when the country is threatened from abroad, national unity, [i.e.] the Reich, is to be preserved in its traditional federal structure.

(2) The rule of law based on liberty is to be completed and secured through guaranteed basic rights, a division of powers and increased protection by the law.

(3) The principle of equality in the sense of an absolute equality of opportunity and a removal of all privileges presupposes that state authority is legitimated from the bottom up: the authoritarian state becomes a people's state.

(4) Within the framework of this equality [postulate] the former class state is to be replaced by a system of social equalisation and social reforms, while avoiding at the same time the emergence of a class dictatorship in reverse: the liberal democratic state is to be capable of developing into a welfare state.

(5) The principles of international law are to become part of the constitution. According to the preamble of the Constitution it is the aim of the [new] state to promote peace among the nations.

The preamble also postulates that the German people should create its own constitution. As Preuß further elaborated: 'The foundation of the entire Weimar Constitution is that this republic is not an association, a league of German states, but that the German state is and shall be the political organisation of the unified German people living within this state'.

Although the Kaiser had disappeared, the new democratic republic continued to call itself 'Reich'. Other titles had been discussed in the Constitutional Committee of the National Assembly, such as 'German Republic' and 'German Federation'. As Dr Cohn, an Independent Socialist deputy, argued, the name itself was to indicate that Germany was a Free State. However, in the end the majority accepted Preuß's proposal to uphold the continuity of the German Reich. He justified this position as follows:

The name 'Reich' is associated with century-old traditions and with the great longing of a splintered German people for national unity; we would, without good reason or purpose, hurt deep-rooted feelings held by very wide circles if we were to deviate from this term, representing as it does a unity which has been hard fought for and which was realised after many disappointments.

Under Art. 2 the federal structure was also retained, albeit with a stronger unitary emphasis. After various territorial reorganisations the Reich finally comprised seventeen states: Prussia, Bavaria, Saxony, Württemberg, Baden, Thuringia, Hesse, Hamburg, Mecklenburg-Schwerin, Oldenburg, Brunswick, Anhalt, Bremen, Lippe, Lübeck, Mecklenburg-Strelitz and Schaumburg-Lippe. However, as further territorial adjustments were expected, the Weimar Constitution does not list these states individually. Such a further reorganisation seemed plausible and Preuß had spoken strongly in its favour. His idea was to hive off from Prussia the territories conquered in the nineteenth century and thus to undermine its overwhelming hegemonic weight. The Reich was to be divided up into larger entities of roughly equal size. In 1918 he produced a memorandum on this question in which he argued that neither culturally nor economically did Prussia form an organic whole. A splitting-up of Prussia would not only give greater equality to the southern German states, but would also allow the smaller states in central and northern Germany to organise themselves into viable communities.

In theory there was much to be said for this solution. But in practice it proved impossible to reduce Prussia to its historically legitimated core. The times simply militated against it, for this was not a period when optimal solutions could be implemented. There was deprivation and revolution at home; no military protection was available along the western frontiers and there was the danger of separatist movements in the Rhineland and on the Saar. In these circumstances it seemed irresponsible to Ebert to do without the well-oiled machinery of the Prussian civil service and police, even temporarily, or to engage in territorial reorganisation experiments. Thus everything remained as it was by force of circumstance, however convincingly Preuß had argued his case for a restructuring of the Reich.

Like the Basic Law of the Federal Republic, the Weimar Constitution also contains a reunification clause (Art. 61). The Reich remains open to union with Austria. As will be remembered, a number of deputies in the Frankfurt Parliament had been advocates of a *großdeutsche* solution (to be inclusive of Austria). They had acquiesced in the *kleindeutsche* solution which finally emerged only because there was no other choice. However, in 1919 when a

fresh democratic start was to be made, Austria was to be included
in the Reich, the more so as she had lost all her former non-
German territories.

As early as 12 November 1918 the new Austrian Republic had
declared itself to be part of the German Republic and Ebert took
up the idea of reunification when he opened the proceedings of
the Weimar Assembly in February 1919. Receiving applause from
all parties, he exclaimed:

> Our brothers, to whom we are linked by ethnicity and common fate, can
> rest assured that we shall welcome them with open arms and hearts in
> the new Reich of the German nation. They belong to us, and we belong
> to them. Perhaps I may also express the expectation that the National
> Assembly will empower a future Reich government to enter into
> negotiations with the German–Austrian Free State about a final union at
> the earliest opportunity. No frontier post shall stand between us there-
> after. We want to be a united people of brothers.

However, the idea failed because of the Allies, although under
the much-vaunted principle of national self-determination unification ought to have been an unobjectionable step. All that remained
therefore was a reunification clause in the Weimar Constitution
which expressly emphasised the right of self-determination.

The Bismarckian Empire had adopted the black–white–red colours, being a combination of the Prussian black–white and the
Brandenburgian white–red. They had symbolised the spirit of Bran-
denburg–Prussia. The Weimar Republic wanted to make a visible
break with this tradition and to proclaim a new political principle
which linked up with the *Vormärz* and the 1848 Revolution.
Speaking before the Constitutional Committee, Preuß put this
point in the following words: 'The black–red–golden colours embody many things that are dear [to us] in the history of our people;
[these are] the colours of the fraternities, [the colours] which are
supposed to represent our unity with Austria'. Meanwhile the
right-wing parties pleaded for a retention of the old colours, while
the radical Left moved to adopt the red flag as the symbol of
socialism. The majority joined Preuß in taking the democratic
middle way. However, when it came to deciding on the flag of the
merchant navy, the Weimar coalition's willingness to compromise
almost reached comic proportions: the old and the new colours
were combined in a special flag (Art. 3).

The first Reich organ to be mentioned in the Weimar Constitution is the Reichstag (Art. 20). The fathers of the Constitution wanted Parliament to be the dominant institution of the political system.

According to Art. 22, all men and women over twenty years of age elected the deputies for four years on the basis of a universal, equal, direct and secret ballot. A new development was the replacement of the former majority principle by a system of proportional representation and election through lists. Moreover the number of votes necessary for obtaining a seat was completely equal. The Bismarckian Empire had been characterised by very marked differences in the size of constituencies. Under the Weimar electoral law 60,000 votes amounted to one constituency seat.

This was a fair procedure. The decision of the voters could not be distorted by the geometry of a constituency or by the retirement of unsuccessful candidates. However, there were drawbacks as well. Thus the existing system interfered with the direct-ballot principle. The voter elected lists of candidates whose selection he could not influence. It is not possible for him to vote for his local constituency candidate. As a result the principles of representation and of independence (Art. 21) were being threatened. Another disadvantage of proportional representation is that it promotes a multi-party system with splinter groups and a constant pressure to form coalition governments.

The Weimar Constitution upheld the principle, established in 1906, of paying the deputies (Art. 40). In 1930 the total sum per deputy was 600 marks, a relatively small amount.

There were a number of powers indicating that the Reichstag was meant to be the power centre in the new democratic state. These were:

(1) For the first time and unlike the solutions found in 1848 and 1871 the Reichstag determined the length of its annual parliamentary sessions.

(2) According to Art. 68, the Reichstag is the central legislative organ. However, the Reichsrat participated in legislation. Under Art. 69 it had the right to initiate legislation and to voice objections (Art. 74). This gave the Reichsrat a strong position which could only be over-ruled by a two-thirds Reichstag majority or by a plebiscite. In accordance with Art. 73 laws could also be approved by plebiscite although in practice no bill ever reached the statute book by this route.

(3) The Reichstag had a co-determining influence upon the

executive. Reich Chancellor and Reich ministers had to have the confidence of Parliament (Art. 54). It can also sue the Reich President and members of the Cabinet before the State Court (Art. 59).

It is one of the tragedies of the Weimar Constitution that what it tried to achieve as the norm frequently proved unrealisable in practice. Indeed, on occasion constitutional practice turned out to be the opposite of what the text envisaged. Thus the Reichstag was to be the central institution of the Reich. However, other clauses of the Constitution tended to weaken this central position in a way which was to prove fateful later on. These clauses were those on proportional representation and the fragmentation of the party spectrum, the strong position of the Reich President, who was endowed with emergency powers under Art. 48 and had the right to dissolve Parliament (Art. 25), the weighty position of the Reichsrat and the possibility of holding a plebiscite. Consequently, no Weimar Reichstag ever saw the end of its alloted four-year term. Elections were always called prematurely.

According to Art. 41, the Reich Presidency was the second major institution of the Weimar Republic. Its incumbent was elected directly by the entire voting population. Partly because of this legitimation and partly because of the powers with which the office was endowed, the Reich President had a very strong constitutional position.

Preuß himself had developed the idea of juxtaposing the Reichstag with a strong presidency. Max Weber, the famous sociologist, who had given Preuß a hand with his draft, even advocated creating a 'plebiscitary dictator of the masses'. Such notions were discussed quite widely at the time among constitutional lawyers. It was not so much that they were looking for an *Ersatzkaiser*, but rather that they adhered to Montesquieu's postulate of the division of powers, according to which parliamentarians themselves were fearful of being all-powerful. As Dr Ablaß, the rapporteur of the Constitutional Committee, put it: 'Both institutions, i.e. Parliament . . . and President, originate from the same source [of legitimacy]: the undiluted will of the people. [The dualism] guarantees that if the will of one of these two peak offices errs in some [wrong] direction, the other [office] has the chance to correct [this mistake]'.

Thus the President was to embody the democratic principle by virtue of his being popularly elected and of this office being open to all citizens. At the same time, however, the democratic presidency, like the Hohenzollern emperor, was to symbolise the unity

The Reichstag Building in Berlin

of the Reich; its incumbent was to be the guardian of the interests of the nation as a whole who stood above the parties; and, in an emergency, he was to be the saviour, which is why he was endowed with wide powers and, because of his popular e.ection, was independent of the Reichstag.

Critics of the Weimar Constitution have often pointed out that the President occupied the position of *Ersatzkaiser* or acted as a regent for the Hohenzollern monarchy. This criticism is a travesty of the actual intentions of the fathers of the Constitution. Not for one moment did they mourn the Kaiser's departure. However, neither did they wish to create a power vacuum at the very top of the state machinery. It is also worth mentioning that the figure of the President became a bulwark against attempts to bring back the monarchy.

According to Art. 75, the Reich President represented the country in international law. He also had the right to nominate and to dismiss the Chancellor and individual Reich ministers (Art. 53), without the involvement of the Reichstag in either a proposing or a consultative capacity. There existed an unwritten rule that he could take the chair at Cabinet meetings. According to Art. 25, he was empowered to dissolve the Reichstag and was hence in a position to force fresh elections at any time. Moreover, under Art. 73 he could suspend legislation passed by Parliament and submit it to a plebiscite. The President was the supreme commander of the armed forces (Art. 47). Under Art. 48 he had wide-ranging emergency powers and could order the Reichswehr to bring a dissident Federal state to heel. Finally, he appointed and dismissed Reich civil servants and officers. His term of office was unusually long, i.e. seven years (Art. 43).

All these privileges, together with his legitimation through a popular vote, gave the President an extremely strong position. Given that the Weimar Republic experienced an almost permanent emergency situation, these constitutional realities further augmented his power, and if the Constitution had intended the President to be a saviour in an euphemeral crisis, the later development of the Republic cast him in this role in perpetuity. In particular, the application of Art. 48, which provided him with dictatorial powers, came to be based on an extraordinarily extensive interpretation of this clause. A threat to public order and security was assumed to exist in the case of economic, financial or social exigencies of all kinds. In this way and for several years in succession, many cases arose in which legislation via the normal parliamentary channels was replaced by emergency decrees issued by the President under Art. 48. The institution which the National Assembly had invented as a check on their own democratic omnipotence grew, in fact, into the superior executive and legislative power of the Weimar period, while the Reichstag lapsed into increasing powerlessness.

Today it is generally accepted that the shaping of the President's position in the Constitution had a disastrous effect on the history of the Weimar Republic. The lessons learned from this were later incorporated into the Basic Law of the Federal Republic.

This was the constitutional background against which, in 1925, the German people elected as President the 76-year-old Paul von Hindenburg, a former Imperial Field Marshal, and re-elected him in 1932. Hindenburg, who remained a monarchist at heart, saw himself as a former Prussian officer to whom politics remained rather a sordid and strange business. Thus it was he who, by then even more tottering than in 1925, appointed Adolf Hitler Reich Chancellor on 30 January 1933.

According to Art. 52, the Reich government consisted of the Chancellor and the Reich ministers. It was a collegiate body in which the Chancellor sat as *primus inter pares*. He also determined the broad guidelines of policy; it was within these guidelines that the ministers led the departments entrusted to them.

The Reich Chancellor was appointed and dismissed by the Reich President and so were the ministers at the Chancellor's suggestion (Art. 56). Moreover, they required the Reichstag's vote of confidence and were obliged to resign if Parliament withdrew its confidence from them (Art. 54).

This dual dependence of the Cabinet on both the President's and the Reichstag's confidence proved to be an unfortunate solution in the light of Weimar political practice. It impeded the formation of cabinets and made government virtually impossible at a time when a strong executive was urgently required. Moreover, apart from his right to select the Chancellor, the President could also influence the guidelines of cabinet policy. Finally, in practice the Chancellors who were supposed to set these guidelines were not the pace-setters of their cabinets; with a multi-party system which required the formation of coalition governments in order to obtain parliamentary majorities, Chancellors found themselves in the position of conciliators and mediators in constant crises between the Coalition parties. It was possible to topple the government simply by finding a 'negative' majority ('destructive vote of no-confidence') so that occasionally even Nazis and Communists could be seen to vote together in order to help bring down a Cabinet. In this way, the Weimar Republic had twenty different governments in the course of its fourteen years of existence. During its final years, the Republic was increasingly a democracy which lacked democratic support. From September 1930 onwards the balance of seats was such that it became impossible to form cabinets which would not have had to include parties fundamentally hostile to the existing constitutional order.

According to Art. 60, the Reichsrat was the representation of the States in matters of legislation and administration. Votes in the Reichsrat were distributed proportionally to the respective populations, but there was an upper and a lower ceiling (Art. 61). Thus the largest State could not have more than two-fifths of the total votes and this was clearly directed against Prussia, which comprised more than three-fifths of Germany's population and hence would have had an absolute majority had it not been for this clause. Moreover, under Art. 63, Prussia was obliged to pass a law stipulating that half of the Prussian votes came from the State's provincial administrations, thereby securing an influence for those parts of

Prussia which had been added in the nineteenth century. In fact there were occasions when the Prussian votes, coming as they did from different parts of the State, cancelled each other out. Nevertheless, the two-fifths rule and this stipulation were the only two elements left of Preuß's idea to reduce Prussian hegemony.

All in all, the powers of the Reichsrat were limited. It could initiate legislation and raise objections to Reichstag bills. But it was not a second chamber; rather its position was comparable to that of the Bündesrat of the Federal Republic.

Articles 109 to 165 of the Weimar Constitution contain an extensive catalogue of 'basic rights and basic obligations of the Germans'. Originally Preuß had been hesitant about including a section on basic rights in his draft. He felt that the historical significance of such a catalogue had diminished in a modern democratic state, since it had originally been conceived as a list of defensive rights against absolutist monarchical power. Nevertheless he was persuaded to include a few fundamental rights because 'a section of this kind . . . should not be missed out as a profession of the general guidelines of the constitutional developments'. In other words, he saw it as a somewhat empty gesture in order to honour the achievements of the movements for emancipation of earlier times.

Dr Friedrich Naumann, a liberal and the rapporteur of the Constitutional Committee was not at all happy with this. Here the liberal academic Preuß encountered the liberal thoroughbred politician Naumann. Naumann criticised the draft for treating the basic rights contained in it like antiquated tomb stones and as museum pieces of an earlier legal culture. Moreover, as incorporated they were not comprehensible to ordinary citizens and out of line with recent developments in political culture. Accordingly Naumann produced an alternative draft in popular language which has since been called a 'people's catechism with catchword-like formulations'. Here are a few examples for Naumann's catalogue:

The preservation of the nation is the *raison d'être* of the State; demographic growth means national strength.
The Fatherland stands above party loyalty. Unity and legality and liberty are a German's Fatherland.
Order and liberty are siblings.
Green light for the fit and able.
Labour power is the uppermost human good. The State has the permanent task to implement the right to work. He who does

not want to work, shall not eat.

The national economy stands above the private economy.

The forest is to be maintained.[!]

Industrial parliamentarism is the natural concomitant of the democratic industrial state.

Nationalisation is a question of utility.

We live in the age of transport. Global transport is *joie de vivre*.

There is to be no more secret diplomacy.

We respect all nations who respect us.

While this may have been a fascinating collection of political aphorisms, Naumann's slogans were not to the liking of the constitutional lawyers. In their view his proposals were a credit to his 'literary taste and patriotic sentiments'; however, they were not thought to be appropriate for a 'codification of basic rights and obligations', as the DNVP deputy Düringer put it in the plenary session. So all of Naumann's most original political ideas were left out and the second main section was put into a form acceptable to the lawyers by Professor Konrad Beyerle, a deputy of the Bavarian People's Party (BVP). He was a legal historian and taught at Munich University.

In the first place, the catalogue of basic rights of the Weimar Constitution is taken essentially from the 1849 constitutional documents. However, given the situation of 1919, the bourgeois deputies inevitably saw this catalogue in a somewhat different light to that of their predecessors of 1848. Many now aimed to build legal dams against all left-wing attempts at revolutionary change. Thus Düringer, speaking in the Constitutional Committee, put the problem as follows: 'I stress the sentence: "Property is inviolable". This sentence has a great significance, particularly at this moment. It is of immediate significance, for example, in connection with the nationalisation question'.

Apart from basic rights, the Weimar Constitution also lays down basic obligations. This was another of Naumann's ideas and is an expression of a novel concept of the democratic state.

The third novel idea relating to the catalogue of basic rights concerns the inclusion of social rights in addition to civil rights. Again Naumann put the point succinctly when he spoke before the Constitutional Committee:

Let us not forget that also in those parties which do not call themselves socialist [similar] questions are being raised; [indeed] the entire nation is, optimistically or fearfully, preoccupied with the problem: What is the State going to say, not to the problems of 1848, but to those of today? . . . What could emerge from the attempt to create constitutional rights in the social sphere is, it appears [to me], a kind of peace based on a reconciliation between capitalism and socialism.

The fruits of this historical compromise, upon which German society rests to this day, were such codes and programmatic declarations as may be found below in Art. 119, 121, 122, 145, 153, 155, 156, 159, 163, 165.

Most of the basic rights of the Weimar Constitution were subject to the possibility of future legislation. They could be limited by simple legislation, and in this sense their protection by the Constitution was qualified. There was also the wide-ranging dictatorial powers encapsulated in Art. 48. Finally it should be pointed out that, in accordance with Art. 76, the basic rights could be changed, albeit by a two-thirds majority. In this sense they were subject to a value relativism. The Weimar Constitution did not establish a catalogue of fundamental norms which were immutable.

There are many factors which explain the failure of the Weimar Republic. To begin with, initial conditions for German democracy were very poor. The Bismarckian Empire of 1871 had emerged from a splendid military victory and had led to rising prosperity. The Weimar Republic was born from a humiliating defeat and amid desperation and mass misery. The reactionary legend of the 'stab in the back' helped to discredit the Republic. By many citizens 'Weimar' was made responsible for what was really the depressing legacy of the Hohenzollern monarchy.

The Western Allies — caught no less by a nationalist myopia than the Germans — made it difficult for the young Republic to develop when they presented it with the Versailles Treaty. According to that Treaty reparation payments would have been due up to the 1980s.

It was also to prove fateful that revolutionaries and Republicans refrained from introducing any changes of personnel in the Army, the administration and the judiciary. The Republic therefore had to rely upon soldiers, civil servants and judges, most of whom bemoaned the disappearance of the monarchy and tacitly despised the Republic. How, in such circumstances, was that reeducation in democracy to succeed which Preuß, following von Stein, had recognised as being essential for a fresh start? As early as during the first Reichstag elections of 6 June 1920, the so-called Weimar Coalition of parties who were absolutely loyal to the Constitution lost the majority gained in the 1919 elections for the National Assembly.

Further reasons for failure were the experience of hyper-inflation and of the 1923 currency reform, both of which impoverished the middle classes and made them amenable to radicalism. From 1929 onwards Germany was hit by the Great Slump which ultimately resulted in some six million unemployed. Some 18 million people had to rely on inadequate social security payments and thus became more receptive to extremist slogans.

The split between Social Democrats and Communists ultimately also emaciated the labour movement as a pillar of Republicanism.

If all these factors are taken together, little room is left for posing the question as to what was the Constitution's share in the downfall of the Republic. It would be over-estimating the significance of constitutions if they are to be made responsible for political developments which undoubtedly stem from political and economic conditions. Hence it is not possible to sustain the argument that the Weimar Constitution failed the Germans. In more normal times a durable democracy could have been established on its foundations, which would have compared not unfavourably with the democratic systems of the West.

Adolf Hitler demonstrated very impressively how little political importance he attached to constitutional law: so little was he bothered by the Weimar Constitution that he did not even see the need to abolish or change it. Formally that Constitution remained in force even during the Nazi dictatorship.

Weimar, whose spirit had pervaded the National Assembly, was one of the first towns to succumb to the new barbarism. In 1926 Hitler held his first Party Rally there. In 1930 the Nazis entered the Thuringian government. From 1932 onwards they controlled the State of Thuringia on their own. In 1937 the Nazis established Buchenwald concentration camp, in which some 240,000 people were tortured and some 56,000 of them murdered; it was no more than a few miles from the town of the German Classical period.

The Basic Law
of the Federal Republic of Germany

Looking back on the Nazi period, it was the German people who
had failed in 1933, rather than the Weimar Constitution, and the
concept of failure would appear to be more appropriate in this
respect than the notion of guilt. The penalties for this failure were
heavy. What the 1848ers had fought for in the 1848 Revolution
and thereafter was lost. The German people lost their freedom,
their national unity, their daily sustenance and their international
reputation.

Many millions of people had been killed. Among them were
over five million Germans, but more than twenty million Russians.
Poland had lost some 20 per cent of its population and there had
been the murder of millions of Jews from all over Europe. The
atrocities inside and outside the camps had destroyed the moral
self-confidence of the Germans and undermined Germany's reputation in the eyes of the world. Allied bombing had flattened many of
the country's cities. Millions of refugees were trekking westwards,
exacerbating the general crisis.

The end of the war was tantamount to the collapse of state
authority at all levels of administration from the centre downwards.
Germany was no more than a geographical concept — whatever
may have become of it as a legal entity. Unconditional surrender
on 8 May 1945 turned the country into a mere object of Allied
policy. Allied troops occupied its remotest regions. The Control
Council took over supreme power in Germany; on it the supreme
commanders of the four occupying powers had equal representation.

The country suffered territorial losses both in the east and in the
west and the rest was divided into four zones of occupation. The
capital city of Berlin was split up into four sectors. The political
aims proclaimed by the Allies were the de-militarisation, de-
Nazification and re-education of the German people. Under various reparations plans parts of German industrial plant and machinery were to be dismantled.

The opposition between the Allies and Germany during the
Second World War and in the period immediately thereafter soon
came to be overlaid by a new antagonism: the East–West Conflict

and the Cold War between the Soviet Union and the West. Germany became both the beneficiary and the victim of this division of the world. She benefited in the sense that she was released, more quickly than had been thought possible in May 1945, from her role of a vanquished and politically disenfranchised country obliged to pay reparations. She became a victim because the Cold War division of the world drew a frontier which ran through the middle of Germany and thus turned the idea of national unity into a distant dream.

The principles which the Allies pursued when they began to re-educate the Germans and to organise a new administration resembled those of the Augsburg Peace of 1648: *cujus regio, ejus religio* (whoever rules, also determines the religious denomination of the inhabitants). The Soviet Union installed the Communist Party (KPD), following its forced merger with the East German Social Democrats in April 1946, as the absolutely dominant political force. Through land reforms, large-scale expropriations in industry and commerce and far-reaching interventions into the educational system and the civil service the Russians created conditions similar to those existing in the Soviet Union. Meanwhile the Western Allies promoted their ideas of democratic government in their zones of occupation and created the preconditions for the establishment of a liberal–capitalist economic system.

The fresh democratic start in the Western zones took very much the form which Hugo Preuß had propagated and desired a half-century or so earlier. The re-establishment of self-administration started from below in the towns and local councils. Here the Allies appointed burgomasters with a democratic record and free elections were held as early as January 1946. About a year later democratic institutions were created at *Land* (State) level. As first proposed by Preuß, the State of Prussia was dissolved. There emerged new *Länder* which, though they had no historical cohesion, nevertheless proved remarkably viable. Diets were elected in these States from the autumn of 1946 onwards and from these emerged democratically legitimated governments. It was solely on the basis of these functioning systems of self-government that the Federal Republic of Germany was built in 1948–9. In other words, the Federal Republic arose from the *Länder* of the Western zones of occupation; it was not shaped by the nation as a whole – or rather: the Western parts of that nation.

In 1946 the US Secretary of State, James Byrnes, seized the

initiative for intensified inter-zonal cooperation and self-administration. His move was propelled by the East–West Conflict as well as by economic pressures and led ultimately to the creation of the Bizone which combined the British and American zones. The American attitude was summed up by Byrnes at the end of his famous speech at Stuttgart on 6 September 1946 when he stated:

> The United States cannot relieve Germany from the hardships inflicted upon her by the war her leaders started. But the United States has no desire to increase those hardships or to deny the German people an opportunity to work their way out of those hardships so long as they respect human freedom and follow the paths of peace.
>
> The American people want to return the government of Germany to the German people. The American people want to help the German people to win their way back to an honorable place among the free and peace-loving nations of the world.*

The Bizone came into operation on 1 January 1947 and facilitated economic cooperation between the British and the American authorities. In June 1947 a central administration for the two zones was established at Frankfurt am Main. The *Verwaltung für Wirtschaft* was given a parliamentary underpinning, the *Wirtschaftsrat*, which was composed of delegates from the Diets of the eight participating *Länder*. Finally a joint bizonal supreme court was set up at Cologne. These were cornerstones upon which a new German central authority could be built.

The three Western zones of occupation were also included in the Marshall Plan aid programme, first announced by the US Secretary of State, George F. Marshall, in June 1947. This reinforced the need for an inter-zonal cooperation of all three economic administrations. The London Conference of the three Western Allies and a subsequent meeting of the Benelux countries cleared the way for the establishment of a West German state. As the recommendation of the London Conference put it, the Germans were to be given an opportunity eventually to regain national unity on the basis of free and democratic government. Meanwhile a constituent assembly was to prepare the way for the creation of a West German state. The population of the three Western zones was to approve, through a ballot, the constitution which the assembly was supposed to draw up.

* Quoted in US Department of State, *Documents on Germany, 1945–1985*, Washington, 1986, p. 99.

The currency reform of 21 June 1948 and the subsequent Soviet blockade of Berlin contributed to moving developments in the direction of a West German state and to reducing the gap between victors and vanquished in the Western zones of occupation.

The minister-presidents of the *Länder* took up the proposals of the London Conference. But they added the following rider: in order to stress the provisional character of the founding of a West German state, a 'Parliamentary Council' rather than a Constituent Assembly was to be elected. The document to be drafted by this Council was to be called 'Basic Law' rather than 'Constitution'. The minister-presidents also rejected the idea of submitting this Basic Law to a plebiscite. They did not wish to give 'a weight to the Basic Law with which only a definitive constitution is to be endowed'. Before the Parliamentary Council assembled a conference of experts was held at Herrenchiemsee in Bavaria on 10 August 1948. Each *Land* sent two delegates. They met for two weeks, discussed all essential questions of the proposed Basic Law and put together a first draft on the basis of which the Parliamentary Council later began its deliberations.

Bonn had been selected to be the seat of the Council by the minister-presidents even while the Herrenchiemsee meeting was going on. Other cities applied to be considered — Celle, Düsseldorf, Frankfurt, Karlsruhe, Koblenz and Cologne. But Bonn without doubt embodied best the provisional character of this first start.

The *Länder* diets elected a total of seventy delegates for the Parliamentary Council. Five of them came from Berlin, but did not have voting rights because of reservations voiced by the Western Allies. The two large parties, the SPD and the Christian Democrats (CDU, together with its Bavarian sister party, the CSU) sent twenty-seven delegates each. The Liberals (FDP) were represented with five members followed by the German Party (DP), the Communists (KPD) and the Centre Party with two members each. Three of the Berlin representatives were Social Democrats, with one each from the CDU and the FDP. Wartime destruction did not make it easy to find a representative building for such a venerable assembly. The only possible choice was the Museum Koenig, which had been spared from major bomb damage. The name was taken from its founder and benefactor, Alexander Koenig (1858–1940), a very wealthy man who had been a great huntsman and collector. It was for his zoological collections that he had built this museum.

Konrad Adenauer, the president of the Parliamentary Council, during the final vote for the ratification of the Basic Law on 8 May 1949

On 1 September 1948 the Parliamentary Council gathered in the glass-covered inner quadrangle of the museum, normally reserved for large stuffed animals. Dr Konrad Adenauer, the chairman of the CDU in the British Zone, was elected president of the Council. Professor Carlo Schmid (SPD) was made chairman of the 21-member Main Committee. Schmid was Justice Minister in the *Land* of Württemberg-Hohenzollern.

The debates proved difficult and slow-moving, above all because the Council did not possess legislative sovereignty. The Allied Military Governors were in the background and on a number of occasions their interventions led to conflicts.

The final draft of the Basic Law was adopted by the Parliamentary Council on 8 May 1949 by 53 votes to 12. Six CSU delegates and those of the Centre Party, the DP and the KPD made up the opposition. The Military Governors gave their approval on 12 May, having registered a number of reservations. Between 18 and 21 May 1949 the *Länder* Diets added their consent with the exception of the Bavarians. The Basic Law was published in the *Bundesgesetzblatt* on 23 May 1949 and came into force at the end of that day.

Constitutions almost invariably document a radical turning away from earlier conditions. They are revolutionary in the sense that the political system is given a completely new form. This was the thrust behind the 1849 Constitution, which was to replace divine law and particularism with a Federal state based on a constitution and the rule of law. It also applied to the Bismarckian Constitution in so far as it realised above all the aim of national unity. The Weimar Constitution, finally, put a republic in the place of the Hohenzollern monarchy. By proclaiming the principle of social rights it abolished, at least in theory, the ostracism of the working class from political and social life.

Hence all three earlier constitutions had been revolutionary. The 1848 Revolution had come from below, 1871 presented a case of a revolution from above and in 1918 a revolution had been unleashed from above and below at the same time. The Bonn Basic Law was ultimately a product of Germany's liberation by the Allies and hence of a 'revolution from the outside', as Alfous Steiniger once put it.

The Parliamentary Council was concerned above all to make a radical break with the conditions which had obtained in Germany under the Nazi dictatorship between 1933 and 1945. In the first instance the Basic Law is therefore an anti-fascist document — a term whose applicability is not invalidated by the fact that it has also been used by the Communists. Never again was the dignity and liberty of men and women to be cast aside as the Nazis had done; never again was a war to be launched from German soil; never again was it to be possible for democracy to be replaced by dictatorship.

The Basic Law is hence the counter-constitution to the unwritten one upon which the Nazi regime had been based. At the same time it is marked by a strangely ambivalent relationship *vis-à-vis* the Weimar Constitution. In large measure both constitutions pursued the same objective, that is, to replace, after a lost war, an authoritarian system by a parliamentary–democratic republic, although one must not go too far in equating the Hohenzollern monarchy with the Hitler dictatorship. Theoretically the Weimar Constitution could therefore have acted as a guideline when it came to founding the Federal Republic. Indeed, prior to the establishment of the Parliamentary Council, a few people had proposed that the Weimar Constitution be revived in modified form. Among them was the former Prussian minister-president Otto Braun. By contrast, the Parliamentary Council distanced itself quite distinctly from the Weimar Constitution. Its passionate rejection of the Nazi dictatorship indirectly also affected its evaluation of constitutional conditions during the Weimar period. As Dr Kroll, a CSU delegate put it: 'A democracy which allows a tyranny to emerge from its midst with so little resistance, does not deserve being recreated for a second time'. And Dr Thomas Dehler, a Liberal and later the Federal Republic's first Justice Minister, on one occasion reproached the members of the Parliamentary Council of behaving 'in haunting fashion, exactly like the people of 1919'. Thus we can detect, apart from an anti-fascist mood, a sentiment among the members of the Council which amounts to a blaming of the Weimar Constitution for the rise of Hitler, even if these feelings were not always clearly expressed. The roots of the Nazi dictatorship are seen, *inter alia*, in the Weimar Constitution. And a constitution which had failed to stop Hitler and, through some of its clauses, even facilitated his rise was to be a model only to the extent that a better framework was to be constructed this time around.

The minister-presidents of the *Länder* had been worried even before the first meeting of the Parliamentary Council that the division of Germany might become exacerbated and the hopes for national unity be dashed if the Council began to draft an explicit *constitution*. This worry also shaped the underlying idea of the Basic Law. Through a preamble all Germans are exhorted to complete the unity and liberty of Germany under the principle of self-determination. And there is also the final article which, instead of containing the customary formula concerning the promulgation of the constitution, refers imploringly to the day when an actual 'constitution' will come into force which in a free vote has received the support of the entire nation.

Because it is enshrined in the Basic Law, the political demand for reunification also gained a legal significance which permeates the public life of the Federal Republic. The Federal Constitutional Court has even gone so far as to derive from this demand a legal obligation by all state institutions 'to strive with all their might for German unity, to train their policies upon this goal and to use, as a yardstick for their political actions, the question of how far they are capable of promoting the attainment of that goal'.

The unspoken premises of the Parliamentary Council also emerge from the name which it gave to the new state. The Weimar Constitution had retained the title 'German Reich'; but now the term 'Reich' was out of the question. It was a term which the country's neighbours associated with aggression. The Herrenchiemsee meeting had proposed the name 'Federation of German *Länder*'. But Dr Theodor Heuß, a liberal and later the first Federal President, thought this to sound too provisional and too haphazard. He felt that it amounted to an 'evasive action before one's own identity' (*ein Ausweichen vor sich selbst*). His proposal was to call the new state the 'Federal Republic of Germany'. This Federal Republic was not to be a fraction of a larger Germany which was constituted as a state; rather it was to be the core of the German nation as a whole.

The salient features of the Basic Law are:

(1) the granting of basic rights and their best possible protection;

(2) the creation of a state which was federally structured and legitimated through parliamentary–democratic institutions; a state which upheld the principles of the rule of law and of social justice;

(3) The preservation of peace and international understanding;

(4) the assertion and safeguarding of these principles against the enemies of the Republic.

No previous rulers in German history had treated human beings with such contempt, terrorised them so much and slaughtered so many of them as the Nazis had done. The establishment of a

catalogue of basic rights at the beginning of the Basic Law was
therefore a demonstrative response to this experience. Carlo
Schmid had announced this idea at the very beginning of the first
substantive discussion of the Parliamentary Council.

> The basic rights must govern the Basic Law; they must not be a mere
> appendix, like the Weimar catalogue of basic rights was an appendix of
> the Constitution. These basic rights are not just to be declamations,
> declarations or directives; [they are] not merely to make demands upon
> the constitutions of the *Länder*; [and] to guarantee the basic rights of
> the *Länder*; rather they are to be Federal law which possesses a direct
> validity and on the basis of which every individual German, every
> individual inhabitant of our country, can initiate a law-suit in the courts.

Indeed no constitution can have a better beginning than the one
found in the Basic Law: 'The dignity of a human being is untouch-
able; to respect and to protect it is the obligation of all state
authority'.

There are a number of other fundamental rights which are not
included in the catalogue of basic rights in the first section of the
Basic Law, but which in their essence must be counted among the
basic rights. These are the privileges of the deputies (Art. 38, 46,
47, 48), the rights of the political parties (Art. 21), the equality of
all Germans (Art. 33), the independence of the courts (Art. 97),
the right to be heard in a properly constituted court and the
banning of retrospective punishment or multiple conviction for
the same crime (Art. 103), protection in case of legal imprisonment (Art. 104) and the rights of religious communities (Art. 140).

The Parliamentary Council turned its special attention also to
provisions designed to protect basic rights. They were guided in
this by the earlier experience of the Weimar Republic when the
possibility of restricting basic rights through parliamentary legislation and the traditional positivism of the German legal profession
had led to a watering down and undermining of basic rights. As a
result, various safeguards were built into the Basic Law, such as the
ban on individual exemptions from the basic rights, the inviolability
of the catalogue's substance, their directly binding force also on
the legislator and their irremovability through government emergency measures. Also, according to Art. 79, the principles enshrined
in Art. 1 and Art. 20 are exempt from constitutional change under
any circumstances. In 1951 legislation was introduced which made
it possible for everyone to submit a Constitutional Complaint

directly to the Federal Constitutional Court if he or she believed they had suffered an infringement of his or her basic rights at the hands of the public authorities.

Like the Weimar Constitution, the Basic Law gives first place to the Bundestag among the organs of the West German state. Thus Parliament is allocated the central position within the Federal system as the representation of the population. To secure this dominant position, the Parliamentary Council, mindful of the experience of the Weimar Republic, has invested the Federal President with powers markedly weaker than those that were available to the Reich President under the Weimar Constitution. Moreover, the plebiscitarian element was restricted to a few rare exceptions.

The Bundestag can call its own meetings and it cannot be dissolved outside the regular four-year term, except in two special cases. It has manifold powers. It ratifies laws (Art. 77) and, through the institution of the *Bundesversammlung*, is prominently involved in the election of the Federal President (Art. 54). The Bundestag elects the Federal Chancellor (Art. 63) and can dismiss him by means of a constructive vote of no-confidence (Art. 67). It also elects half of the members of the Federal Constitutional Court (Art. 94) and controls the budget (Art. 110). Finally, Parliament has other means of co-determining domestic and foreign policy which are not specifically mentioned in the Basic Law.

The members of the Bundestag are elected on the basis of a universal, direct, free, equal and secret ballot (Art. 38). The details are laid down in a special electoral law. Because of its sophisticated blending of direct and proportional principles, this law amounts to a combination of the systems of the Imperial and the Weimar periods. However, there is also the Five Per Cent Clause which is designed to block splinter parties from gaining just a few seats; it is intended to promote the formation of working majorities capable of producing a government. It was a matter of dispute even in the Parliamentary Council as to whether this was a lesson to be learned from the Weimar period. Dehler vehemently argued against such a clause, asserting that the Council was still traumatised by Nazi slogans:

> Hitler grew big in his struggle against the small parties. He created a party based on the claim that our nation was disastrously divided and had to overcome this fragmentation. This is how things developed in terms of propaganda. Reality was quite different [though]. Our Weimar democracy did not suffer damage because of the small parties which had

no more than a limited influence in the Reichstag and certainly not a corrosive one; what damaged it was the centrifugal development of the parties and the ominous growth of the large extremist parties. If a party represents a particular intellectual idea, it also has the right of co-participation, even if there are only a few [deputies].

The Communist deputy Karl Renner reminded his colleagues that the SPD, too, had started as a splinter party in the Parliament of the North German Federation; it had no more than one deputy, and his name was August Bebel.

Constitutional practice has endowed the political parties with the monopoly of fielding candidates. For the first time in German constitutional history these parties are deemed worthy of a positive mention in the Basic Law (Art. 21). For almost a century monarchist and anti-parliamentary traditions in Germany had succeeded in portraying a supra-party attitude as something positive and work in or for a particular party as something negative. This prejudice against party politics can be discerned to this day, even though it has been an iron law since the 1860s that a democratic system in a large territorial state cannot do without political parties. Even the members of the National Assembly were unconsciously influenced by this stance and hence mentioned parties only once and in a negative context (see Art. 130 of the Weimar Constitution).

Like all earlier constitutions the Basic Law guarantees the independence of members of the Bundestag (Art. 38). In other words, there is no imperative mandate. Of course, there exists a certain tension between the parties' monopoly in the selection of candidates and the independent mandate principle; however it is a feature of parliamentary democracies to resolve such antinomies through compromise.

According to Art. 50, the *Länder* participation in the legislative process and the administration of the Federation is through the Bundesrat. Although it is composed of members of the *Länder* governments, the Bundesrat is an organ of the Federation. The *Länder* representatives shape Federal policy in it and they are under an obligation to act loyally towards the Federation. They are not representatives of the individual states working in opposition to the centre.

The Weimar Assembly had created a strong President because its members wished to uphold the principle of the division of powers and were concerned not to accumulate too much power in the hands of the Reichstag. These arguments re-emerged in the course of the discussions in the Parliamentary Council. As the Christian Democrat Dr Süsterhenn put it, he had no desire to create 'a constitution à la Rousseau' in which all power lay with Parliament. Rather, 'with Montesquieu we shall also have to take account of the idea of a division of powers. We believe any concentration of power in the hands of one institution to be an evil'.

Dr Dehler (FDP) added the further consideration that it was important to build in braking mechanisms against the proliferation of legislation and the belief that miracles could be achieved by pressing every aspect of life into legal norms.

Very different proposals were put forward when it came to the question of how these aims were to be achieved in detail. The Social Democrats favoured a US-style Senate, that is, a second chamber composed of senators who were elected on a *Land* basis and in equal number for each *Land*. The Christian Democrats, on the other hand, advocated the principle of delegations sent by the *Länder* governments. Voting rights in the Bundesrat were to depend on the population size of the individual *Länder*. The formula found in the Basic Law represented a compromise between widely divergent ideas. According to Art. 51 the difference in the weighting of Bundesrat votes is small in relation to the relative population size of various *Länder*. This chimes in with the tasks which the Parliamentary Council wanted the Bundesrat to fulfil. Carlo Schmid put this point by stating that he found it difficult to see why 'the accumulated administrative experience of Württemberg-Baden should be given a much higher specific weight than that of [the city-states of] Hamburg or Bremen'. Accordingly, it is not the task of the Bundesrat to represent the entire country or to reflect a particular power-ratio between the political parties.

The main powers of the Bundesrat consist of its right to initiate legislation (Art. 76) and to participate in Federal legislation. Some legislative items require its consent: it can raise objections in the case of other specified items (Art. 77). Changes in the Basic Law require a two-thirds majority in both the Bundestag and the Bundesrat (Art. 79). Certain decrees and administrative rulings by the Federal government also require Bundesrat participation (Art. 80, 84, 85, 108). It is expected to elect half of the members of the Federal Constitutional Court. So far it has not been necessary to invoke the Bundesrat's emergency powers under Art. 37 and 81.

In terms of official protocol, the special position of the Bundesrat is reflected in the fact that its president acts as deputy to the head of state (Art. 57).

When shaping the institution of the Federal presidency, the Parliamentary Council diverged most markedly from the Weimar model which, it was felt, had contributed to the downfall of the Weimar Republic. To repeat: the Reich President was elected by the entire population for seven years. He appointed the Chancellor without having to consult the Reichstag and possessed emergency powers for use in times of crisis which in practice amounted to dictatorial rights. He could rid himself of the Reichstag at any time by dissolving it.

All these powers were no longer to be. The Federal President was to be neither the democratic counter-weight of Parliament nor the guardian of the constitution. These roles were now to be fulfilled by the Bundesrat and the Federal Constitutional Court respectively. But what *was* this office to be? Dr Süsterhenn (CDU) characterised the Federal President as a head of state who had political and ceremonial functions which, he thought, were important from the point of view of 'popular psychology'.

If the President was to be the dignified representative of the Federal Republic, it made no sense to elect him by plebiscite. What emerged in the end was a weak institution whose incumbents are elected by the *Bundesversammlung* composed of Federal and *Länder* deputies who are assumed to give adequate representation to the views of the people (Art. 54). There are no historical precedents for the *Bundesversammlung*, which originated in a proposal made by Dr Dehler. The Herrenchiemsee draft had envisaged that the Bundestag and the Bundesrat would cast their votes separately. The powers of the President are limited essentially to the task of representing the Federal Republic in international law (Art. 59) and of appointing and dismissing civil servants and judges. He also exercises the right of pardon (Art. 60), the right of proposing the candidate for the election of the Chancellor by the Bundestag (Art. 63) and the right to dissolve Parliament in a few cases of extreme emergency (Art. 63, 68).

Apart from their concern about the wide powers of the Reich President under the Weimar Constitution, the memory of twenty Reich governments having been overturned within thirteen years constituted the other key experience of democratic politicians during the postwar period. Hence there existed a general agreement in the Parliamentary Council that, firstly, the President had to be excluded from the process of cabinet formation and, secondly, that it was to be made impossible for a negative majority among the Bundestag parties to topple the government. Because of its conscious dissociation from the Weimar experience, the Parliamentary Council cleared the way for giving added strength to the position of the Federal government.

The Chancellor is the dominant figure of the Cabinet. He determines the broad outlines of policy-making; he also decides who is to be appointed as a minister and who must vacate his ministerial seat. In this respect the Chancellor's position within the division of powers is reminiscent of the Bismarckian Constitution.

The Chancellor is elected by the Bundestag, and the President's right to propose him does not constitute a major privilege during the first ballot (Art. 63). He can be toppled only by a Bundestag majority simultaneously electing his successor (Art. 67). This idea, which was novel in German constitutional history — the so-called constructive vote of no-confidence — provides the government with considerable stability and forces Parliament to use its control functions in a spirit of constructive criticism.

The anti-fascist mood in the Parliamentary Council to prevent 'things from ever happening again' led the fathers of the Basic Law to create a democracy which is capable of defending itself (*wehrhafte Demokratie*). The Federal Republic was not only to be the complete antithesis of the Nazi state, but it was also to be safeguarded, in so far as the available constitutional means made this possible, against a relapse into autocracy.

As Carlo Schmid explained in a major speech on 8 September 1948:

> It is my view that it is not part of the concept of democracy that it creates the preconditions of its own destruction. I would even like to go further. I would like to say: democracy is more than a product of utilitarian considerations only in those places where the courage exists to believe in it as something that is indispensable for the dignity of man. If this courage exists, we should also have the courage to be intolerant towards those who wish to use a democratic system in order to kill it off.

This idea of intolerance towards the enemies of democracy emerges clearly in the Basic Law. Thus Art. 18 envisages the forfeiture of certain basic rights in cases where these rights are being misused in a struggle against the existing democratic order. According to Art. 21 those political parties are unconstitutional which aim to restrict or destroy that order. In both cases the decision lies with the Federal Constitutional Court. Owing to its manifold powers, especially in respect of the protection of basic rights, this court has emerged as the actual 'guardian of the Constitution'.

In March 1933 the Reichstag had voted in favour of Hitler's Enabling Act and thereby sealed the self-dissolution of the Weimar Republic. This case had demonstrated that *in extremis* a parliamentary–democratic system could not be sure of its own Parliament. The members of the Parliamentary Council were painfully aware of these depressing events, hence the attempt to protect the principles of the Basic Law against dismantling by the Bundestag. Art. 20 obliges all legislation to conform to the existing constitutional order and Art. 79 blocks certain changes in the Basic Law altogether. Thus it is impossible to change the division of the Federation into *Länder* or to exclude the *Länder* from the legislative process. It is also unconstitutional to try and touch the principles laid down in Art. 1 and 20.

During the discussions in the Constitutional Committee of the Parliamentary council, Dr Hans Seebohm, a member of the German Party, had proposed to incorporate an individual right of resistance. The idea was rejected. In particular Carlo Schmid, as chairman, did not think much of it.

However, in 1968 a fourth section was added to Art. 20 by which all Germans were given a right of resistance against anyone who aims to destroy the existing constitutional order, but only if all alternative avenues are found to be closed. This means that all contingencies have been covered by the Basic Law. All we can hope for is that we shall also have the courage to resist, should serious resistance become necessary. It is even better to hope that, unlike our ancestors, we shall never have to face that test.

In the thirty-five years during which the Basic Law has been in force, the Federal Republic of Germany has developed into an unshakeable democracy. Our Basic Law has proved its worth. It is the fruit of a hundred years of German constitutional history, combining within it the merits of the three previous constitutions, and at the same time avoiding their weaknesses.

With its unwavering commitment to basic human rights, the Basic Law continues the tradition of the Paulskirche. From the Reich Constitution of Weimar, it has borrowed the historic compromise — to be seen in the 'social State' principle — between liberalism and socialism. Nor, finally, has our constitution failed to inherit from Otto von Bismarck a sense of what is essential to the organisation of a stable State — a practical sense, free of all illusions, and finding its expression in the Reich Constitution of 1871.

The 1849 Constitution

Reichs-Gesetz-Blatt.

16tes Stück. Ausgegeben Frankfurt a. M., den **28.** April. **1849.**

Verfassung des deutschen Reiches.

Die deutsche verfassunggebende Nationalversammlung hat beschlossen, und verkündigt als Reichsverfassung:

Verfassung des deutschen Reiches.

Abschnitt I. Das Reich.

Artikel I.

§. 1.

Das deutsche Reich besteht aus dem Gebiete des bisherigen deutschen Bundes.

Die Festsetzung der Verhältnisse des Herzogthums Schleswig bleibt vorbehalten.

§. 2.

Hat ein deutsches Land mit einem nichtdeutschen Lande dasselbe Staatsoberhaupt, so soll das deutsche Land eine von dem nichtdeutschen Lande getrennte eigene Verfassung, Regierung und Verwaltung haben. In die Regierung und Verwaltung des deutschen Landes dürfen nur deutsche Staatsbürger berufen werden.

Die Reichsverfassung und Reichsgesetzgebung hat in einem solchen deutschen Lande dieselbe verbindliche Kraft, wie in den übrigen deutschen Ländern.

§. 3.

Hat ein deutsches Land mit einem nichtdeutschen Lande dasselbe Staatsoberhaupt, so muß dieses entweder in seinem deutschen Lande residiren, oder es muß auf verfassungs-

mäßigem

The German Constituent National Assembly has resolved, and proclaims as the Reich Constitution:

Constitution of the German Reich

PART I
The Reich

Section I

Art. 1
The German Reich consists of the territory of the former German Federation. The position of the Duchy of Schleswig remains to be determined.

Art. 2
Where a German state has the same head of state as a non-German state, this German state is to have a constitutional government and administration of its own which is separate from that of the non-German state. Only German citizens may be nominated to become members of the government and administration of the German state.

The Reich Constitution and Reich legislation have the same binding force in such a German state as in the other German States.

Art. 3
Where a German state has the same head of state as a non-German state, he shall either reside in his German territories or as regent shall be instituted by constitutional means to which only Germans may be nominated.

Art. 4
Apart from the links between German and non-German states which are already in existence, no head of state of a non-German state shall assume the government of a German state; nor shall a prince who rules in Germany accept a foreign crown without giving up his German office.

Art. 5

The individual German states retain their independence in so far as it is not limited by the Reich Constitution; they have all the sovereign powers and rights of a state in so far as these have not been explicitly transferred to the Reich authority.

PART II
The Reich Authority

Section I

Art. 6

The Reich Authority alone exercises Germany's representation in its international relations as well as that of the individual German states *vis-à-vis* foreign countries.

The Reich Authority employs the Reich envoys and the consuls. It conducts the diplomatic intercourse, concludes alliances and treaties with foreign countries, in particular commercial and shipping agreements, as well as treaties of extradition. It makes rulings on all matters relating to international law.

Art. 7

The individual German governments do not have the right to receive permanent foreign envoys or to accredit them.

Nor are they allowed to accredit special consuls. Consuls of foreign states obtain their accreditation from the Reich Authority.

The individual governments are at liberty to send plenipotentiaries to the Head of the Reich.

Art. 8

The individual German governments have the right and competence to conclude treaties with other German governments. Their right and competence to conclude treaties with non-German governments is restricted to matters of civil law, of neighbourly traffic and of policing.

Art. 9

All treaties which do not concern purely matters of civil law and which a German government concludes with another German or non-German one, are to be notified to the Reich Authority and, in so far as Reich interests are involved, to be submitted for confirmation.

Section II

Art. 10

The Reich Authority has the exclusive right of decision on whether to declare war or to stay at peace.

Section III

Art. 11

The Reich Authority has at its disposal the entire armed force of Germany.

Art. 12

The Reich Army consists of the total land forces of the individual German states which are earmarked for the purpose of war. The strength and the composition of the Reich Army shall be determined by a law concerning the military constitution. Those states which have fewer than 500,000 inhabitants shall be combined by the Reich Authority into larger military entities which will then be under the immediate leadership of the Reich Authority; or they are to be linked to a neighbouring larger state.

The more detailed conditions of such a unification are to be laid down in both cases by the states involved with the mediation and approval of the Reich Authority.

Art. 13

The Reich Authority above has the legislative and organisational authority in respect of the Army; it supervises the implementation in the individual states through constant control. The individual states have the right to develop their military organisation on the basis of Reich law and the directives of the Reich Authority and, respectively, within the limits of agreements concluded in accordance with Art. 12. They have disposal over their armed forces in so far as these are not being called upon for Reich service.

Art. 14

The obligation to be loyal to the Head of the Reich and the Reich Constitution is to be given top priority in the military oath.

Art. 15

All expenditures which arise from the use of troops for Reich purposes and which exceed the peacetime levels as laid down by the Reich shall be debited to the Reich.

Art. 16

A special Reich law is to be promulgated concerning a general military constitution which applies to the whole of Germany.

Art. 17

The appointment of their troops' commanders and officers, in so far as these are required by virtue of their strength, is left to the governments of the individual states.

The Reich Authority shall appoint a joint commander of those larger military entities into which the troops of several states have been combined.

In case of war, the Reich Authority shall appoint the commanding generals of the independent corps as well as the personnel of the Headquarters.

Art. 18

The Reich Authority is authorised to build Reich fortifications and coastal defences and, in so far as the security of the Reich so demands, to declare existing fortifications as Reich fortifications in return for fair compensation, in particular for war materials held there.

Reich fortifications and Reich coastal defences shall be maintained at Reich cost.

Art. 19

The Navy is a matter exclusively for the Reich. No individual state may keep its own warships or issue letters of marque.

The personnel of the Navy represents part of the armed forces. It is independent of the land force.

The crews which an individual state provides for the Navy shall be deducted from the number of land forces to be kept in service by it. The details of this as well as of the equalisation of costs between the Reich and the individual states shall be determined by a Reich law.

The Reich alone deals with the appointment of the officers and civil servants of the Navy.

The Reich Authority is to look after the equipment, the training and the maintenance of the Navy ports and the naval arsenals.

Reich laws shall be ratified to determine the expropriations necessary for the building of Navy ports and naval establishments. They are also to determine the rights of the Reich officers employed for this purpose.

Section IV

Art. 20

Shipping installations along the seaboards and in the estuaries of German rivers (ports, buoys, lightships, pilots, shipping channels etc.) remain in the hands of the individual shore states. The shore states shall maintain these installations through their own budget.

A Reich law shall determine how far the estuaries of individual rivers are to be counted.

Art. 21

The Reich Authority has the oversight over these establishments and installations. It is empowered to direct the states concerned properly to maintain them [and] also to increase and to extend them with the help of Reich funds.

Art. 22

Charges which are paid to the seaboard states for the use of shipping installations by ships and their cargoes may not exceed the costs necessary for the maintenance of these installations. They are subject to approval by the Reich Authority.

Art. 23

All German ships and their cargoes are to be treated equally in respect of these charges.

Only the Reich Authority may initiate the introduction of higher charges for foreign shipping. The higher charge paid by foreign shipping shall be due to the Reich Treasury.

Section V

Art. 24

The Reich Authority has the right to legislate for, and exert the oversight over, the rivers and lakes which are navigable and pass through, or border on, several states. The same applies to the estuaries of the tributaries lying in these states as well as to the shipping and rafting on these.

A Reich law shall determine in what ways the navigability of these rivers can be upheld or improved.

The remaining waterways shall be looked after by the individual states. However, the Reich Authority has the right, if this is deemed necessary in the interest of general traffic, to issue general regulations on shipping and rafting and to give the same status under the same conditions as has been given to the above-mentioned joint rivers.

The Reich Authority is empowered to require of the individual states the proper maintenance of the navigability of these waterways.

Art. 25

All German rivers shall be free of river duties for German shipping. Rafting, too, is not to be subjected to such charges on navigable stretches. A Reich law will determine the details.

Where rivers flow through, or border on, several states the lifting of these river duties shall be replaced by a fair compensation.

Art. 26

Charges for the use of ports, cranes, weighbridges, storage, locks etc. which are being raised on jointly used rivers or at the mouths of the tributaries which flow into them, may not exceed the costs necessary for the maintenance of such installations. They are subject to approval by the Reich Authority.

As far as these charges are concerned, no members of one German state may be favoured over those of others.

Art. 27

Only the Reich Authority may impose river duties and river shipping charges upon foreign ships and their cargoes.

Section VI

Art. 28

The Reich Authority has the oversight and legislative right over the railways and their operation in so far as the protection of the Reich and general transport interests demand this. A Reich law shall determine which aspects are to be considered part of this.

Art. 29

The Reich Authority has the right in so far as it is deemed necessary for the protection of the Reich or in the interest of general transport, to approve the construction of railways, and to build them on its own initiative if the individual state in whose territory construction is to take place, itself refuses the building of these railways. The Reich Authority may use, at any time and against an indemnity, the railways for Reich purposes.

Art. 30

If individual states build or approve railways, the Reich Authority has the right and competence to represent the protection of the Reich and the interest of general transport.

Art. 31

The Reich Authority has the oversight and legislative right over the roads in so far as the protection of the Reich and general transport interests demand this. A Reich law shall determine which aspects are to be considered part of this.

Art. 32

The Reich Authority has the right to decree, in so far it is deemed necessary for the protection of the Reich or in the interest of general traffic, that overload roads and canals be built, rivers be made navigable or their navigability be extended.

The order to construct the works necessary for this shall be issued by the Reich Authority after prior consultations with the individual states concerned.

The construction and maintenance of the new installations takes place under the auspices of the Reich and at the Reich's expense if no accord can be achieved with the individual states.

Section VII

Art. 33

The German Reich shall constitute a single customs and trading area, surrounded by a common customs border with all internal customs being abolished.

To the Reich Authority is reserved the right to exclude individual places or territories from the customs area.

To the Reich Authority is moreover reserved the right to include, by means of special treaties, countries or parts thereof which do not belong to the Reich in the German customs area.

Art. 34

The Reich Authority has the exclusive right to legislate in all customs matters and in matters of common taxes on production and consumption. Reich legislation shall determine which taxes on production and consumption are to be common ones.

Art. 35

The levying and administration of customs and of common taxes on production and consumption shall be undertaken in accordance with the directives and under the oversight of the Reich Authority.

A certain portion of the gains shall be set aside for Reich expenditure as laid down in the ordinary budget; the rest shall be distributed to the individual states.

A special Reich law shall determine the details of this arrangement.

Art. 37

The individual German states have no right and competence to impose customs on goods which enter or leave via the Reich borders.

Art. 38

The Reich Authority has the right to pass legislation relating to trade and shipping and supervises the execution of the Reich laws promulgated for this purpose.

Art. 39

The Reich Authority has the power to promulgate Reich laws concerning trades and industry and to supervise their execution.

Art. 40

Patents on inventions shall be granted exclusively under the auspices of the Reich and on the basis of a Reich law; the Reich Authority also has the exclusive right to legislate against the reprinting of books, against all unauthorised imitations of works of art, logos, samples and forms and against other interference with intellectual property.

Section VIII

Art. 41

The Reich Authority has legislative rights and an oversight concerning the postal services, in particular in respect of their organisation, charges, transit, the apportioning of income from stamps and relations between individual post office administrations.

By means of executive decrees the Reich Authority also looks after the even-handed applications of the laws and supervises their implementation in the individual states through constant controls.

The Reich Authority may regulate, in the interest of general traffic, the movement of mail within several postal regions.

Art. 42

Post agreements with foreign postal agencies may be concluded only by the Reich Authority or with its permission.

Art. 43

The Reich Authority has the right and competence, in so far as this is deemed necessary, to take over the German postal services on account of the Reich and in accordance with a Reich law, provided fair compensation is paid to those holding the legal entitlement.

Art. 44

The Reich Authority has the right and competence to instal telecommunication lines and to use existing ones against a fee or to acquire existing lines by means of expropriation.

Further regulations relating thereto and to the use of telegraphs by private users shall be reserved to the ratification of a Reich law.

Section IX

Art. 45

The Reich Authority has exclusive legislative rights and an oversight over the monetary system. It is charged with introducing a uniform system for the whole of Germany. It has the right to mint Reich coins.

Art. 46

The Reich Authority is charged with establishing in the whole of Germany a uniform system of weights and measures, as well as of standards for gold and silver ware.

Art. 47

The Reich Authority has the right to regulate banking and the issue of paper money through legislation. It supervises the execution of the Reich laws ratified for this purpose.

Section X

Art. 48

The costs of all measures taken, and of institutions established, on Reich authority shall be defrayed by the Reich Authority from Reich funds.

Art. 49

In order to pay for its expenditure, the Reich has in the first instance, to rely on its share in the income raised from tariffs and from joint producers' and consumers' taxes.

Art. 50

The Reich Authority has the right to raise matricular contributions [from the states] where the other income is insufficient.

Art. 51

In exceptional circumstances, the Reich Authority has the right and competence to impose and raise or order to raise Reich taxes: it may also take up loans or enter into debt agreements.

Section XI

Art. 52

The extent of the Reich's judiciary rights is laid down in the section relating to the Reich Court.

Section XII

Art. 53

The Reich Authority is charged to overlook the preservation of the rights which are guaranteed to all Germans through the Reich Constitution.

Art. 54

The Reich Authority is charged with the preservation of the peace of the Reich.

It is to take the measures necessary for the maintenance of law and order at home:

(1) if a German state is disturbed or endangered in its peace by another German state;

(2) if the natives or aliens in a German state disturb or endanger law and order. However, in this case the Reich Authority shall intervene only if the state government directly asks for an intervention, except where the latter is known to be incapable of making this request or where the peace of the Reich in general appears threatened;

(3) if the constitution of a German state is suspended or changed by force or unilaterally and no immediate help can be effected by going to the Reich Court.

Art. 55

Measures which can be taken by the Reich Authority for the preservation of the peace of the Reich are: (1) decrees; (2) the sending of commissars; (3) the use of armed force.

A Reich law shall define the principles according to which the costs are to be borne which arise from such measures.

Art. 56

The Reich Authority is charged with defining through a Reich law the cases and forms in which armed force is to be used against disturbances of public order.

Art. 57

The Reich Authority is charged with fixing the legal norms relating to the acquisition and loss of Reich and citizens' rights.

Art. 58

The Reich Authority has the power to legislate on the right of domicile and to supervise the execution of such legislation.

Art. 59

The Reich Authority has the power to legislate on rights of association, irrespective of the right of free association and assembly guaranteed by the [catalogue of] basic rights.

Art. 60

Reich legislation shall lay down such criteria for the drafting of public documents as are required to give them recognition of their authenticity in the whole of Germany.

Art. 61

The Reich Authority has the right and competence to decree general rules for the health service in the interests of the commonweal.

Section XIII

Art. 62

The Reich Authority has the right of legislation in so far as this is required for the execution of the powers with which it is endowed under the Constitution and for the protection of the institutions over which it has charge.

Art. 63

Should the Reich Authority deem it necessary to establish common institutions and rules in the interest of the whole of Germany, it has the right and competence to promulgate the required laws for their establishment within the guidelines laid down for constitutional amendments.

Art. 64

The Reich Authority is charged with establishing a uniform legal system among the German people by promulgating general codes relating to civil law, commercial and banking law, criminal law and legal procedure.

Art. 65

All laws and decrees by the Reich Authority obtain their binding force through their proclamation on behalf of the Reich.

Art. 66

Reich laws override laws of the individual states unless they are explicitly said to have a subsidiary validity.

Section XIV

Art. 67

The Reich employes the public servants of the Reich. The service conditions of the Reich shall be determined by a Reich law.

PART III
The Head of the Reich

Section I

Art. 68

The title of Head of the Reich shall be given to a ruling German prince.

Art. 69

This title shall be hereditary within the House of the prince to whom it has been given. It is inherited in the male line according to the right of primogeniture.

Art. 70

The Head of the Reich shall bear the title: Kaiser of the Germans.

Art. 71

The Kaiser's residence shall be at the seat of the Reich government. The Kaiser will reside there permanently at least for the duration of the Reichstag [sessions]. Whenever the Kaiser is absent from the seat of the Reich government, one of the Reich ministers must be among his immediate entourage.

The regulations concerning the seat of the Reich government shall be left to [the ratification of] a Reich law.

Art. 72

The Kaiser draws upon a civil list to be fixed by the Reichstag.

Section II

Art. 73

The person of the Kaiser is inviolable.

The Kaiser exercises the powers given to him through responsible ministers who are nominated by him.

Art. 74

To be valid, all acts of government by the Kaiser require the counter-signature of at least one Reich minister who thereby assumes the responsibility.

Section III

Art. 75

The Kaiser represents the German Reich and the individual German states in international law. He employs the Reich envoys and consuls and conducts the diplomatic intercourse.

Art. 76

The Kaiser declares war and concludes peace.

Art. 77

The Kaiser concludes alliances and treaties with foreign powers, the Reichstag being involved in so far as its participation is reserved under the Constitution.

Art. 78

All treaties which are not of a purely private character and which the German governments conclude among themselves or with foreign governments, shall be notified to the Kaiser and, in so far as

Reich interests are involved, shall be submitted for confirmation.

Art. 79

The Kaiser opens and closes the Reichstag; he has the right to dissolve the Popular Assembly.

Art. 80

The Kaiser has the right to propose legislation. He exercises his legislative power jointly with the Reichstag and under the limitations imposed by the Constitution. He proclaims Reich laws and issues the decrees necessary for execution of the same.

Art. 81

In criminal matters, which fall into the sphere of the Reich Court, the Kaiser has the right of pardon and of mitigation. Only with the Reichstag's consent can the Kaiser prohibit the opening or the continuation of criminal investigations.

The Kaiser may exercise his right of pardon and of mitigation in the case of a Reich minister who has been sentenced on grounds of his public conduct only if the House which initiated the suit tables a motion to this effect. He has no such right in respect of ministers of individual states.

Art. 82

The Kaiser is charged with the preservation of Reich peace.

Art. 83

The Kaiser disposes over the armed forces.

Art. 84

Generally speaking, the Kaiser has governmental power in all Reich affairs in accordance with the Reich Constitution. He, as the bearer of this power, may claim all rights and competences which the Reich Constitution has laid into the hands of the Reich Authority and which have not been allocated to the Reichstag.

PART IV
The Reichstag

Section I

Art. 85

The Reichstag is made up of two houses, the State House and the Popular Asssembly.

Section II

Art. 86

The State House is constituted by the representatives of the German states.

Art. 87

The number of members is decided according to the following key:

Prussia	40 members
Austria	38 "
Bavaria	18 "
Saxony	10 "
Hanover	10 "
Württemberg	10 "
Baden	9 "
Kurhessen	6 "
Grand Duchy of Hesse	6 "
Holstein (= Schleswig, see Section I, Art. 1)	6 "
Mecklenburg-Schwerin	4 "
Luxemburg-Limburg	3 "
Nassau	3 "
Brunswick	2 "
Oldenburg	2 "
Saxe-Weimar	2 "
Saxe-Coburg-Gotha	1 member
Saxe-Meiningen Hildburghausen	1 "
Saxe-Altenburg	1 "
Mecklenburg-Strelitz	1 "
Anhalt-Dessau	1 "

Anhalt-Bernburg	1	"
Anhalt-Köthen	1	"
Schwarzburg-Sondershausen	1	"
Schwarzburg-Rudolstadt	1	"
Hohenzollern-Hechingen	1	"
Liechtenstein	1	"
Hohenzollern-Sigmaringen	1	"
Waldeck	1	"
Reuß ältere Linie	1	"
Reuß jüngere Linie	1	"
Schaumburg-Lippe	1	"
Lippe-Detmold	1	"
Hesse-Homburg	1	"
Laüenburg	1	"
Lübeck	1	"
Frankfurt	1	"
Bremen	1	"
Hamburg	1	"

192 members

So long as the German–Austrian lands do not take part in the federal state, the following states shall be given a larger number of votes in the State House, i. e.:

Bavaria	20
Saxony	12
Hanover	12
Württemberg	12
Baden	10
Grand Duchy of Hesse	8
Kurhessen	7
Nassau	4
Hamburg	2

Art. 88

Half the members of the State House are to be nominated by the government, the other half by the popular assembly of the states concerned.

In those German states which are composed of severaⅼ provinces or regions with their own constitution and administration, the members of the State House who are to be nominated by the popular assemblies of that State shall not be selected by the representation of the State as a whole, but by the representatives of the individual regions or provinces (provincial estates).

It is left to State legislation to decide on the proportion according to which the number of deputies due to these States shall be divided up among the individual regions and provinces. Where there exist two chambers and there is no representation in accordance with provinces, the two chambers shall make the elections in a joint session and with absolute majorities.

Art. 89

In those States which have only one seat in the State House the government shall put forward three candidates from among whom the popular representative shall be elected by an absolute majority.

The same procedure shall apply to the last member being elected by those states which have an odd number of candidates.

Art. 90

If several German states combine to become a whole, a Reich law shall determine the changes in the composition of the State House which may be necessary as a result of this change.

Art. 91

Only those can be a member of the State House who:
  (1) possess the citizenship of the sending state;
  (2) are over 30 years of age;
  (3) enjoy the full use of citizens' rights.

Art. 92

The members of the State House shall be elected for six years. Half of the membership is to be renewed every three years.

A Reich Law will have to determine by which method one-half of the members is to retire after the first three years. Those leaving may be re-elected at any time.

If an extraordinary Reichstag meeting is called between the completion of the first three years and the completion of fresh elections, the former members shall be called if fresh elections have not yet taken place.

Section III

Art. 93

The Popular Assembly consists of the representatives of the German People.

Art. 94

The members of the Popular Assembly shall be elected for four years in the first round, thereafter election shall invariably be for three years.

Elections shall be held in accordance with the rules contained in the Reich Electoral Law.

Section IV

Art. 95

Members of the Reichstag receive, from the Reich Treasury, a regular daily allowance and a reimbursement of their travelling expenses. The details shall be determined by a Reich law.

Art. 96

No member of the two Houses may be bound by instructions.

Art. 97

No one may be a member of both Houses at the same time.

Section V

Art. 98

For either House to be quorate it is necessary for at least half of the legal number of members for a simple majority to be present. If there is a tied vote, the motion is to be regarded as defeated.

Art. 99

Either House has the right to propose legislation, to make a complaint, to petition and to launch a fact-finding investigation, as well as to initiate criminal proceedings against a minister.

Art. 100
A Reichstag resolution can be brought about only with the consent of both Houses.

Art. 101
A Reichstag resolution which does not gain the consent of the Reich government may not be reintroduced again during the same session.

If the Reichstag has passed without amendment the same resolution in three ordinary consecutive sessions, it shall become law at the end of the third Reichstag period, even if government approval was not given. An ordinary session which does not last a minimum of four weeks, shall not be counted as part of this sequence.

Art. 102
A Reichstag resolution is required in the following instances:
(1) if Reich laws are to be ratified, abolished, amended, or interpreted;
(2) if the Reich Budget is to be determined, if loans are to be taken up, if the Reich introduces expenditures not provided for in the Budget or if matricular contributions or taxes are to be levied;
(3) if foreign sea- or river-going shipping is to be burdened with higher charges;
(4) if *Land*-owned fortifications are to be declared as Reich fortifications;
(5) if trade, shipping and extradition treaties with foreign countries are to be concluded as well as treaties in international law in so far as they impose burdens on the Reich;
(6) if States or parts of States which do not belong to the Reich are to be incorporated into the German customs area, or if individual places or regions are to be excluded from it;
(7) if German territories are to be ceded or if non-German territories are to be incorporated into the Reich or to be linked to it by some other means.

Art. 103
The following rules shall obtain regarding the ratification of the Reich Budget:
(1) all bills by the Reich government relating to finance shall first be sent to the Popular Assembly;
(2) approval of expenditure may occur only if a government

motion has been tabled to that effect and only in relation to that motion. Each appropriation shall be valid for the special purpose only for which the expenditure has been ear-marked. It may be used exclusively within the limits of the appropriation;

(3) the financial year and the period of appropriation shall be twelve months;

(4) the budget relating to regular Reich expenditure and to the contingency reserve as well as to the funds to cover both shall be ratified in the first Reichstag through a Reichstag resolution. An increase in this Budget at subsequent Reichstag meetings equally requires a Reichstag resolution.

(5) this ordinary Budget shall be submitted to the Popular Assembly in the first instance during each Reichstag session [the Popular Assembly shall examine and approve or reject in whole or in part the Budget under its various titles and in accordance with the explanations and supporting evidence which the Reich government is required to submit];

(6) the Budget is to be sent on to the State House after the Popular Assembly has completed its examination and approval. The former merely has the right to formulate reminders and representations within the overall allocation in the Budget which has been made by the first Reichstag or through subsequent Reichstag resolutions; [it is] for the Popular Assembly to arrive at a final decision [over these representations];

(7) all extraordinary expenditures and their cover require, like increases in the ordinary Budget, ratification by the Reichstag;

(8) the accounts relating to the use of Reich funds shall be submitted to the Reichstag, and to the Popular Assembly in the first instance, for scrutiny and final approval.

Section VI

Art. 104

The Reichstag shall meet every year at the seat of the Reich government. In so far as the date of the meeting is not fixed by a Reich law, it is to be announced by the Head of the Reich when the Reichstag is called. The Reichstag may, moreover, be called together at any time by the Head of the Reich for extraordinary meetings.

Art. 105

The ordinary meetings of the Diets of the individual states shall, as a rule, not coincide with those of the Reichstag. The details are to be reserved to the ratification of a Reich law.

Art. 106

The Popular Assembly may be dissolved by the Head of the Reich. If the Reichstag has been dissolved, it shall be reconvened within three months.

Art. 107

As a consequence of a dissolution of the Popular Assembly the State House meetings shall be adjourned at the same time until the Reichstag has been called again.

The parliamentary sessions of both Houses are the same.

Art. 108

The end of a Reichstag session is to be determined by the Head of the Reich.

Art. 109

An adjournment of the Reichstag or of one of the two Houses by the Head of the Reich requires the consent of the Reichstag or of the House concerned if it is to last for more than a fortnight after the opening of the session.

The Reichstag and either of its two Houses may adjourn for a fortnight on its own account.

Section VII

Art. 110

Each of the two Houses elects its own president, vice-presidents and secretaries.

Art. 111

The meetings of both Houses are public. The Standing Orders of each House shall determine under what circumstances confidential meetings may be held.

Art. 112

Each House examines its members' credentials and decides on their admission.

Art. 113

Each member shall, when first taking up his seat, swear the [following] oath: 'I swear loyally to observe and to uphold the German Reich constitution, so help me God'.

Art. 114

Each House has the right to punish and *in extremis* exclude its members because of dishonourable conduct. The Standing Orders of each House shall determine the details. A member can be excluded only if a two-thirds majority of the votes so decides.

Art. 115

No petitioners and deputations in general shall be admitted to appear before both Houses.

Art. 116

Each House has the right to give itself its own Standing Orders. The parliamentary relations between the two Houses shall be regulated through an agreement between the two Houses.

Section VIII

Art. 117

A member of the Reichstag, unless he is caught *in flagrante delicto*, may not be arrested or taken in for questioning on criminal charges during a parliamentary session without the consent of the House concerned.

Art. 118

The House concerned shall be notified immediately of the measures taken if an *in flagrante delicto* arrest is made.

Art. 119

Each House has the same competence in respect of the arrest or investigation of a member which was ordered at the time of his election or between his election and the opening of the parliamentary session.

Art. 120

No member of the Reichstag may at any time be prosecuted by judicial or disciplinary measures or be charged outside the assembly because of how he voted or because of statements made in the execution of his duties.

Section IX

Art. 121

Reich ministers have the right to attend the meetings of either of the two Reichstag Houses and must be heard by them at any time.

Art. 122

Reich ministers are obliged to appear and to answer questions before either of the two Reichstag Houses, if this is requested, or they have to state the reason why [a particular piece of information] cannot be given.

Art. 123

Reich ministers cannot be a member of the State House.

Art. 124

If a member of the Popular Assembly accepts a Reich office or a promotion, he must submit to a fresh election; he retains his seat until this by-election has taken place.

PART V
The Reich Court

Section I

Art. 125

Jurisdiction which is to be reserved for the Reich shall be exercised by a Reich Court.

Art. 126

The Reich Court has jurisdiction over:

(a) suits by an individual state against the Reich Authority alleging a violation of the Reich Constitution due to the promulgation of Reich laws or to measures taken by the Reich government; [conversely] suits by the Reich Authority against an individual state alleging a violation of the Reich Constitution;

(b) disputes between the State House and the Popular Assembly or between one of these and the Reich government relating to an interpretation of the Reich Constitution, should the two sides to the disputes agree to turn to the Reich Court for a decision;

(c) political or civil law disputes of all kinds between the individual German states;

(d) disputes concerning successions to the throne, a prince's capacity to rule or the institution of a regent in the individual states;

(e) disputes between the governments of an individual state and its popular assembly concerning the validity and interpretation of a State constitution;

(f) suits by members of an individual state against their government alleging a suspension or an illegal change of the State constitution. Suits by members of an individual state against their government alleging a violation of the State constitution may only be brought if the means of redress listed in the State constitution cannot be invoked;

(g) suits by German citizens alleging a violation of the rights granted to them under the Reich Constitution. Reich legislation shall determine the details relating to the extent of this judicial right and the ways and means by which it may be exercised;

(h) complaints relating to a refusal or a blocking of judicial channels, provided that the means of obtaining redress under State law have been exhausted;

(i) criminal review in the case of accused Reich ministers, in so far as the charges relate to their ministerial responsibility;

(k) criminal review in the case of accused ministers in the individual states in so far as the charges relate to their ministerial responsibility;

(l) criminal review in cases of high treason against the Reich.

Subsequent Reich laws shall determine if other crimes against the Reich are also to be made part of the criminal review proceedings of the Reich Court;

  (m) suits against the Reich Treasury;

  (n) suits against individual German states where the obligation to fulfil the law is in doubt or in dispute between several states; [the same applies to the suit] against several states alleging a common obligation.

Art. 127

The Reich Court alone shall decide on the question of whether a case is subject to a decision by the Court.

Art. 128

A special law shall be promulgated to regulate the institution and organisation of the Reich Court, its procedures and the implementation of its decisions and rulings.

To this law shall also be reserved the regulation of whether and in which cases a verdict of the Reich Court shall be based on jurors.

The same applies to [the question of] whether and how far this law is to be regarded as an organic part of the Constitution.

Art. 129

It is reserved to Reich legislation to institute admiralty and maritime courts as well as to establish regulations concerning jurisdiction over Reich envoys and consuls.

PART VI
The Basic Rights of the German People

Art. 130

The German people shall possess the following fundamental rights. These rights shall serve as a standard for the individual German states, and no constitution or legislation of a German state shall abolish or circumscribe them.

Section I

Art. 131

The German people consists of the citizens of the states which make up the Reich.

Art. 132

Every German has the right of German Reich's citizenship. He can exercise this right in every German state. Reich franchise legislation shall provide for the right of the individual to vote for members of the national assembly.

Art. 133

Every German has the right to live or reside in any part of the Reich's territory, to acquire and dispose of property of all kinds, to pursue his livelihood, and to win the right of communal citizenship.

The terms for living and residence shall be established by a law of settlement; trade regulations shall be established by regulations affecting trade and industry; both to be set by the Reich Authority for all of Germany.

Art. 134

No German state is permitted to make a distinction between its citizens and other Germans in civil, criminal and litigation rights which relegates the latter to the position of foreigners.

Art. 135

Capital punishment for civil offences shall not take place, and, in those cases where condemnation has already been made, shall not be carried out, in order not to infringe upon the hereby acquired civil law.

Art. 136

Freedom of emigration shall not be limited by any state; emigration levies shall not be established.

All matters of emigration remain under the protection and care of the Reich.

Section II

Art. 137

There are no class differences before the law. The rank of nobility is abolished.

All special class privileges are abolished.

All Germans are equal before the law.

All titles, in so far as they are not bound with an office, are abolished and never again shall be introduced.

No citizen shall accept a decoration from a foreign state.

Public office shall be open to all men on the basis of ability.

All citizens are subject equally to military service; there shall be no draft substitutions.

Section III

Art. 138

The freedom of man shall be inviolable.

The arrest of a person, with the exception of one caught in the act, shall take place only under a legally-executed warrant. This warrant must be served on the arrested person at the moment of the arrest or within the next twenty-four hours.

The police authority must, in the course of the following day, either release or present to a court any person which it has taken into custody.

Any suspect shall be released from custody against bail, the size of which is to be determined by the courts, unless he is under urgent suspicion of a serious crime.

In case of an imprisonment which has been decreed or extended illegally, those responsible and, if necessary, the state are obliged to make amends and to offer compensation.

The modifications of these regulations necessary for the army and navy shall be covered by special laws.

Art. 139

Capital punishment, with the exception of cases prescribed by martial law or maritime law concerning mutiny, is abolished, as are sentences to public whipping, branding and bodily punishment.

Art. 140

The house of every German shall be inviolable. A search is admissible only:

(1) if there is a court order setting out the reasons which shall be handed to the person affected either at once or within the next twenty-four hours;

(2) in case of an *in flagrante delicto* prosecution by the legally authorised civil servant;

(3) in cases and contingencies in which the law exceptionally permits certain officers [to make a search] even without a court order.

Any search must take place, when practicable, in the presence of other inhabitants.

The inviolability of homes shall provide no hindrance to apprehending a fugitive from justice.

Art. 141

The confiscation of letters and papers, except at an arrest or house search, can take place with a legally executed warrant, which must be served on the arrested person at once or within the next twenty-four hours.

Art. 142

The privacy of posts is guaranteed.

Necessary exceptions in cases of criminal investigation and in the event of war shall be established by legislation.

Section IV

Art. 143

Every German shall have the right freely to express his opinion through speech, writing, publication and illustration.

Under no circumstances shall the freedom of the press be suspended through preventive measures, namely, censorship, concessions, security orders, imposts, limitation of publication or bookselling, postal bans or other restraints.

Jury courts shall deal with press offences which are made the subject of an official prosecution.

The Reich shall promulgate a press law.

Section V

Art. 144

Every German has complete freedom of religion and conscience.

No one is required to reveal his religious convictions.

Art. 145

Every German possesses the unlimited right for the private or public exercise of his religion.

Any crimes or acts which prevent the exercise of freedom of religion shall be punished by law.

Art. 146

The enjoyment of civil liberties is neither preconditioned nor limited by religious denomination.

Art. 147

All religious communities regulate and administer their own affairs, but remain subject to the general laws of the State.

No religious community shall enjoy privileges granted by the State over others; nor does a state church exist.

New religious communities may establish themselves; there is no need for their faith to be recognised by the State.

Art. 148

No one may be forced to participate in a religious act or celebration.

Art. 149

The oath formula shall henceforth be: 'So help me God'.

Art. 150

The validity of marriage in civil law is only dependent on the completion of the civil registration. A church wedding may take place only after the completion of the civil registration.

Adherence to a different religious faith is no obstacle to civil marriage.

Art. 151

The marriage registers shall be kept by the civil authorities.

Art. 152

Arts and science, and their teaching, shall be free.

Art. 153

Teaching and education remain under the authority of the state, and, with the exception of religious instruction, are removed from the authority of the clergy.

Art. 154

Every German is free to establish and to direct institutions of instruction and education and to teach in them, if he has demonstrated his ability to do so to the state authority concerned.

There is no restriction on private tuition at home.

Art. 155

The education of the German youth shall be looked after everywhere and sufficiently through state schools. Parents or their representatives may not leave their children or wards without the kind of instruction which is prescribed for primary schools.

Art. 156

Teachers at state schools enjoy the rights of civil servants.

The State employs primary school teachers from among the number of examined candidates, with the legally regulated participation of the local authorities.

Art. 157

There shall be no fees for instruction in primary schools and lower-level vocational schools. Those without means shall be given a free education at all institutions of public instruction.

Art. 158

Every person is free to choose his trade, occupation or profession, and to prepare himself for it wherever and however he wishes.

Section VII

Art. 159

Every German possesses the right of written petition to the authorities, to the representatives of the people and to the Reichstag.

This right may be exercised by individuals as well as by associations and by several people jointly; however, disciplinary regulations must be followed as far as the army and navy are concerned.

Art. 160
It is not necessary to obtain prior permission of the authorities in order to prosecute public servants on account of their official actions.

Section VIII

Art. 161
All Germans have the right to assemble peaceably and without arms; special permission for this is not needed.

Association of people outdoors can be forbidden in the event that it endangers public order and security.

Art. 162
All Germans have the right to form associations. This right shall not be restricted by any preventive regulation.

Art. 163
The principles contained in Articles 161 and 162 extend to the army and navy inasmuch as rules of military discipline do not countermand them.

Section IX

Art. 164
Property is inviolable.

Expropriation of property may take place only if necessary for the commonweal, only on a legal basis and against fair compensation.

Intellectual property shall be protected by Reich legislation.

Art. 165
All owners of landed property may sell their property in their lifetime or upon death. It is up to the individual states to facilitate, through transitional legislation, the implementation of the principle that all landed property is divisible. It is permissible to

legislate in the interests of public welfare that the church is restricted in its rights to acquire land and to dispose over them.

Art. 166
All associations of bondage and serfdom shall be disbanded for ever.

Art. 167
The following shall be terminated without compensation:
(1) patrimonial justice and police powers of the landlord, including the competences, exemptions and incomes stemming from these rights;
(2) the personal receipts and services stemming from a feudal and patrimonial association.

The counter-services and burdens which those who held these rights hitherto were expected to render shall lapse together with their privileges.

Art. 168
All deliveries and services resting on land, and tithes in particular, are redeemable; legislation by individual states shall determine whether this may be done only by the person owing such deliveries and services or equally by the recipient and in what way [this may be effected].

Henceforth no piece of land shall be burdened with deliveries or services which are not redeemable.

Art. 169
Land holding includes hunting rights on one's own property.

Hunting rights on foreign land, hunting services and compulsory services as well as other services for hunting purposes are abolished without compensation.

However, hunting rights are redeemable if they can be demonstrated to have been acquired through a burdensome agreement signed with the owner of the land so affected; state legislation shall determine the details of how and in what ways redemption can be gained.

State legislation has the right to regulate the exercise of hunting rights on grounds of public security and the commonweal.

Hunting rights on foreign land must not in future be instituted as a patrimonial privilege.

Art. 170

Entailed family holdings are to be dissolved. Legislation of the individual states shall determine the character and the conditions of this dissolution.

Regulations concerning the entailed family holdings of the ruling houses are to be reserved for legislation by the states.

Art. 171

All vassal associations are to be abolished. Legislation by the individual states shall direct the details concerning the ways and means of implementing [this rule].

Art. 172

There shall be no penalty resulting in a confiscation of property.

Art. 173

Taxation shall be regulated in such a way that an end is put to all favouritism of individual classes or individual large-scale landed estates at national and local level.

Section X

Art. 174

All jurisdiction emanates from the State. There shall be no patrimonial courts.

Art. 175

The courts shall exercise their judicial powers independently. Justice via the Cabinet or the ministry is not permissible.

Nobody may be given dispensation from facing his legal judge. Never shall there be special courts.

Art. 176

There shall be no judiciary for privileged persons or goods.

Military justice is to be restricted to the meting out of punishments for military crimes and offences as well as for violations of the code of military discipline, with [special] rules for the officer corps.

Art. 177

No judge may be removed from his office or be treated in a way prejudicial to his rank or salary, except on the basis of a court decision based on the law.

No suspension shall occur without a judicial decision.

No judge may be transferred, against his will, to another post or be retired early, except by a judicial decision within the case law and the framework defined by the law.

Art. 178
Court proceedings shall be public and oral. A law shall determine exceptions from the publicity [requirement] in the interests of morality.

Art. 179
In criminal matters there shall be trial by public prosecution.

Jury courts shall sit in judgment over all more serious criminal matters and over all political offences.

Art. 180
Justice requiring special professional experience shall be administered or co-administered by judges who are expert and are freely elected by their peers.

Art. 181
The judiciary and the general administration shall be separate and independent of each other. Conflicts over competences between administrative and judiciary authorities in the individual states shall be decided by a court to be set up through legislation.

Art. 182
Justice under the auspices of the administration shall cease; courts are to decide in all matters of violations of the law.

The police have no powers of criminal justice.

Art. 183
Valid judgments of German courts shall apply and be ratifiable equally in all German lands. A Reich law shall determine the details.

Section XI

Art. 184

Every community shall have as fundamental rights of its constitution:

- (a) election of its chairman and representatives;
- (b) independent control of its communal affairs including the local police under legal supervision of the state;
- (c) publication of its budget;
- (d) public consideration of its affairs as a rule.

Art. 185

All plots of land shall be part of a communal association. Restrictions relating, to forests and wastelands remain the preserve of legislation by the individual states.

Section XII

Art. 186

Every German state shall have a constitution with a popular assembly.

Ministers are responsible to the people.

Art. 187

These assemblies have the decisive voice in respect of legislation, of taxation and of the structuring of the Budget. Where a two-chamber system is in operation, they also have the right — each chamber independently — to propose legislation, to make a complaint, to petition and to initiate proceedings against ministers. The meetings of the diets are, as a rule, public.

Section XIII

Art. 188

The non-German speaking people of Germany are guaranteed their national development, namely, equal rights for their languages, in so far as they exist in their territories, in ecclesiastical matters, in education, in administration of local affairs and of justice.

Section XIV

Art. 189

Every German citizen abroad stands under the protection of the Reich.

PART VII
Guarantee of the Constitution

Section I

Art. 190

If not already assembled, the Reichstag shall meet after every change of government in the same composition as the previous time. The Kaiser, when assuming office, takes an oath to the Reich Constitution in front of both Houses of the Reichstag which have been convened in a joint session.

The oath shall read: 'I swear to shield the Reich and the rights of the German People, to maintain the Reich Constitution and to implement it conscientiously, so help me God'.

Only after taking the oath is the Kaiser authorised to engage in acts of government.

Art. 191

Reich civil servants are obliged to take an oath to the Reich Constitution when they assume their office. The details are to be determined by the civil service regulations of the Reich.

Art. 192

A Reich law shall be promulgated relating to the responsibility of the Reich ministers.

Art. 193

The pledge to the Reich Constitution shall be combined with a pledge to the state constitution in the individual states and shall precede the latter.

Section II

Art. 194

No clause in the constitution or the laws of an individual state may stand in contradiction to the Reich Constitution.

Art. 195

A change of the form of government in an individual state may be effected only with the consent of the Reich Authority. This consent must be given in line with the procedures prescribed for [such] changes of the Reich Constitution.

Section III

Art. 196

Changes to the Reich Constitution may be made only by means of a resolution of both Houses and with the consent of the Head of the Reich.

In order to pass such a resolution, each of the two Houses requires:

(1) the presence of at least two-thirds of their members;
(2) two separate votes, between which there shall be an interval of at least eight days;
(3) an at least two-thirds majority of the members present at each of the two votes.

The consent of the Head of the Reich is not necessary if the same Reichstag motion has been passed unchanged by three consecutive ordinary meetings. An ordinary session which lasts less than four weeks shall not be counted as part of this sequence.

Section IV

Art. 197

The clauses relating to basic rights about arrest, search and assembly may be temporarily suspended in individual districts by the Reich government or by the government of an individual state in case of war or riot; however, [this may occur] only under the following conditions:

(1) the decree must in all cases emanate from the entire Reich

Cabinet or the Cabinet of the individual state concerned;

(2) the Reich Cabinet must obtain without delay the consent of the Reichstag, the State Cabinet and that of the [respective] diet, if these happen to be meeting at the time. If these are not in session, the decree may not be operative for more than a fortnight without the [respective] popular assemblies being convened and the measures taken being submitted to them for approval.

Further regulations shall be reserved to a Reich law.

The existing legal regulations are to remain in force as far as the proclamation of the state of siege in fortresses is concerned.

The Reich Constitution of 1871

Bundes-Gesetzblatt

des

Deutschen Bundes.

№ 16.

(Nr. 628.) Gesetz, betreffend die Verfassung des Deutschen Reichs. Vom 16. April 1871.

Wir Wilhelm, von Gottes Gnaden Deutscher Kaiser, König von Preußen 2c.

verordnen hiermit im Namen des Deutschen Reichs, nach erfolgter Zustimmung des Bundesrathes und des Reichstages, was folgt:

§. 1.

An die Stelle der zwischen dem Norddeutschen Bunde und den Großherzog-thümern Baden und Hessen vereinbarten Verfassung des Deutschen Bundes (Bundesgesetzbl. vom Jahre 1870. S. 627. ff.), sowie der mit den Königreichen Bayern und Württemberg über den Beitritt zu dieser Verfassung geschlossenen Verträge vom 23. und 25. November 1870. (Bundesgesetzbl. vom Jahre 1871. S. 9. ff. und vom Jahre 1870. S. 654. ff.) tritt die beigefügte

Verfassungs-Urkunde für das Deutsche Reich.

§. 2.

Die Bestimmungen in Artikel 80. der in §. 1. gedachten Verfassung des Deutschen Bundes (Bundesgesetzbl. vom Jahre 1870. S. 647.), unter III. §. 8. des Vertrages mit Bayern vom 23. November 1870. (Bundesgesetzbl. vom Jahre 1871. S. 21. ff.), in Artikel 2. Nr. 6. des Vertrages mit Württemberg vom 25. November 1870. (Bundesgesetzbl. vom Jahre 1870. S. 656.), über die Einführung der im Norddeutschen Bunde ergangenen Gesetze in diesen Staaten bleiben in Kraft.

Die dort bezeichneten Gesetze sind Reichsgesetze. Wo in denselben von dem Norddeutschen Bunde, dessen Verfassung, Gebiet, Mitgliedern oder Staaten, Indigenat, verfassungsmäßigen Organen, Angehörigen, Beamten, Flagge u. s. w. die Rede ist, sind das Deutsche Reich und dessen entsprechende Beziehungen zu verstehen.

　　　　　Das-

Ausgegeben zu Berlin den 20. April 1871.

Constitution of the German Reich
Berlin, 16 April 1871

His Majesty the King of Prussia in the name of the North German Federation, His Majesty the King of Bavaria, His Majesty the King of Württemberg, His Royal Highness the Grand Duke of Baden and His Royal Highness the Grand Duke of Hesse and by Rhine, for those parts of the Grand Duchy of Hesse which are south of the river Maine, conclude an everlasting Federation for the protection of the territory of the Federation and the rights thereof, as well as to care for the welfare of the German people. This Federation will bear the name 'German Reich', and is to have the following

CONSTITUTION.

Section I. Territory of the Federation

Art. 1

The territory of the Federation is comprised of the States of Prussia with Lauenburg, Bavaria, Saxony, Württemberg, Baden, Hesse, Mecklenburg-Schwerin, Saxe-Weimar, Mecklenburg, Strelitz, Oldenburg, Brunswick, Saxe-Meiningen, Saxe-Altenburg, Saxe-Coburg-Gotha, Anhalt, Schwarzburg-Rudolstadt, Schwarzburg-Sondershausen, Waldeck, Reuss Elder Line, Reuss Younger Line Schaumburg-Lippe, Lippe, Lübeck, Bremen, and Hamburg.

Section II. Legislature of the Reich

Art. 2

Within this federate territory the Reich exercises the right of legislation according to the stipulations of this Constitution, and with the effect that the Reich laws take precedence of the laws of the States. The Reich laws receive their binding power by their publication in the name of the Reich, which takes place by means of a *Reich Law Gazette*. If the date of its first coming into force is not otherwise fixed in the published law, it comes into force on the 14th day after the close of the day on which the part of the *Reich Law Gazette* which contains it is published in Berlin.

121

Art. 3

For the whole of Germany one common nationality exists with the effect that every person (subject, State citizen) belonging to any one of the federated States is to be treated in every other of the federated States as a born native and accordingly must be permitted to have a fixed dwelling, to trade, to be appointed to public offices, to acquire property, to obtain the rights of a State citizen, and to enjoy all other civil rights under the same presuppositions as the natives, and likewise is to be treated equally with regard to legal prosecution or legal protection.

No German may be restricted from the exercise of this right by the authorities of his own State or by the authorities of any of the other federated States.

Those regulations which have reference to the care of the poor and their admission into local communities are not affected by the principles set down in the first paragraph.

Until further notice the Treaties likewise remain in force which have been entered into by the particular States of the Federation regarding the reception of persons expelled, the care of sick persons, and the burial of deceased persons belonging to the States.

What is necessary for the fulfilment of military duty in relation to the native country will be ordered by Reich legislation.

Every German has the same claim to the protection of the Reich with regard to foreign nations.

Art. 4

The following affairs are subject to the superintendence and legislation of the Reich:

  (1) the regulations as to freedom of movement, domicile and settlement affairs, right of citizenship, passport and police regulations for aliens, and as to transacting business including insurance affairs in so far as these objects are not already provided for by Art. 3 of this Constitution. In Bavaria, however, the domicile and settlement affairs, and likewise the affairs of colonisation and emigration to foreign countries, are herefrom excluded;

  (2) the customs and commercial legislation and the taxes which are to be applied to the requirements of the Reich;

  (3) the regulation of the system of coinage, weights and measures, likewise the establishment of the principles for the issue of funded and unfunded paper money;

(4) the general regulations as to banking;

(5) the granting of patents for inventions;

(6) the protection of intellectual property;

(7) the organisation of the common protection of German commerce in foreign countries, of German vessels and their flags at sea, and the arrangement of a common consular representation, which is to be salaried by the Reich;

(8) railway affairs — excepting in Bavaria the arrangements in Art. 46 — and the construction of land and water communications for the defence of the country and for general transport;

(9) the rafting and navigation affairs on waterways belonging in common to several of the States, and the condition of the waterways, and likewise the river or other water dues;

(10) postal and telegraphic affairs; in Bavaria and Württemberg, however, only with reference to the provisions of Art. 52;

(11) regulations as to the reciprocal execution of judgments in civil affairs and the settlement of requisitions in general;

(12) likewise as to the verification of public documents;

(13) the general legislation as to obligatory rights, penal law, commercial and bill of exchange laws, and judicial procedure;

(14) the military and naval affairs of the Reich;

(15) the measures of medicinal and veterinary police;

(16) the regulations for the press and for associations.

Art. 5

The legislation of the Reich is carried on by the Federal Council and the Reichstag. The accordance of the majority of votes in both Assemblies is necessary and sufficient for a law of the Reich.

In projects of law on military affairs, on naval affairs, and on the taxes mentioned in Art. 35 the President has the casting vote in cases where there is a difference of opinion, if his vote is in favour of the maintenance of the existing arrangements.

Section III. The Federal Council

Art. 6

The Federal Council consists of the representatives of the members of the Federation, amongst which the votes are divided in such ε manner that Prussia has, with the former votes of Hanover, Electoral Hesse, Holstein, Nassau, and Frankfurt,

	17 votes	
Bavaria	6	"
Saxony	4	"
Württemberg	4	"
Baden	3	"
Hesse	3	"
Mecklenburg-Schwerin	2	"
Saxe-Weimar	1	"
Mecklenburg-Strelitz	1	"
Oldenburg	1	"
Brunswick	2	"
Saxe-Meiningen	1	"
Saxe-Altenburg	1	"
Saxe-Coburg-Gotha	1	"
Anhalt	1	"
Schwarzburg-Rudolstadt	1	"
Schwarzburg-Sondershausen	1	"
Waldeck	1	"
Reuss Elder Line	1	"
Reuss Younger Line	1	"
Schaumburg-Lippe	1	"
Lippe	1	"
Lübeck	1	"
Bremen	1	"
Hamburg	1	"

Total 58 votes

Each member of the Federation can nominate as many plenipotentiaries to the Federal Council as it has votes, but the totality of such votes can only be given in one sense.

Art. 7

The Federal Council determines:

(1) what Bills are to be brought before the Reichstag and on the resolutions passed by the same;

(2) as to the administrative regulations and institutions necessary for the general execution of the Reich legislation, in so far as no other Reich law has decreed to the contrary;

(3) as to defects which have made themselves manifest in the

execution of the Reich laws or the above-mentioned measures and arrangements.

Every member of the Federation has the right to propose Bills and to recommend them, and the Presidency is bound to bring them under debate.

The decisions take place by simple majority, with the reservation of the stipulations in Art. 5, 37 and 78. Non-represented votes or votes without instructions are not counted. In equal divisions the Presidential is the casting vote.

In decisions upon affairs wherein, according to the rules of this Constitution, the whole Reich has not a common interest, only the votes of those federated States are counted which are interested in common.

Art. 8

The Federal Council forms permanent Committees from its own members:

(1) for the army and fortresses;
(2) for naval affairs;
(3) for customs and taxes;
(4) for commerce and communications;
(5) for railways, post and telegraphs;
(6) for affairs of justice;
(7) for finances.

In each of these Committees, besides the Presidency, at least four of the federated States will be represented, and in the same each State has only one vote. In the Committee for the army and fortresses, Bavaria has a perpetual seat, the other members thereof as well as the members for the Naval Committee are nominated by the Emperor; the members of the other Committees are elected by the Federal Council. The composition of these Committees is to be renewed for every session of the Federal Council or every year, when the outgoing members may be re-elected.

Besides these in the Federal Council, a Committee for Foreign Affairs will be formed, comprised of the representatives of the Kingdoms of Bavaria, Saxony and Württemberg, and of two other representatives of other federated States, who will be elected each year by the Federal Council, in which Committee Bavaria will occupy the chair.

The necessary officials will be placed at the disposal of these Committees.

Art. 9

Every member of the Federal Council has the right to appear in the Reichstag, and must at his desire at all times be heard, in order to represent the views of his government, even when these views have not been adopted by the majority of the Federal Council. No one may at the same time be a member of the Federal Council and of the Reichstag.

Art. 10

The Emperor is bound to afford the usual diplomatic protection to the members of the Federal Council.

Section IV. The Presidency

Art. 11

The Presidency of the Federation belongs to the King of Prussia, who bears the name of German Emperor. The Emperor has to represent the Reich internationally, to declare war and to conclude peace in the name of the Reich, to enter into alliances and other treaties with foreign powers, to accredit and to receive ambassadors.

The consent of the Federal Council is necessary for the declaration of war in the name of the Reich, unless an attack on the territory or the coast of the Federation has taken place.

In so far as treaties with foreign states have reference to affairs which, according to Art. 4, belong to the jurisdiction of the legislation, the consent of the Federal Council is requisite for their conclusion, and the sanction of the Reichstag for their coming into force.

Art. 12

The Emperor has the right to summon, to open, to prorogue and to close both the Federal Council and the Reichstag.

Art. 13

The summoning of the Federal Council and of the Reichstag takes place once each year and the Federal Council can be called together for preparation of business without the Reichstag being likewise summoned, whereas the latter cannot be summoned without the Federal Council.

Art. 14
The Federal Council must be summoned whenever one-third of the votes require it.

Art. 15
The presidency of the Federal Council and the direction of the business belongs to the Reichskanzler, who is to be appointed by the Emperor.

The Reichskanzler can be represented, on his giving written notification thereof, by any other member of the Federal Council.

Art. 16
The requisite Bills, in accordance with the votes of the Federal Council, will be brought before the Reichstag in the name of the Emperor, where they will be supported by members of the Federal Council, or by particular commissioners nominated by the latter.

Art. 17
The expedition and proclamation of the laws of the Reich, and the care of their execution, belongs to the Emperor. The Orders and Decrees of the Emperor are issued in the name of the Reich and require for their validity the counter-signature of the Reichskanzler, who thereby undertakes the responsibility.

Art. 18
The Emperor nominates the Reich officials, causes them to be sworn for the Reich and, when necessary, decrees their dismissal.

The officials of any state of the Federation, when appointed to any Reich office, are entitled to the same rights with respect to the Reich as they would enjoy from their official position in their own country, excepting in such cases as have otherwise been provided for by the Reich legislation before their entrance into the service of the Reich.

Art. 19
Whenever members of the Federation do not fulfil their constitutional duties towards the Federation, they may be constrained to do so by way of a warrant. Such warrant must be decreed by the Federal Council and be carried out by the Emperor.

Section V. The Reichstag

Art. 20

The Reichstag is elected by universal and direct election with a secret ballot.

Until the legal arrangement reserved in §5 of the Election Laws of 31 May 1869 (*Federal Law Gazette*, 1869, p. 145) has been made, there are to be elected: in Bavaria, 48; in Württemberg, 17; in Baden, 14; Hesse, south of the Main, 6 members; the total number of the members consists, therefore, of 382.

Art. 21

Officials do not require any leave of absence on entering into the Reichstag.

If any member of the Reichstag accepts any salaried appointment of the Reich, of any State of the Federation, or enters into any Reich or State office to which a higher rank, or higher salary is attached, he loses his seat and service in the Reichstag, and can only regain his position in the same by re-election.

Art. 22

The proceedings of the Reichstag are public.

Truthful reports of the proceedings in the public sittings of the Reichstag are free from any responsibility.

Art. 23

The Reichstag has the right to propose laws within the competency of the Reich, and to forward petitions which have been addressed to it either to the Federal Council or to the Reichskanzler.

Art. 24

The legislative period of the Reichstag is three years. For a dissolution of the Reichstag within this time, a resolution of the Federal Council, with the assent of the Emperor, is requisite.

Art. 25

In case of a dissolution of the Reichstag, the meeting of the electors must be called within a period of sixty days after such dissolution, and within a period of ninety days the Reichstag must be summoned.

Art. 26

Without the assent of the Reichstag the prorogation of the same may not be extended over thirty days, and it can never be repeated during the same session.

Art. 27

The Reichstag scrutinises the legality of the credentials of its members and decides thereon. It regulates its own method of business and discipline by means of a standing order and elects its President, Vice-Presidents, and Secretaries.

Art. 28

The Reichstag decides by an absolute majority of votes. The presence of a majority of the legal number of the members is necessary for the validity of a resolution.

In voting on a matter which, according to the stipulations of this Constitution, is not common to the whole Reich, only the votes of those members will be counted who have been elected in those federate States to which the matter is common.

Art. 29

The members of the Reichstag are representatives of the entire people and are not bound by orders and instructions.

Art. 30

No member of the Reichstag can at any time be proceeded against either judicially or by way of discipline, on account of his votes, or for statements made in the exercise of his functions, nor can he be made responsible in any other way out of the Assembly.

Art. 31

Without the assent of the Reichstag no member of the same may be placed under examination or arrested during the period of the session for any punishable deed except when taken in the fact or in the course of the following day.

The same assent is needful in arrest for debt.

At the demand of the Reichstag every correctional procedure against a member of the same and all investigations or civil arrests must be relinquished for the duration of the period of the session.

Art. 32

The members of the Reichstag must not receive any salary or

expenses in that capacity.

Section VI. Customs and Commercial Affairs

Art. 33
Germany forms one customs and commercial territory surrounded by a common customs frontier. Those separate parts of territory are excluded, which from their position are not adapted for inclusion in the customs area.

All articles of free trade in any one of the States of the Federation may be introduced into any other State of the Federation, and can only be subjected to a duty in the latter in so far as similar articles produced in that State are subject to a home duty.

Art. 34
The Hanseatic towns of Bremen and Hamburg, with so much of their own or of the adjacent territory as may be needful for the purpose, remain as free ports outside the common customs area until they apply to be admitted therein.

Art. 35
The Reich has the sole right of legislation in all customs affairs, in the taxation of salt and tobacco produced in the territories of the Federation, beer and spirits and sugar and syrup or other home productions made from beetroot, in the reciprocal protection of consumption duties raised in the separate States of the Federation against defraudations, as well as in such measures as the Customs' Committees may find requisite for the security of the common customs frontier.

In Bavaria, Württemberg and Baden, the taxation of the native spirits and beer remains for the present subject to the laws of the land. But the States of the Federation will direct their efforts to bring about an assimilation in the taxation of these articles likewise.

Art. 36
The collection and administration of the duties and consumption taxes (Art. 35) remain in the hands of each State of the Federation, within its own territory, in so far as they have hitherto been so.

The Emperor watches over the observance of the legal procedure through Reich officials, whom he attaches to the customs or excise offices, and to the directing authorities of the separate States according to the advice of the Committee of the Federal Council for customs and excise affairs.

Information given by these officials as to defects in the execution of the common legislation (Art. 35) will be laid before the Federal Council for decision.

Art. 37

In decisions relative to the administrative instructions and arrangements (Art. 35) for the execution of the common legislation, the Presidency has the easting vote, when it is given for the maintenance of the existing instruction or arrangement.

Art. 38

The revenue from the duties or other taxes mentioned in Art. 35, the latter in so far as they are subject to Reich legislation, flows into the Reich Treasury.

This revenue consists of the whole income arising from the duties and other taxes after the deduction of:

(1) the tax compensations and abatements according to the laws or the general administrative regulations;

(2) the repayments for incorrect levies;

(3) the expenses of collection and administration, as follows:

   (a) for the customs, the expenses which are requisite for the protection and the collection of the duties in that part of the frontiers situated towards foreign countries and in the border district;

   (b) for the salt tax, the expenses which are incurred for the salaries of the officials who are employed in the salt works to collect and control that tax;

   (c) for the beet-sugar and tobacco tax, the compensation which, according to the decisions of the Federal Council from time to time, has to be made to the several Federal governments for the expenses incurred in the administration of these taxes;

   (d) for the other duties, 15 per cent of the total income.

The territories situated outside the common customs frontier pay an agreed sum towards defraying the expenses of the Reich.

Bavaria, Württemberg and Baden do not participate in the income flowing into the Reich Treasury from the taxes on spirits and beer, nor in the corresponding part of the above-mentioned agreed payment.

Art. 39

The quarterly extracts which are to be made at the end of each quarter of the year by the collecting authorities of the Federal States, and the final statements to be made at the end of the year and the close of the books, on the income from duties and from consumption dues flowing into the Reich Treasury according to Art. 38, falling due during the quarter or during the financial year, are to be collected into chief summaries, after previous examination, by the directing authorities of the Federal States, and therein each duty is to be separately shown; these summaries are to be sent in to the Committee of the Federal Council for financial affairs.

On the basis of these summaries the said Committee makes out preliminarily, every three months, the amount due from the Treasury of each State of the Confederation, to the Reich Treasury, and communicates these amounts to the Federal Council and to the States of the Federation; it also presents the final statement of these amounts every year, with remarks, to the Federal Council. The Federal Council decides on this statement.

Art. 40

The stipulations in the Zollverein Treaty of 8 July 1867 remain in force in so far as they have not been altered by the provisions of this Constitution, and so long as they are not altered in the way pointed out in Art. 7 or Art. 78.

Section VII. Railways

Art. 41

Railways which are considered necessary for the defence of Germany or for the sake of common transport may, by virtue of a Reich law and even against the opposition of the members of the Federation whose territory is intersected by the railways, but without prejudice to the prerogatives of the country, be constructed on account of the Reich, or concessions to execute the works may be granted to private contractors, with the right of expropriation.

Every existing railway board of direction is bound to consent to the junction of newly-constructed railways at the expense of the latter.

The legal enactments which have granted a right of denial to existing railway undertakings against the construction of parallel or competing lines are hereby, without prejudice to rights already gained, repealed for the whole of the Reich. Nor can such a right of denial be ever granted again in concessions to be issued hereafter.

Art. 42

The governments of the States bind themselves to manage the German railways as a uniform network in the interest of common transport, and likewise for this purpose to have all new railways which are to be made, constructed and fitted up according to uniform rules.

Art. 43

For this purpose corresponding working arrangements are to be adopted with all possible dispatch, particularly with regard to railway police regulations. The Reich has likewise to take heed that the railway boards keep the lines at all times in such a state of repair as to ensure safety, and that they provide them with the working material necessary for the traffic.

Art. 44

The railway boards are bound to introduce the necessary passenger trains of the proper speed for through traffic and for the arrangement of corresponding journeys, also the requisite trains to provide for goods traffic; likewise to arrange direct despatches for passengers and goods traffic, with permission for conveying the means of transport from one line to the other for the usual payments.

Art. 45

The Reich exercises control over the tariffs and will especially operate to the end:
  (1) that working regulations, in conformity with each other, be introduced as soon as possible on all German railways;
  (2) that the greatest possible equalisation and reduction of the tariffs shall take place and, for greater distances, an abatement of the tariffs for the transport of coals, coke, timber, ores, stones, salt, raw iron, fertilisers and similar articles, so as to be more in proportion to the necessities of agriculture and industry, and that the one pfennig tariff may be introduced as speedily as possible.

Art. 46

In times of crisis, and particularly when an unusual rise in food prices occurs, the railway boards are bound to introduce a temporary special lower tariff for the transport of grain, flour, pulses and potatoes, according to the necessity, as will be determined by the Emperor on the proposal of the respective committee of the Federal Council, which tariff, however, must not be lower than the lowest rate already existing for raw produce on the respective line.

The above, as well as the stipulations made in Art. 42 to Art. 45, are not applicable to Bavaria.

However, the Reich has the right in regard to Bavaria likewise to lay down, by way of legislation, uniform rules for the construction and fitting up of those railways which are of importance for the defence of the country.

Art. 47

The requisitions of the authorities of the Reich relative to making use of the railways for the purpose of the defence of Germany, must be obeyed without question by all the railway boards. In particular, the military and all materials of war are to be conveyed at equally reduced rates.

Section VIII. Postal and Telegraphic Affairs

Art. 48

The postal and telegraphic affairs will be arranged and administered for the entire German Reich as uniform institutions for State intercourse.

The legislation of the Reich in postal and telegraphic affairs, as provided in Art. 4, does not extend to those objects, the regulation of which, according to the principles which govern the North German postal and telegraph administration, has been left to definitive rules or administrative directions.

Art. 49

The revenues of the postal and telegraphic service are in common for the entire Reich. The expenses will be defrayed from the common revenues. The surpluses flow into the Reich Treasury (Section XII).

Art. 50

The supreme authority over the postal and telegraphic administration is in the hands of the Emperor. The officials appointed by him have the duty and the right to take care that uniformity in the organisation of the administration and in carrying on the service, as well as in the qualification of the officials, be introduced and maintained.

The issue of definitive rules and general administrative directions, as well as the exclusive right to deal with other postal and telegraphic offices, belongs to the Emperor.

All the officials of the postal and telegraph administration are bound to obey the directions of the Reich. This obligation is to be recorded in the oath of service.

The appointment of the requisite higher officials for the administrative authorities of the postal and telegraphic service in the various districts (such as directors, counsellors, chief-inspectors), likewise the appointment of the officials acting as the organs of the before-mentioned public servants, in the service of supervision, etc., in the separate districts (such as inspectors, controllers), proceeds, for the whole territory of the German Reich, from the Emperor, to whom these officials render the oath of service. Timely notice of the appointments in question, for governmental approbation and publication, will be given to the governments of the several States, so far as their territory is thereby concerned.

The other officials necessary for the postal and telegraphic service, as well as all those required for the local or technical business, therefore the officials, etc., acting at the actual places of business, will be appointed by the respective State governments.

Where there is no independent State post or telegraph administration, the provisions of the special treaties form the rule.

Art. 51

In making over the balance of the postal administration for general Reich purposes (Art. 49), in consideration of the previous difference in the net incomes obtained by the State postal administrations of the separate territories, the following procedure is to be observed for the purpose of a corresponding arrangement during the undermentioned period of transition:

From the postal balances which have accrued in the separate postal districts during the five years from 1861 to 1865, an average yearly balance will be calculated, and the share which each separate postal district has had in the postal balance thus shown for the whole territory of the Reich, will be fixed according to percentages.

According to the proportion ascertained in this manner, the separate States will be credited for the next eight years after their entrance into the postal administration of the Reich, with such quotas as accrue to them from the postal balances produced in the Reich, in account with their other contributions for purposes of the Reich.

At the expiration of the eight years all distinctions cease, and the postal balances will flow in undivided account into the Reich Treasury, according to the principle set forth in Art. 49.

From the quotas of the postal surplus thus ascertained during the before-mentioned eight years for the Hanseatic towns, one-half will be placed beforehand every year at the disposal of the Emperor, for the purpose, in the first place, of paying therefrom the expenses for the establishment of normal postal institutions in the Hanseatic towns.

Art. 52

The stipulations in the foregoing Art. 48 to Art. 51 have no application to Bavaria and Württemberg. In their place the following stipulations are in force for those two States of the Federation.

To the Reich alone belongs the legislation as to the postal and telegraphic privileges, as to the legal relations between both institutions and the public, as to exemptions from postage and rates of postage, exclusively, however, of the rules and tariff regulations for the home circulation of Bavaria, and of Württemberg respectively, likewise under similar reservation the settlement of the fees for telegraphic correspondence;

In the same manner the regulation of the postal and telegraphic communication with foreign countries belongs to the Reich, excepting the direct communication of Bavaria and of Württemberg themselves with the neighbouring States which do not belong to the Reich, regulations as to which remain as stipulated in Art. 49 of the Postal Treaty of 23 November 1867;

Bavaria and Württemberg do not participate in the income flowing into the Treasury from the postal and telegraphic services.

Section IX. Shipping and Navigation

Art. 53

The war navy of the Reich is one united navy under the chief command of the Emperor. The organisation and composition thereof is the business of the Emperor, who appoints the naval officers and officials and into whose service they and the men are to be sworn.

The harbour of Kiel and that on the Jade Bight are military harbours of the Reich.

The necessary expenses for the establishment and maintenance of the war fleet, and the institutions in connection therewith, are paid from the Reich Treasury.

The whole of the maritime population of the Reich, including engineers and shipwrights, are free from service in the land forces but, on the other hand, are bound to serve in the Reich Navy.

The apportionment of the recruits is arranged according to the number of the maritime population, and the quota which each State thus contributes is deducted from the contingent to the land army.

Art. 54

The merchant vessels of all the States of the Federation form one unified commercial navy.

The Reich has to determine the method of ascertaining the burden of sea-going vessels, to grant bills of admeasurement, as well as to regulate the ship certificates and to determine the conditions upon which the permission to command a sea-going vessel depends.

The commercial ships of all the States of the Federation will be admitted and treated on equal terms in the sea harbours and in all the natural and artificial waterways of the separate States of the Federation. The dues to be levied in the sea ports from sea-going vessels or their cargoes for using the navigation installations must not exceed the expenses which are requisite for the maintenance and ordinary repairs of those appliances.

On all natural waterways dues may be levied only for the use of such installations as are intended especially for aiding traffic. These dues, as well as the dues payable for making use of such artificial waterways as are State property, must not exceed the expenses which are requisite for the maintenance and ordinary repairs of such erections and works. These regulations are also applicable to rafting so far as it takes place on navigable waterways.

The imposition of other or higher dues on foreign ships or their cargoes than those paid by the ships of the Federal States does not belong to any single State, but solely to the Reich.

Art. 55

The flag of the navy and of the merchant shipping is black–white–red.

Section X. Consular Service

Art. 56

The whole of the Consular service of the German Reich is under the superintendence of the Emperor, who appoints the Consuls after consultation with the Committee of the Federal Council for Commerce and Traffic.

Within the official district of the German Consuls no new Consulates for separate States may be erected. The German Consuls exercise the functions of a national Consul for any State of the Federation not represented in their district. All the existing Consulates for separate States are to be abolished as soon as the organisation of the German Consulates is so completed that the representation of the interests of all the States of the Confederation is recognised by the Federal Council as secured by the German Consulates.

Section XI. Military Affairs of the Reich

Art. 57

Every German is liable to military service and cannot have that service performed by a substitute.

Art. 58

The expenses and burdens of the whole of the military affairs of the Reich are to be borne equally by all of the States of the Federation and those belonging to them, so that no preferences, or overburdening of any single States or classes, are in principle admissible. Where an equal division of the burdens is not practicable *in natura*, without prejudice to the public welfare, the matter is to be arranged on the principles of equity by means of legislation.

Art. 59

Every German capable of service belongs for seven years to the standing army, as a rule from the completion of the twentieth to the commencement of the twenty-eighth year of his age; that is, for the first three of these years with the standards, and for the last four years in the reserve; then for the following five years of his life to the Landwehr. In those States of the Federation wherein hitherto a longer period than twelve years of service altogether has been legal, the gradual reduction of such service can take place only in so far as regard for the readiness for war of the Reich army permits it.

With respect to the emigration of the reserve men only those regulations are to be applied which are in force for the emigration of the Landwehr men.

Art. 60

The effective strength of the German army in peace is fixed until 31 December 1871 at 1 per cent of the population of the year 1867, and the separate States of the Federation supply it pro rata thereof. Subsequently the effective strength of the army in peace will be determined by legislation of the Reichstag.

Art. 61

After the publication of this Constitution the whole Prussian Military Code is to be introduced throughout the Reich without delay, both the laws themselves and the regulations, instructions and rescripts issued for the explanation and completion thereof, especially therefore the Military Penal Code of 3 April 1845; the Military Court Martial Regulations of 3 April 1845; the Ordinance upon Courts of Honour of 20 July 1843; the regulations as to recruiting, time of service, allowance and maintenance affairs, billeting, compensations for damages to agriculture mobilisation, etc., for war and peace. The military church ritual is, however, excluded.

After the uniform war organisation of the German army has been effected, a comprehensive military law for the Reich will be laid before the Reichstag and the Federal Council for their constitutional decision.

Art. 62

To cover the outlay necessary for the entire German army and the arrangements appertaining thereunto until 31 December 1871, there are yearly to be placed at the disposal of the Emperor as many times 225 thalers (in words, two hundred and twenty-five thalers) as the poll number of the peace strength of the army amounts to, according to Art. 60. See Section XII.

After 31 December 1871 these contributions must continue to be paid to the Reich Treasury by each State of the Federation. For the calculation thereof the effective peace-time strength, as provisionally settled in Art. 60, will be taken as the basis until it is altered by legislation of the Reichstag.

The expenditure plan of this sum for the entire army of the Reich and its arrangements will be determined on by the Estimate Law.

In settling the estimates of the military expenses the legal organisation of the Reich army, as laid down in this Constitution, will be taken as the basis.

Art. 63

The entire land force of the Reich will form a single army which in war and peace is under the command of the Emperor.

The regiments, etc., bear running numbers for the entire German Army. For their clothing, the ground colours and fashion of the Royal Prussian army are to be the model. It is left to the chiefs of the respective contingents to determine the insignia (cockades, etc.).

It is the duty and the right of the Emperor to take care that all the divisions of troops within the German army are numerically complete and utilisable for war, and that unity in the organisation and formation, in the armament and command, in the training of the men, as well as in the qualifications of the officers, be established and maintained. For this purpose the Emperor has the right to convince himself of the condition of the separate contingents at all times by inspection, and to order the reformation of any defects thereby discovered.

The Emperor determines the effective strength, the division and arrangement of the contingents of the Reich army, as well as the organisation of the Landwehr; he also has the right to determining the garrisons within the territories of the Federation and to order the embodiment of any part of the army in a state of preparation for war.

For the purpose of keeping up the indispensable uniformity in the administration, maintenance, armament and equipment of all the divisions of troops of the German army, the orders issued thereon in future for the Prussian army will be communicated in a suitable manner, through the committee for the land army and fortresses mentioned in Art. 7 (1), to the commanders of the other contingents for observance.

Art. 64

All German troops are bound to obey the commands of the Emperor unconditionally. This duty is to be specified in the banner-oath.

The Commander-in-Chief of a contingent, likewise all officers who command troops of more than one contingent and all commanders of fortresses are appointed by the Emperor. The officers appointed by the Emperor take the banner-oath to him. The appointments of Generals and officers acting as Generals within the contingents are at all times subject to the approbation of the Emperor.

The Emperor has the right, for purposes of transfer with or without promotion, to select, for such appointments as are to be made by him in the service of the Reich, whether in the Prussian army or in other contingents, from the officers of all the contingents of the army of the Reich.

Art. 65

The right of erecting fortresses within the territories of the Federation belongs to the Emperor, who proposes, according to Section XII, the grant of the necessary means for the purpose, in so far as they are not provided for in the ordinary estimates.

Art. 66

Where nothing to the contrary is stipulated by particular conventions, the sovereign heads of the Federation or the senates appoint the officers of their respective contingents, subject to the restriction of Art. 64. They are the chiefs of all the divisions of troops belonging to their territories, and enjoy the honours connected therewith. They have especially the right of inspection at all times and receive, besides the regular reports and announcements of alterations which take place, timely information, for the purpose of governmental publication, of all promotions or nominations among the respective troops.

Likewise they have the right to make use, for purposes of policing, not only their own troops, but also to make requisition for any other division of troops of the Reich army which may be located in their territories.

Art. 67

Savings from the military estimate do not belong under any circumstances to a single government, but at all times to the Reich Treasury.

Art. 68

The Emperor may, when public safety is threatened in the territories of the Federation, declare any part thereof to be in a state of war. Until the promulgation of a Reich law which fulfils the preconditions, the form of publication and the effects of such a declaration, the rules of the Prussian law of 4 June 1851 remain in force. (*Collection of Laws for 1851*, pp. 451ff.)

Final Stipulation to Section XI

The provisions contained in this section come into force in Bavaria according to the special stipulations of the Treaty of Confederation, of 23 November 1870 (*Federal Law Gazette*, 1871, p. 9), under II, §5, and in Württemberg according to the special stipulations of the Military Convention of 21–25 November 1870 (*Federal Law Gazette*, 1870, p. 658).

Section XII. Finances of the Empire

Art. 69

All the receipts and disbursements of the Reich must be estimated for each year, and be brought into the Reich estimates. These are to be fixed by a law before the beginning of the financial year, according to the following principles.

Art. 70

To provide for all common expenses, any balances of the preceding year are first of all employed, and likewise the common revenues derived from the duties, the common consumption taxes, and from the postal and telegraphic services. In so far as they cannot be provided for by these revenues they are, as long as Reich taxes are not introduced, to be met by contributions from the single States of the Federation, in proportion to their population, which contributions to the amount estimated in the budget will be assessed by the Reichskanzler.

Art. 71

The common disbursements are, as a rule, voted for one year; they may, however, in particular cases, be voted for a longer period.

During the time of transition mentioned in Art. 60, the estimates of the expenditure for the army, arranged under heads, are to be laid before the Federal Council and the Reichstag, only for their information and as a reminder.

Art. 72

The Reichskanzler is to give account yearly to the Federal Council and to the Reichstag of the application of all the incomes of the Reich, for discharge of responsibility.

Art. 73

In cases of extraordinary requirements the contracting of a loan, also the undertaking of a guarantee on account of the Reich, may take place in the way of Reich legislation.

Final Stipulation to Section XII.

To the expenditure for the Bavarian army Art. 69 and Art. 71 are applicable only in conformity with the stipulations of the Treaty of 23 November 1870, mentioned in the final stipulation to Section XI, and Art. 72 only so far that the assignment to Bavaria of the sums necessary for the Bavarian army is to be notified to the Federal Council and to the Reichstag.

Section XIII.
Settlement of Differences and Penal Stipulations

Art. 74

Any action against the existence, the integrity, the safety or the Constitution of the German Reich, finally, insulting the Federal Council or the Reichstag, or a member of the Federal Council or of the Reichstag or any authority, or a public servant of the Reich whilst in the exercise of their vocation, or in reference to their vocation, by word, in writing, printing, symbolic, figurative or other representation, will be sentenced and punished in the separate States of the Federation according to the existing law, or the laws which may in future be enacted there, in pursuance of which a similar offence committed against that separate State of the Federation, its Constitution, its Chambers, or Diet, the members of its Chambers, or Diet, its authorities and functionaries, would be punished.

Art. 75

For those actions against the German Reich, mentioned in Art. 74, which, if they had been undertaken against one of the separate States of the Federation, would be qualified as high treason or treason against the country, the Common Upper Court of Appeal of the three free and Hanseatic towns at Lübeck, is the competent deciding authority in the first and any instance.

The special regulations as to the competency and the procedure of the Upper Court of Appeal are to be settled by way of Reich legislation. Until the promulgation of a Reich law, the competency of the courts in the separate States of the Federation and the provisions relative to the procedure of these courts, remain as they have hitherto been.

Art. 76

Differences between various States of the Federation, in so far as they are not of a private legal nature and therefore to be decided by the competent judicial authorities, will, at the suit of one of the parties, be settled by the Federal Council.

Constitutional differences in those States of the Federation in whose constitution no authority for settling such disputes is provided, are to be amicably arranged by the Federal Council at the suit of one of the parties, or if this should not succeed, they are to be settled by way of Reich legislation.

Art. 77

If, in a State of the Federation, the case of a refusal of justice should occur and sufficient aid cannot be obtained by way of law, it is the duty of the Federal Council to take cognizance of the complaints as to the refused or hindered administration of the law when proved according to the Constitution and existing laws of the respective State of the Federation, and thereupon to cause the government of the federate State which has given occasion for the complaint, to afford judicial aid.

Section XIV. General Stipulations

Art. 78

Alterations in the Constitution take place by way of legislation. They are considered as rejected if they have 14 votes of the Federal Council against them.

Those provisions of the Constitution of the Reich by which certain rights are established for separate States of the Federation in their relation to the community, can only be altered with the consent of the State of the Federation entitled to those rights.

The Weimar Constitution of 1919

— 1383 —

Reichs-Gesetzblatt

Jahrgang 1919

Nr. 152

Inhalt: Die Verfassung des Deutschen Reichs. S. 1383.

(Nr. 6982) Die Verfassung des Deutschen Reichs. Vom 11. August 1919.

Das Deutsche Volk, einig in seinen Stämmen und von dem Willen beseelt, sein Reich in Freiheit und Gerechtigkeit zu erneuen und zu festigen, dem inneren und dem äußeren Frieden zu dienen und den gesellschaftlichen Fortschritt zu fördern, hat sich diese Verfassung gegeben.

Erster Hauptteil
Aufbau und Aufgaben des Reichs
Erster Abschnitt
Reich und Länder
Artikel 1

Das Deutsche Reich ist eine Republik.
Die Staatsgewalt geht vom Volke aus.

Artikel 2

Das Reichsgebiet besteht aus den Gebieten der deutschen Länder. Andere Gebiete können durch Reichsgesetz in das Reich aufgenommen werden, wenn es ihre Bevölkerung kraft des Selbstbestimmungsrechts begehrt.

Artikel 3

Die Reichsfarben sind schwarz-rot-gold. Die Handelsflagge ist schwarz-weiß-rot mit den Reichsfarben in der oberen inneren Ecke.

Artikel 4

Die allgemein anerkannten Regeln des Völkerrechts gelten als bindende Bestandteile des deutschen Reichsrechts.

Ausgegeben zu Berlin den 14. August 1919.

Constitution of the German Reich
of 11 August 1919

The German people, united in every branch and inspired by the determination to renew and establish its realm in freedom and justice, to be of service to the cause of peace at home and abroad, and to further social progress, has given itself this Constitution.

PART I
Organisation and Functions of the Reich

Section I. The Reich and the States

Art. 1

The German Reich is a Republic.
All state authority emanates from the people.

Art. 2

The territory of the Reich consists of the territories of the German States. Other territories may, by a law of the Reich, be incorporated in the Reich if their population so desires in virtue of the right of self determination.

Art. 3

The colours of the Reich are black, red and gold. The commercial flag is black, white and red, with the colours of the Reich in the upper inside corner.

Art. 4

The generally recognised rules of International Law are valid as binding constituent parts of the Law of the German Reich.

Art. 5

State authority is exercised in the affairs of the Reich through the institutions of the Reich on the basis of the Constitution of the Reich and in State affairs by the institutions of the States on the basis of the Constitutions of the States.

Art. 6

The Reich has exclusive legislative power as regards:

    (1) foreign relations;

    (2) colonial affairs;

    (3) nationality, freedom of domicile, immigration, emigration, and extradition;

    (4) military organisation;

    (5) monetary system;

    (6) customs, as well as uniformity in the sphere of customs and trade, and freedom of commercial intercourse;

    (7) posts and telegraphs, including telephones.

Art. 7

The Reich has legislative power as regards:

    (1) civic rights;

    (2) penal law;

    (3) judicial procedure, including the carrying out of sentences, as well as official cooperation between public authorities;

    (4) passports and the police supervision of foreigners;

    (5) poor relief and vagrancy;

    (6) the Press, associations and assemblies;

    (7) population questions and the care of motherhood, infants, children and young persons;

    (8) public health and veterinary matters, and the protection of plants against disease and pests;

    (9) labour laws, the insurance and protection of workers and employees, together with labour bureaux;

  (10) the institution of vocational representative bodies for the territory of the Reich;

  (11) the care of persons who took part in the war, and of their dependants;

  (12) the law of expropriation;

  (13) the formation of associations for dealing with natural resources and economic undertakings, as well as the production, preparation, distribution and determination of prices of economic commodities for common use;

  (14) commerce, the system of weights and measures, the issue of paper money, banking affairs and the system of exchange;

  (15) traffic in foodstuffs and luxuries, as well as in articles of daily necessity;

(16) industry and mining;
(17) insurance matters;
(18) navigation, deep sea and coastal fishery;
(19) railways, inland navigation, motor traffic by land, water and air, as well as the construction of high-roads, so far as this is concerned with general traffic and home defence;
(20) theatres and cinemas.

Art. 8

Further, the Reich has legislative power as regards taxes and other revenues in so far as they are appropriated wholly or in part to its purposes. Should the Reich appropriate taxes or other revenues hitherto appertaining to the various States, it must take into consideration the maintenance of the vitality of those States.

Art. 9

Where there is need for the issue of uniform regulations, the Reich has legislative power as regards:
(1) sanitary administration;
(2) the maintenance of public order and security.

Art. 10

The Reich may by legislation lay down fundamental principles governing:
(1) the rights and duties of religious associations;
(2) education, including higher education and scientific literature;
(3) the law as to the conditions of service of officials of all public bodies;
(4) the land laws, the distribution of land, land settlement and small holdings, the tenure of landed property;
(5) burial of the dead.

Art. 11

The Reich may by legislation lay down fundamental principles governing the admissibility and mode of collection of State taxes, in so far as they are requisite either for the purpose of preventing:
(1) loss of revenue or injury to the commercial relations of the Reich;
(2) double taxation;
(3) charges for the use of public means of communication and their accessories, which are excessive and constitute a

hindrance to traffic;
(4) assessments which are prejudicial to imported goods, as opposed to home products, in dealings between the separate States and parts of a State;
(5) bounties on exportation, or for the purpose of protecting important social interests.

Art. 12

So long and in so far as the Reich does not make use of its legislative power, the States retain that power for themselves. This does not apply to the exclusive legislative power of the Reich.

The Government of the Reich has the right of veto in respect of any laws of a State which refer to subjects included in Art. 7 (13), in so far as the welfare of the Reich as a whole is thereby affected.

Art. 13

The law of the Reich overrides the law of a State.

Where there exists any doubt or difference of opinion as to whether any provision of State law is compatible with the law of the Reich, an appeal may be made by the competent Reich or State authorities to the decision of the Supreme Court of the Reich in accordance with the more detailed provisions to be prescribed by a law of the Reich.

Art. 14

Laws of the Reich are carried into execution by the State authorities, unless these laws decree otherwise.

Art. 15

The Government of the Reich exercises control in those affairs in which the Reich has legislative power.

In so far as laws of the Reich are carried into execution by State authorities, the Government of the Reich may issue general instructions. For the purpose of supervision of the execution of laws of the Reich, the Government is empowered to despatch commissioners to the State central authorities, and, with their consent, to the subordinate authorities.

It is the duty of the State Governments, at the request of the Government of the Reich, to remedy defects observed in the execution of laws of the Reich. In case of differences of opinion, both the Government of the Reich and the State Government may appeal to the decision of the Supreme Court, save where appeal to another Court has been prescribed by law of the Reich.

Art. 16

Officials entrusted with the direct administration of the Reich in the various States shall, as a rule, be citizens of the State in question. Officials, employees and workmen of the administration of the Reich shall, if they desire it, be employed as far as possible in their native districts, unless consideration of training or the exigencies of the service are opposed to this course.

Art. 17

Each state must have a republican constitution. The representatives of the people must be elected by the universal, equal, direct and secret suffrage of all men and women of the German Reich, upon the principles of proportional representation. The State Government must enjoy the confidence of the people's representatives.

The principles governing elections of the people's representatives apply also to elections to local bodies. By a State law the qualification for a vote may, however, be declared conditional upon a year's residence in the district.

Art. 18

The organisation of the Reich into States shall serve the highest economic and cultural interests of the people with all due consideration for the will of the population concerned. Alteration of the territory of the States, and the formation of new States within the Reich, shall be effected by means of a law of the Reich amending the Constitution.

Where the States concerned give their direct consent, a simple law of the Reich suffices.

A simple law of the Reich suffices also, in a case where the consent of one of the States concerned has not been obtained, but where an alteration of territory or reorganisation is demanded by the will of the population and required by paramount interests of the Reich.

The will of the population is ascertained by plebiscite. The Government of the Reich orders the taking of a plebiscite when demanded by one-third of those inhabitants of the territory to be separated who are entitled to vote for the Reichstag.

For the determination of an alteration or reorganisation of territory, the proportion of votes required is three-fifths of the number cast, or, at least, a majority of the votes of persons qualified. Even when it is a question only of the separation of a portion of a Prussian administrative area (*Regierungsbezirk*), a Bavarian district (*Kreis*) or of a corresponding administrative district (*Verwaltungsbezirk*) in other States, the will of the population of the whole district in question shall be ascertained. Should the area of the territory to be separated and that of the whole district (*Bezirk*) not coincide, the will of the population of the former may by means of a special law of the Reich be declared sufficient.

The consent of the population having been obtained, the Government of the Reich shall lay before the Reichstag a law in accordance with the decision.

In the case of union or separation, should any dispute arise on the question of arrangements as to the property, the decision on such points shall be given, upon an application from one party, by the Supreme Court of the German Reich.

Art. 19

Constitutional controversies within a State in which no court exists for their settlement, and disputes, not of a private nature, between different States or between the Reich and a State, are decided, upon an application from one of the parties, by the Supreme Court of the German Reich unless another Court of the Reich is competent.

The President of the Reich carries out the decision of the Supreme Court.

Section II. The Reichstag

Art. 20

The Reichstag is composed of the Deputies of the German people.

Art. 21

The Deputies are representatives of the whole people. They are subject to their conscience only, and are not bound by any instructions.

Art. 22

The Deputies are elected by the universal, equal, direct and secret suffrage of all men and women above the age of twenty, upon the principles of proportional representation. Elections must take place on a Sunday, or a public holiday.

Details are determined by the election law of the Reich.

Art. 23

The Reichstag is elected for four years. New elections must take place not later than sixty days after the expiration of its term of office.

The Reichstag must hold its first meeting not less than thirty days after the election.

Art. 24

The Reichstag assembles annually on the first Wednesday in November at the seat of the Government of the Reich. The President of the Reichstag must summon it earlier if requested by the President of the Reich or by at least one-third of the members.

The Reichstag determines the conclusion of the session and the day of re-assembly.

Art. 25

The President of the Reich may dissolve the Reichstag, but only once for any one reason.

The new elections must take place not later than sixty days after the dissolution.

Art. 26

The Reichstag elects its Chairman, Deputy-Chairman and Secretaries. It determines its own rules of procedure.

Art. 27

Between two sessions or elective periods the Chairman and Vice-Chairman of the last session continue to discharge their duties.

Art. 28

The Chairman exercises domestic and police authority within the Reichstag buildings. He is responsible for the administration of the House; regulates receipts and expenditure within the limits fixed by the Budget of the Reich, and represents the Reich in all the legal business and legal proceedings connected with his administration.

Art. 29
The Reichstag conducts its business in public. Upon the motion of fifty members, supported by a two-thirds majority, the public may be excluded.

Art. 30
Accurate reports of deliberations in the public sessions of the Reichstag, of a State Diet, or of their Committees are privileged.

Art. 31
A Court of Inquiry into Elections is established in connection with the Reichstag. It also decides the question as to whether a Deputy has forfeited his membership.

The Court consists of members of the Reichstag, chosen by it for the electoral period, and of members of the Administrative Court of the Reich, appointed by the President of the Reich, upon the motion of the presiding officer of that Court.

The Court gives judgment after public *viva voce* investigation by three members of the Reichstag and two judicial members.

Apart from the investigation before this Court, the proceedings are conducted by an official of the Reich, appointed by the President of the Reich. Further provisions as to procedure are determined by the Court.

Art. 32
For a decision of the Reichstag, a simple majority of votes is required, where no other proportion of votes is prescribed by the Constitution. The rules of procedure may permit exceptions in the case of elections to be undertaken by the Reichstag.

The number required to form a quorum is regulated by the rules of procedure.

Art. 33
The Reichstag and its Committees may require the attendance of the Chancellor of the Reich and of any Ministers of the Reich.

The Chancellor and the Ministers of the Reich, and officials appointed by them, have access to the sittings of the Reichstag and its Committees. The States are entitled to send plenipotentiaries to these sittings, for the purpose of stating the point of view of their Government with regard to the subject under discussion.

At their request, Government representatives must be heard during the debate, and the representatives of the Government of the Reich must be heard without regard to the Order of the Day. Such representatives are subject to the authority of the Chair.

Art. 34

The Reichstag has the right to appoint Committees of Inquiry and must do so on the motion of one-fifth of its members. These Committees examine in open session such evidence as may be considered necessary by the Committee or by the movers of the motion for their appointment. The public may be excluded by resolution of the Committee of Inquiry supported by a two-thirds majority. The rules of procedure prescribe the procedure of the Committee and determine the number of its members.

The Courts and administrative authorities are bound to comply with the request of such Committees for the production of evidence; the official documents of the authorities must be laid before them if desired. The regulations as to criminal procedure are applicable in principle to the investigations of the Committees and of the authorities applied to by them, but the privacy of correspondence and of postal, telegraphic and telephonic communications must be respected.

Art. 35

The Reichstag appoints a Standing Committee for Foreign Affairs which may also continue its work beyond the sessions of the Reichstag and after the expiration of the term of office or the dissolution of the Reichstag, until the assembly of the new Reichstag. The sittings of this Committee are not public, unless so decided by the Committee upon a two-thirds majority.

The Reichstag also appoints a Standing Committee for the Protection of the Rights of the Representatives of the People as against the Government of the Reich, for the period when the Reichstag is not in session, and after the expiration of its term of office.

These Committees have the same rights as Committees of Inquiry.

Art. 36

No judicial or administrative proceedings may be taken at any time against any Member of the Reichstag or of any State Diet, on account of any vote he has given, or of any utterances made in the exercise of his functions, nor may he be called to account in any other way outside the House.

Art. 37

No member of the Reichstag or of a State Diet may be summoned for examination or arrested for any action involving criminal proceedings during the period of a session, without the consent of the House of which he is a member, unless the member be apprehended at the time of the act or, at the latest, in the course of the following day.

The same consent is requisite for any other limitation of personal liberty which might hinder a Deputy in the exercise of his functions.

Any criminal proceedings against a Member of the Reichstag or of a State Diet and any arrest or other limitation of personal freedom shall, upon demand of the House of which he is a member, be suspended for the duration of the Session.

Art. 38

Members of the Reichstag or a State Diet are entitled to refuse evidence with regard to persons who have confided any facts to them in their capacity as Deputies, or to whom they, in the exercise of their functions as Deputies, have made confidential statements; they may likewise refuse to give evidence as to such facts. With regard also to the sequestration of documents, they are in the position of persons who have a legal right to refuse evidence.

No search or sequestration may be carried out upon the premises of the Reichstag or of a State Diet without the consent of the Chairman.

Art. 39

Officials and members of the Military Forces do not require leave of absence in order to exercise their functions as Members of the Reichstag or of a State Diet. If they are candidates for a seat in these bodies, they shall be granted the requisite leave in order to prepare for the election.

Art. 40

Members of the Reichstag are entitled to travel free on all German railways, and to receive allowances as determined by a law of the Reich.

Section III
The President of the Reich and the Government of the Reich

Art. 41

The President of the Reich is elected by the whole German people.

Every German who has completed his thirty-fifth year is eligible. Details shall be determined by a law of the Reich.

Art. 42

The President of the Reich when entering upon his office takes the following oath before the Reichstag: 'I swear to dedicate my powers to the welfare of the German people, to augment their prosperity, to guard them from injury, to maintain the Constitution and the laws of the Reich, to fulfil my duties conscientiously, and to do justice to every man'.

The addition of a religious asseveration is permissible.

Art. 43

The President of the Reich holds office for seven years. Re-election is permissible.

The President of the Reich may, upon the motion of the Reichstag, be removed from office before the expiration of his term by the vote of the people. The resolution of the Reichstag must be carried by a two-thirds majority. Upon the adoption of such a resolution, the President of the Reich is prevented from the further exercise of his office. Refusal to remove him from office, expressed by the vote of the people, is equivalent to re-election, and entails the dissolution of the Reichstag.

Penal proceedings may not be taken against the President of the Reich without the consent of the Reichstag.

Art. 44

The President of the Reich may not at the same time be a member of the Reichstag.

Art. 45

The President of the Reich represents the Reich in international relations. He concludes alliances and other treaties with Foreign Powers in the name of the Reich. He accredits and receives ambassadors.

The declaration of war and the conclusion of peace are dependent upon the passing of a law of the Reich.

Alliances and treaties with foreign states which refer to matters in which the Reich has legislative power require the consent of the Reichstag.

Art. 46

The President of the Reich appoints and dismisses officials and officers of the Reich, where no other system is determined by law. He may delegate his right of appointment and dismissal to other authorities.

Art. 47

The President of the Reich has Supreme Command over all the Armed Forces of the Reich.

Art. 48

In the event of a State not fulfilling the duties imposed on it by the Constitution or the laws of the Reich, the President of the Reich may make use of the armed forces to compel it to do so.

Where public security and order are seriously disturbed or endangered within the Reich, the President of the Reich may take the measures necessary for their restoration, intervening in case of need with the help of armed forces. For this purpose he is permitted, for the time being, to abrogate either wholly or partially the fundamental rights laid down in Arts. 114, 115, 117, 118, 123, 124, and 153.

The President of the Reich must, without delay, inform the Reichstag of any measures taken in accordance with paragraph 1 or 2 of this Article. Such measures shall be abrogated upon the demand of the Reichstag.

Where there is danger in delay, the State Government may take provisional measures of the kind indicated in paragraph 2, for its own territory. Such measures shall be abrogated upon the demand of the President of the Reich or the Reichstag.

Details are to be determined by a law of the Reich.

Art. 49

The President of the Reich exercises the right of pardon for the Reich.

The grant of amnesty by the Reich requires to be effected by a law of the Reich.

Art. 50

All orders and decrees of the President of the Reich, including those relating to the armed forces, require for their validity the counter-signature of the Chancellor or the competent Minister of the Reich. The counter-signature entails the undertaking of responsibility.

Art. 51

In case of any disability the President of the Reich is represented in the first instance by the Chancellor of the Reich. Should it be probable that the disability might continue for some time, his representative shall be appointed by a law of the Reich.

The same applies to the case of premature vacancy in the office of President pending the carrying out of the new election.

Art. 52

The Government of the Reich consists of the Chancellor of the Reich and the Ministers of the Reich.

Art. 53

The President of the Reich appoints and dismisses the Chancellor of the Reich and, on the latter's recommendation, the Ministers of the Reich.

Art. 54

The Chancellor of the Reich and the Ministers of the Reich require the confidence of the Reichstag in the administration of their office. Any one of them must resign should the confidence of the Reichstag be withdrawn by an express resolution.

Art. 55

The Chancellor of the Reich presides over the Government of the Reich and directs its business, according to rules of procedure drawn up by the Government of the Reich and approved by the President of the Reich.

Art. 56

The Chancellor of the Reich determines the main lines of policy, for which he is responsible to the Reichstag. Within these main lines each Minister of the Reich directs independently the department entrusted to him, for which he is personally responsible to the Reichstag.

Art. 57

The Ministers of the Reich must submit to the Government for consideration and decision the drafts of all Bills and other matters for which such a course is prescribed by the Constitution or by law, as well as differences of opinion upon questions affecting the sphere of action of more than one Minister of the Reich.

Art. 58

The Government of the Reich comes to a decision by a majority of votes. In case of an equality of votes the presiding member gives the casting vote.

Art. 59

The Reichstag may arraign the President of the Reich, the Chancellor and the Ministers before the Supreme Court of the German Reich for culpable violation of the Constitution or of a law of the Reich. The motion for the arraignment must be signed by at least one hundred members of the Reichstag, and requires the assent of the majority prescribed for alterations of the Constitution. Details are to be regulated by the law of the Reich as to the Supreme Court.

Section IV. The Reichsrat

Art. 60

A Reichsrat is formed in order to represent the German States in the legislation and administration of the Reich.

Art. 61

In the Reichsrat, each State has at least one vote. In the larger States, one vote is assigned for each million inhabitants. Any surplus not less than the total population of the smallest State is reckoned as a full million. No State may be represented by more than two-fifths of all the votes.

German Austria will, after her union with the German Reich, acquire the right of participation in the Reichsrat, with the number of votes corresponding to her population. Until that time, the representatives of German Austria have an advisory voice.*

The number of votes shall be readjusted by the Reichsrat after each general census of the population.

Art. 62

In Committees appointed by the Reichsrat from its members no State shall have more than one vote.

Art. 63

The States are represented in the Reichsrat by members of their Governments. However, one-half of the Prussian votes shall be assigned, according to a State law, to representatives of Prussian provincial administrations.

The States are entitled to send to the Reichsrat as many representatives as they have votes.

Art. 64

The Government of the Reich must convene the Reichsrat upon the demand of one-third of its members.

Art. 65

The Reichsrat and its Committees are presided over by a member of the Government of the Reich. The members of the latter are entitled and, if requested, are bound, to take part in the deliberations of the Reichsrat and its Committees. They must be heard upon their demand at any time during the debate.

Art. 66

The Government of the Reich and each member of the Reichsrat are authorised to lay proposals before the Reichsrat.

The Reichsrat regulates the conduct of its business by rules of procedure.

The plenary sessions of the Reichsrat are public. The public may be excluded during the discussion of certain subjects, in accordance with the rules of procedure.

For a decision a simple majority of the votes is required.

---

* According to Art. 80 of the Treaty of Peace between the Allied and Associated Powers and Germany, signed at Versailles on 28 June 1919: 'Germany acknowledges and will respect strictly the independence of Austria, within the frontiers which may be fixed in a Treaty between that State and the Principal Allied and Associated Powers; she agrees that this independence shall be inalienable, except with the consent of the Council of the League of Nations'. A declaration that all the provisions of this Constitution which were found to be in contradiction with the terms of the Treaty of Peace would be null and void was signed on 22 September 1919 at Paris by the acting Head of the German delegation.

Art. 67

The Reichsrat shall be kept informed by the Ministries of the Reich of the progress of affairs in the Reich. Upon important subjects the Committees of the Reichsrat concerned shall be called into consultation by the Ministries of the Reich.

Section V. Legislation of the Reich

Art. 68

Bills are introduced by the Government of the Reich or by members of the Reichstag.

The laws of the Reich are passed by the Reichstag.

Art. 69

The introduction of Bills by the Government of the Reich requires the consent of the Reichsrat. Should the Government and the Reichsrat not be in agreement, the former may nevertheless introduce the Bill but, in doing so, must state the divergent view of the Reichsrat.

Should the Reichsrat adopt a Bill to which the Government does not agree, the latter must introduce the Bill in the Reichstag with a statement of its own point of view.

Art. 70

The President of the Reich shall prepare for publication the laws which have been adopted in accordance with the Constitution and, within the period of one month, shall promulgate them in the *Reichsgesetzblatt* (*Journal of Laws of the Reich*).

Art. 71

Laws of the Reich come into force, unless otherwise provided therein, fourteen days from the day on which the *Reichsgesetzblatt* is published in the capital.

Art. 72

The promulgation of a law of the Reich shall be deferred for two months, if one-third of the Reichstag so demands. Laws which the Reichstag and the Reichsrat declare to be urgent may, however, be promulgated by the President of the Reich, notwithstanding such a demand.

Art. 73

A law passed by the Reichstag shall, before its promulgation, be submitted to the decision of the people, if the President of the Reich so determines within one month.

A law the promulgation of which is deferred on the motion of at least one-third of the Reichstag shall be submitted to the decision of the people, if desired by one-twentieth of those entitled to the franchise.

There may also be an appeal to the decision of the people if one-tenth of those entitled to the franchise initiate a request for the introduction of a Bill. This popular initiative must be based on a complete draft of the Bill. It shall be submitted to the Reichstag by the Government, accompanied by a statement of the Government's attitude in regard to it. The appeal to the decision of the people shall not take place if the proposed Bill is accepted without amendment by the Reichstag.

The President of the Reich alone is entitled to institute an appeal to the decision of the people on the Budget and on laws dealing with taxation and decrees as to payments to employees.

The procedure in connection with the appeal to and initiative by the people is to be regulated by a law of the Reich.

Art. 74

The Reichsrat may enter an objection against a law passed by the Reichstag.

This objection must be lodged with the Government of the Reich within two weeks after the final vote in the Reichstag, and must be supported by reasons, presented at latest within a further two weeks.

When an objection is entered, the law shall be brought before the Reichstag for further consideration. Should the Reichstag and the Reichsrat not arrive at an agreement the President of the Reich may, within three months, order an appeal to the people upon the subject in dispute. Should the President not make use of this right, the law shall not come into operation. Should the Reichstag decide by a two-thirds' majority against the objection of the Reichsrat, the President must, within three months, either promulgate the law in the form approved by the Reichstag or order an appeal to the people.

Art. 75

A decision of the Reichstag can be annulled by the decision of the people only when a majority of those entitled to the franchise take part in the vote.

Art. 76

The Constitution may be amended by legislation. But decisions of the Reichstag as to such amendments come into effect only if two-thirds of the legal total of members be present, and if at least two-thirds of those present have given their consent. Decisions of the Reichsrat in favour of amendments of the Constitution also require a majority of two-thirds of the votes cast. Where an amendment of the Constitution is decided by an appeal to the people as the result of a popular initiative, the consent of the majority of the voters is necessary.

Should the Reichstag have decided upon an alteration of the Constitution in spite of the objection of the Reichsrat, the President of the Reich shall not promulgate the law if the Reichsrat, within two weeks, demands an appeal to the people.

Art. 77

The Government of the Reich issues the general administrative instructions necessary for the execution of the laws of the Reich, unless otherwise provided by law. For this purpose, the Government needs the assent of the Reichsrat when the execution of the law of the Reich is the business of the authorities of the State.

Section VI. Administration of the Reich

Art. 78

The conduct of foreign affairs is the exclusive concern of the Reich.

In affairs regulated by State legislation, the States may conclude agreement with foreign States. These agreements require the consent of the Reich.

Conventions with foreign States as to the alteration of the frontiers of the Reich are concluded by the Reich, with the consent of the State concerned. Alterations in the frontier may be effected only by a law of the Reich, except in the case of a simple rectification of the borders of uninhabited portions of a district.

In order to guarantee representation of the interests of individual

States arising from their special economic relations with foreign States or their proximity thereto, the Reich undertakes the requisite arrangements and measures in agreement with the State concerned.

Art. 79
The defence of the Reich is a matter for action by the Reich. The military organisation of the German people is regulated uniformly by means of a law of the Reich, regard being had to the individual conditions of each State.

Art. 80
Colonial affairs are exclusively the business of the Reich.

Art. 81
All German merchant shipping constitutes a united commercial fleet.

Art. 82
Germany forms one customs and commercial district, enclosed by one common customs frontier.

The customs frontier coincides with the foreign frontier. To seaward it is formed by the shore of the mainland, with the islands belonging to the territory of the Reich. On the sea or on other bodies of water, deviations may be made in the course of the customs frontier.

The territories or portions of the territories of a foreign State may be included in the customs district by State treaties or by agreement.

In cases of special necessity certain areas may be excluded from the customs district. In the case of free ports, exclusion can be set aside only by means of a law amending the Constitution.

Places excluded from the customs district may join a foreign customs district by means of a State treaty or by agreement.

All natural products as well as products of manufacture and industry in which there is free trade within the Reich may be imported, exported or sent in through transit across the frontiers of the States and local authorities. Exceptions may be allowed by a law of the Reich.

Art. 83

Customs and duties upon articles of consumption are administered by authorities of the Reich.

In the administration of taxes by the authorities of the Reich arrangements shall be made so as to ensure to the various States the protection of special State interests within the domain of agriculture, trade, manufacture and industry.

Art. 84

The Government of the Reich regulates by law:

(1) the organisation of the administration of taxes in the States, so far as is required for the purpose of uniform and equal execution of the laws of the Reich on taxation;

(2) the organisation and powers of the authorities entrusted with the superintendence of the execution of the laws of the Reich on taxation;

(3) the settlement of accounts with the States;

(4) the reimbursement of expenses of administration in the execution of the laws of the Reich on taxation.

Art. 85

All receipts and expenditures of the Reich must be estimated for each financial year and be shown in the Budget.

The Budget must be passed into law before the opening of the financial year.

Items of expenditure shall normally be granted for one year; in special cases, they may be granted for a longer period. In general, provisions in the Budget law of the Reich which extend beyond the financial year or do not refer to the receipts and expenditure of the Reich or their administration are inadmissible.

The Reichstag may neither increase items of expenditure nor include new ones in the draft of the Budget without the consent of the Reichsrat.

Failing the consent of the Reichsrat the provisions of Art. 74 apply.

Art. 86

In order to secure discharge of the responsibility of the Government of the Reich, the Minister of Finance for the Reich shall, in the following financial year, submit to the Reichstag and the Reichsrat an account of the expenditure out of all revenues of the Reich. The auditing of accounts shall be regulated by law of the Reich.

Art. 87

Funds may be obtained by way of loan in case of special necessity and, as a rule, only for expenditure on productive undertakings. Such a proceeding, as well as the giving of a security on behalf of the Reich, may be effected only upon the authority of a law of the Reich.

Art. 88

The postal and telegraph services, together with the telephone services, are exclusively the affairs of the Reich.

Postage stamps are uniform for the whole Reich.

The Government of the Reich, with the consent of the Reichsrat, issues the instructions which determine the conditions and charges for the use of the means of communication. With the consent of the Reichsrat, the Government may transfer these powers to the Minister of Posts.

For the purpose of consultative cooperation in matters connected with postal, telegraphic and telephonic communications and the charges therefore the Government of the Reich shall, with the consent of Reichsrat, establish an Advisory Council.

Treaties referring to means of communication with foreign countries are concluded only by the Government of the Reich.

Art. 89

It is the duty of the Government of the Reich to assume ownership of the railways serving for general traffic, and to manage them on a uniform traffic system.

The rights of States to acquire private railways shall be transferred upon demand, to the Government of the Reich.

Art. 90

With the transfer of the railways, the Reich assumes the power of expropriation and the sovereign rights of the States as regards the railway service. The Supreme Court, decides, in case of dispute, as to the extent of such rights.

Art. 91

The Government of the Reich, with the consent of the Reichsrat, issues orders for regulating the construction, management and working of the railways. With the consent of the Reichsrat, the Government may delegate these powers to the competent Minister of the Reich.

Art. 92

Notwithstanding the incorporation of their budget and accounts with the general Budget and accounts of the Reich the railways of the Reich shall be administered as an independent economic undertaking responsible for defraying its own expenses, inclusive of interest and a sinking-fund for the railway debt, and also for accumulating a reserve. The amount of the sinking-fund and reserve, as well as the purpose to which the reserve is to be applied, shall be regulated by means of a special law.

Art. 93

For the purpose of consultative cooperation in matters concerning railway traffic and rates, the Government of the Reich shall, with the consent of the Reichsrat, establish Advisory Councils for the Railways of the Reich.

Art. 94

Where the Government of the Reich has taken over in a certain district the railways serving for general traffic, new railways serving the same purpose may be constructed within this district only by the Reich, or with its consent. Should the construction of new or the alteration of existing railways by the Reich affect the sphere of activity of the police authorities of a State, the Railway Administration of the Reich must consult the State Authorities before coming to a decision.

Where the Reich has not yet taken over the railways, it may, on the authority of a law of the Reich, construct at its own expense, or permit another body to construct (subject when necessary to reservation of the right of expropriation), railways considered necessary for general traffic or for the defence of the territory, even without the consent of the States through the territory of which the railway is to run, but without prejudice to the sovereign rights of the States.

Every railway system must permit other railways to make junctions with it at the cost of the latter.

Art. 95

Railways for general traffic which are not under the administration of the Reich are subject to its supervision.

Railways subject to such supervision shall be constructed and equipped upon the principles laid down by the Reich. They must be maintained in good working order, and developed in accordance with the requirements of traffic. Both passenger and goods traffic must be attended to and organised in accordance with their needs.

In the supervision of rates, uniform and low railway rates are to be aimed at.

Art. 96

All railways, including those not serving for general traffic, must comply with the requirements of the Reich as to the use of railways for the purpose of State defence.

Art. 97

It is the duty of the Reich to acquire and administer waterways serving for general traffic.

After this transfer, waterways serving for general traffic may be constructed or extended only by or with the consent of the Reich.

In the administration, extension or construction of waterways, the requirements of agriculture and the water supply must be safeguarded, in agreement with the States. Their improvement must also be taken into consideration.

Every waterways administration must permit junctions with its system to be made by other inland waterways, at the expense of the latter. The same obligation extends to the establishment of a connection between inland waterways and railways.

With the transfer of the waterways, the Reich assumes authority as to expropriation, and the fixing of rates, as well as the control of river and shipping police.

The business of the River Development Association in relation to the development of natural waterways in the Rhine, Weser and Elbe districts is to be taken over by the Reich.

Art. 98

For the purpose of cooperation in matters concerning waterways, Advisory Councils shall be established with the consent of the Reichsrat, in accordance with detailed regulations by the Government of the Reich.

Art. 99

In connection with natural waterways, dues may be levied only in respect of such works, appliances and other installations as are intended for the facilitation of traffic.

Expenses of the establishment and maintenance of installations not intended exclusively for the facilitation of traffic, but intended also for other purposes, may be defrayed only up to a proportionate amount by means of dues on navigation. Interest and sinking-fund on the capital expended shall be reckoned as expenses of establishment.

The provisions of the previous paragraph apply only to dues levied for artificial waterways, as well as to installations in connection therewith and in the ports.

In the sphere of inland navigation, the basis for the assessment of navigation dues may be the total expenses of a waterway, a river-district, or a system of waterways.

These provisions apply also in respect of timber rafts upon navigable waterways.

The imposition of taxes upon foreign ships and their cargoes, different from or higher than those levied upon German ships and cargoes, is a question for the Reich alone.

The Reich may, by means of a law, require contributions in other ways from parties concerned in navigation, for the provision of funds for the maintenance and development of the German system of waterways.

Art. 100

For the purpose of meeting the expenses of maintenance and development of inland waterways, a law of the Reich may provide for contributions from those who profit in any other way than by navigation in the construction of dams, in cases where several States have shared in, or where the Reich alone has borne the expenses of construction.

Art. 101

It is the duty of the Reich to assume ownership and administration of all navigation marks, particularly lighthouses, light-ships, buoys, barrels and beacons. After such transfer, marks may be constructed and extended only by, or with the consent of, the Reich.

Section VII. Administration of Justice

Art. 102

Judges are independent and subject only to the law.

Art. 103

The ordinary jurisdiction is exercised by the High Court of the Reich and the Courts of the States.

Art. 104

The judges of the ordinary Courts are appointed for life. They may be removed from office, permanently or temporarily transferred to another position or retired only on the authority of a judicial decision, and only upon the grounds and by the methods of procedure fixed by law. Age limits may be fixed by legislation, upon reaching which judges shall retire.

Provisional removal from office when authorised by law is not affected by the above.

In the case of a rearrangement of the Courts or their circuits, the State Administration of Justice may order compulsory transfer to another court, or removal from office, but only on condition of the retention of full salary.

These provisions do not apply to commercial judges, assessors and jurymen.

Art. 105

Extraordinary Courts are prohibited. No one may be withdrawn from his legal judge. Legal regulations regarding Courts-Martial and Summary Military Courts are not affected by the above. Military Courts of Honour are abolished.

Art. 106

Military jurisdiction is abolished, except in time of war and on board warships. Details are regulated by a law of the Reich.

Art. 107

In the Reich and the States, administrative courts shall be established by law for the protection of individuals against regulations and decrees of the administrative authorities.

Art. 108

A Supreme Court for the German Reich shall be established by law of the Reich.

PART II
Fundamental Rights and Duties of Germans

Section I. The Individual

Art. 109
All Germans are equal before the law.

Men and women have fundamentally the same civic rights and duties.

Public legal privileges or disadvantages of birth or rank shall be abolished. Titles of nobility shall be simply a part of the name, and may no longer be conferred.

Titles may be conferred only when they indicate an office or calling; academic degrees are not hereby affected.

Orders and badges of honour may not be conferred by the State.

No German is permitted to accept a title or order from a foreign Government.

Art. 110
Nationality in the Reich and the States is acquired and terminated as may be provided by the law of the Reich. Every subject of a State is also a subject of the Reich.

Every German has the same rights and duties in any State of the Reich as the subjects of that State.

Art. 111
All Germans enjoy the right of change of domicile within the whole Reich. Everyone has the right to stay in any part of the realm that he chooses, to settle there, acquire landed property and pursue any means of livelihood. Restrictions may be imposed only by law of the Reich.

Art. 112
Every German is entitled to emigrate to countries outside the Reich. Emigration may be restricted only by law of the Reich.

All nationals of the Reich within and beyond its territory are entitled to claim the protection of the Reich in relation to a foreign power.

No German may be handed over to a foreign Government for prosecution or punishment.

Art. 113

Sections of the population of the Reich speaking a foreign language may not be restricted, whether by way of legislation or administration, in their free racial development; this applies specially to the use of their mother tongue in education, as well as in questions of internal administrations and the administration of justice.

Art. 114

Personal liberty is inviolable. No encroachment on or deprivation of personal liberty by any public authority is permissible except in virtue of a law.

Persons who have been deprived of their liberty shall be informed — at the latest on the following day — by what authority and on what grounds the deprivation of liberty has been ordered; opportunity shall be given them without delay to make legal complaint against such deprivation.

Art. 115

The residence of every German is an inviolable sanctuary for him; exceptions are admissible only in virtue of laws.

Art. 116

No punishment may be inflicted for any action unless the action was designated by law as punishable, before it was committed.

Art. 117

The secrecy of correspondence and of the postal, telegraph and telephone services, is inviolable. Exceptions may be permitted only by law of the Reich.

Art. 118

Every German has the right, within the limits of general laws, to express his opinion freely, by word of mouth, writing, printed matter or picture, or in any other manner. This right must not be affected by any conditions of his work or appointment, and no one is permitted to injure him on account of his making use of such rights.

No censorship shall be enforced, but restrictive regulations may be introduced by law in reference to cinematograph entertainment. Legal measures are also admissible for the purpose of combating bad and obscene literature, as well as for the protection of youth in public exhibitions and performances.

Section II. The Life of the Community

Art. 119

Marriage, as the foundation of family life and as the preservation and growth of the nation, is under the special protection of the Constitution. It rests upon the equal rights of both sexes.

The preservation of the purity and health of the family and its social advancement is the task both of the State and of the local authorities. Families with a large number of children have a right to corresponding provision.

Motherhood has a claim upon the protection and care of the State.

Art. 120

The rearing of the rising generation in physical, mental and social efficiency is the highest duty and natural right of the parents, the accomplishment of which is watched over by the community of the State.

Art. 121

By means of legislation, opportunity shall be provided for the physical, mental and social nurture of illegitimate children, equal to that enjoyed by legitimate children.

Art. 122

Young persons shall be protected against exploitation as well as against moral, spiritual or bodily neglect. Both the State and the local authorities must undertake the necessary arrangements.

Protective measures of a compulsory character may only be imposed by virtue of a law.

Art. 123

All Germans have the right without notification or special permission to assemble peacefully and unarmed.

Open-air meetings may be made notifiable by a law of the Reich, and in case of direct danger to public security may be forbidden.

Art. 124

All Germans have the right to form unions and associations for purposes not in contravention of the penal laws. This right may not be restricted by preventive regulations. The same provisions apply to religious unions and associations.

Every union is at liberty to acquire legal rights in accordance with the provisions of the Civil Code. These rights shall not be refused to a union on the ground that its objects are of political, social-political, or religious nature.

Art. 125
The freedom and the secrecy of elections are guaranteed. Details are to be determined by electoral laws.

Art. 126
Every German has the right to address written petitions or complaints to the competent authorities or the representatives of the people. This right may be exercised by individuals, and by several persons in common.

Art. 127
Communes and associations of Communes have the right to administer their own affairs within the limits of the laws.

Art. 128
All citizens of the State, without distinction, are eligible for public office, as provided by law and in accordance with their qualifications and abilities.

All exceptional provisions against women officials are annulled.

The conditions of employment of officials shall be determined by law of the Reich.

Art. 129
Officials are appointed for life, save as may be otherwise provided by law. Pensions and provision for surviving dependants shall be regulated by law. Rights duly acquired by officials are inviolable. Officials may have recourse to legal proceedings in respect of financial claims.

Officials may not be provisionally removed from office, or provisionally or permanently retired, or transferred to another post with a lower salary, save in accordance with and in the manner determined by law.

Every penalty inflicted on an official must be subject to appeal and the possibility of revision. Unfavourable entries may not be made in the personal record of an official unless he has been given an opportunity to reply to them. Officials have the right to examine their personal records.

The inviolability of duly acquired rights and opportunity to have recourse to legal proceedings in respect of financial claims are also specially guaranteed to professional soldiers. In other respects their status shall be determined by law of the Reich.

Art. 130

Officials are servants of the community and not of any party.

Freedom of political opinions and the free right of association are guaranteed to all officials.

Officials have special service representation, details in regard to which shall be determined by law of the Reich.

Art. 131

Should an official, in the exercise of the public authority conferred upon him, neglect an official duty incumbent upon him in relation to a third party, the responsibility as a matter of principle falls upon the State or the corporate body in whose service the official is acting. Their right to take retributory action is reserved. Recourse to the ordinary process of law must not be excluded.

More detailed regulations shall be prescribed by legislation by the appropriate authority.

Art. 132

It is the duty of every German to undertake the duties of honorary offices according to the provisions of the laws.

Art. 133

All citizens are bound, according to the provisions of the laws, to undertake personal service for the State and the local authorities.

Military service is organised in accordance with the terms of the Military Defence Law of the Reich. This Law determines also to what extent certain fundamental rights must be restricted for members of the armed forces to ensure the fulfilment of their duties and the maintenance of military discipline.

Art. 134

All citizens, without exception, contribute in proportion to their means to all public taxes, in accordance with the provisions of the laws.

Section III. Religion and Religious Associations

Art. 135

All inhabitants of the Reich enjoy full liberty of faith and of conscience. The undisturbed practice of religion is guaranteed by the Constitution and is under State protection. The general laws of the State shall remain unaffected hereby.

Art. 136

Civil and political duties are neither dependent upon nor restricted by the practice of religious freedom.

The enjoyment of civil and political rights, as well as admission to official posts, are independent of religious creed.

No one is bound to disclose his religious convictions. The authorities have the right to make enquiries as to membership of a religious body only when rights and duties depend upon it or when the collection of statistics ordered by law requires it.

No one may be compelled to take part in any ecclesiastical act or ceremony, or to participate in religious practices or to make use of any religious form of oath.

Art. 137

There is no State Church.

Freedom of association is guaranteed to religious bodies. The union of religious bodies within the territory of the Reich is subject to no restriction.

Every religious body regulates and administers its affairs independently, within the limits of the laws applicable to all. It appoints its officers without cooperation of the State or of the local authorities.

Religious bodies acquire legal status in accordance with the general regulations of the civil code.

Religious bodies remain legal corporations in so far as they have been so up to the present. Equal rights shall be granted to other religious bodies upon application if their constitution and the number of their members offer a guarantee of permanence. Where several such religious bodies which are legal corporations combine to form one union, this union becomes a legal corporation.

Religious bodies which are legal corporations are entitled to levy taxes on the basis of the civic tax-rolls, in accordance with the provisions of the laws of the States.

Associations devoting themselves to the common promotion of a world philosophy shall be placed upon equal footing with religious bodies.

So far as further regulations may be necessary for the carrying out of these provisions, they shall be prescribed by legislation of the States.

Art. 138

Outstanding State liabilities to religious bodies, whether founded upon legislation, contract or exceptional legal title, shall be redeemed by legislation by the States. The governing principles of such legislation shall be prescribed by the Reich.

The property and other rights of religious bodies and unions in respect of their institutions, foundations and other property devoted to public worship, education and social welfare, are guaranteed.

Art. 139

Sundays and holidays recognised by the State shall remain under legal protection as days of rest and spiritual improvement.

Art. 140

The members of the armed forces are guaranteed the necessary free time for the performance of their religious duties.

Art. 141

Religious bodies have the right of entry for religious purposes into the army, hospitals, prisons, or other public institutions, so far as is necessary for the conduct of public worship and religious ministrations, but any form of compulsion is forbidden.

Section IV. Education and Schools

Art. 142

Art and science, and the teaching thereof, are free.

The State guarantees their protection and participates in furthering them.

Art. 143

Provision shall be made for the education of the young by means of public institutions. The Reich, the States and the local authorities shall cooperate in their organisation. The training of teachers shall be regulated in a uniform manner for the whole Reich, on the general lines laid down for higher education.

Teachers in public schools have the rights and duties of State officials.

Art. 144

The whole system of education is under the supervision of the State, which may assign a share in such work to the local authorities. School inspection is carried out by competent, trained and expert officials of high rank.

Art. 145

School attendance is compulsory for all. The fulfilment of this obligation is provided for by primary schools, with at least an eight years' course, followed by continuation schools with a course extending to the completion of the eighteenth year of age.

Instruction and all accessories are free of charge in the primary and continuation schools.

Art. 146

The public system of education shall be developed organically. Upon the basis of primary schools common to all shall be built up a system of secondary and higher education. The governing consideration in the building up of this system shall be the diversity of vocations and, as regards the admission of a child into any particular school, its capacity and inclination, not the economic and social standing of its parents.

Upon the request of persons responsible for the education of children, however, primary schools in accordance with their religious creed or philosophic views may be established in a locality, so far as is possible without interference with the orderly development of the school system, especially as regards the general principles of the first paragraph of this Article. The wishes of persons responsible for the education of children shall be taken into account as far as possible. Further details shall be determined by legislation by the States in accordance with principles laid down by a law of the Reich.

Public provision shall be made by the Reich, the States and the local authorities, for the admission of persons of small means to secondary and higher educational institutions; in particular, educational assistance grants shall be provided for the parents of children considered suitable for education in secondary and higher schools until the completion of their education.

Art. 147

Private schools, as a substitute for public schools, require the approval of the State, and are subject to the laws of the States. Approval may be granted when the private schools are not inferior to the public schools in their educational aims and organisation, nor in the professional qualifications of their teaching staff; further, there must be no segregation of pupils based upon the means of their parents. Approval shall be refused when the economic and legal position of the teaching staff is not sufficiently assured.

Private primary schools are permissible only when there is in a locality no public primary school corresponding to the religious creed or philosophic views of a minority of persons responsible for the education of children whose desires must be taken into consideration in accordance with Art. 146, para. 2, or when the educational administrative authorities recognise that special educational interest is involved.

Primary preparatory schools are to be abolished.

Private schools not serving as substitutes for public schools retain their existing legal rights.

Art. 148

All schools shall aim at inculcating moral character, a civic conscience, personal and vocational efficiency, imbued with the spirit of German nationality and international goodwill.

In giving instruction in public schools, care must be taken not to give offence to the susceptibilities of those holding different opinions.

The duties of citizenship and technical education are subjects of instruction in the schools. Upon the completion of the period of school attendance, every pupil receives a copy of the Constitution.

The Reich, the States and the local authorities shall promote the organisation of popular culture, including popular high schools.

Art. 149

Religious instruction is a regular subject in schools, with the exception of undenominational (secular) schools. The giving of such instruction shall be regulated in accordance with legislation upon schools. Religious instruction shall be given in accord with the principles of the religious body concerned, without prejudice to the right of State supervision.

The giving of religious instruction and the undertaking of spiritual duties are subject to the declared assent of the teacher; participation in religious instruction and in religious rites and ceremonies is subject to the declared assent of the person responsible for the religious education of the child.

The theological Faculties in the Universities shall continue to be maintained.

Art. 150

Monuments of artistic, historic, and natural interest, and exceptional landscapes are under the protection and care of the State.

It is the business of the Reich to prevent the removal of German art treasures into foreign countries.

Art. 151

The organisation of economic life must ·correspond to the principles of justice, and be designed to ensure for all a life worthy of a human being. Within these limits the economic freedom of the individual must be guaranteed.

Legal compulsion is permissible only in order to enforce rights which are threatened, or to subserve the preeminent claims of the common weal.

Freedom of trade and industry is guaranteed in accordance with the provisions of laws of the Reich.

Art. 152

Freedom of contract shall prevail in economic relations, subject to the provisions of the laws.

Usury is forbidden. Contracts opposed to morality are void.

Art. 153

Property is guaranteed by the Constitution. Its extent and the restrictions placed upon it are defined by law.

Expropriation may be effected only for the benefits of the general community and upon the basis of law. It shall be accompanied by due compensation, save in so far as may be otherwise provided by a law of the Reich. In case of dispute as to the amount of compensation, resort may be had to legal proceedings in the ordinary course, unless a law of the Reich otherwise determines. Property of the States, local authorities and public utility associations may be expropriated by the Reich only on payment of compensation.

The ownership of property entails obligations. Its use must at the same time serve the common good.

Art. 154

The right of inheritance is guaranteed in accordance with the provisions of the Civil Law.

The share in any inheritance which accrues to the State is determined by law.

Art. 155

The distribution and use of land shall be supervised by the State in such a way as to prevent abuse and with a view to ensuring to every German a healthy dwelling and to all German families, particularly those with many children, a dwelling and economic homestead suited to their needs. Special consideration shall be given in the framing of the Homestead Laws to persons who have taken part in the war.

Landed property may be expropriated when required to meet the needs of housing, or for the purpose of land settlement, the bringing of land into cultivation or the improvement of husbandry. Testamentary trusts are to be terminated.

The cultivation and full utilisation of the land is a duty the landowner owes to the community. Increment in the value of landed property, not accruing from any expenditure of labour and capital upon the land, shall be devoted to the uses of the community.

All riches in the soil and all natural sources of power of economic value shall be under the control of the State. Private royalties shall be transferred to the State by legislation.

Art. 156

The Reich may, by legislation, without prejudice to the payment of compensation and subject to appropriate application of the provisions governing expropriation, transfer to public ownership private economic undertakings which are suitable for socialisation. It may itself undertake, or assign to the States or local authorities a share in the management of such undertakings and associations, or otherwise ensure to itself a determining influence therein.

Further, the Reich may by legislation, in case of pressing necessity and in the economic interests of the community, oblige economic undertakings and associations to combine, on a self-governing basis, for the purpose of ensuring the cooperation of all productive factors of the nation, associating employers and employees in the management, and regulating the production, manufacture, distribution, consumption, prices and the import and export of commodities upon principles determined by the economic interest of the community.

Industrial and agricultural cooperative societies and federations thereof may be incorporated into the public economic system, at their own request and with due regard to their constitution and special characteristics.

Art. 157
Labour is under the special protection of the Reich.

The Reich will frame a uniform labour code.

Art. 158
Intellectual work, the rights of discoverers, inventors and artists are under the protection and care of the Reich.

By means of international agreements, recognition and protection must be ensured abroad for the products of German science, art, and technical skill.

Art. 159
Freedom of association for the maintenance and improvement of labour and economic conditions is guaranteed to everyone and for all occupations. All agreements and measures tending to restrict or obstruct such freedom are illegal.

Art. 160
Every person in the position of an employee or workman has a right to such free time as is necessary for the exercise of his civic rights and, in so far as the business in which he is employed will not be seriously injured thereby, for the discharge of honorary public duties entrusted to him. Legislation shall determine how far such a person may be entitled to claim compensation.

Art. 161
The Reich will, with the full cooperation of insured persons, create a comprehensive system of insurance for the maintenance of health and fitness for work, the protection of motherhood and provision for the economic consequences of old age, infirmity and the vicissitudes of life.

Art. 162
The Reich will initiate international regulation of the legal conditions

of workers, with a view to securing for the working class of the world a universal minimum of social rights.

Art. 163

It is the moral duty of every German, without prejudice to his personal liberty, to make such use of his mental and bodily powers as shall be necessary for the welfare of the community.

Every German must be afforded an opportunity to gain his livelihood by economic labour. Where no suitable opportunity of work can be found for him, provision shall be made for his support. Details shall be determined by special laws of the Reich.

Art. 164

The independent middle class in agriculture, industry and commerce, shall be encouraged by legislative and administrative measures and shall be protected against exploitation and oppression.

Art. 165

Workers and salaried employees are called upon to cooperate with equal rights in common with the employers in the regulation of wages and conditions of labour and in the general economic development of the forces of production. The organisations on both sides and the agreements made by them shall be recognised.

For the protection of their social and economic interests, workers and salaried employees shall have legal representation in Workers' Councils for individual undertakings and in District Workers' Councils grouped according to economic districts and in a Workers' Council of the Reich.

The District Workers' Council and the Workers' Council of the Reich shall combine with representatives of the employers and other classes of the population concerned so as to form District Economic Councils and an Economic Council of the Reich, for the discharge of their joint economic functions and for cooperation in the carrying out of laws relating to socialisation. The District Economic Councils and the Economic Council of the Reich shall be so constituted as to give representation thereon to all important vocational groups in proportion to their economic and social importance.

All Bills of fundamental importance dealing with matters of social and economic legislation shall, before being introduced, be submitted by the Government of the Reich to the Economic Council of the Reich for its opinion thereon. The Economic

Council of the Reich shall have the right itself to propose such legislation. Should the Government of the Reich not agree with any such proposal, it must nevertheless introduce it in the Reichstag, accompanied by a statement of its own views thereon. The Economic Council of the Reich may arrange for one of its own members to advocate the proposal in the Reichstag.

Powers of control and administration in any matters falling within their province may be conferred upon Workers' Councils and Economic Councils.

The constitution and functions of the Workers' and Economic Councils and their relations with other autonomous social organisations are within the exclusive jurisdiction of the Reich.

Provisional and Concluding Arrangements

Art. 166
Until the establishment of the Administrative Court of the Reich its place shall be taken, as regards the formation of the Court of Inquiry into Elections, by the High Court of the Reich.

Art. 167
The provisions of Art. 18, paras. 3 to 6, shall not come into force until two years after the publication of the Constitution of the Reich.

Art. 168
Until the promulgation of the State law provided for in Art. 63, but at the longest for the period of one year, all Prussian votes in the Reichsrat may be exercised by members of the Government.

Art. 169
The date on which the provisions of Art. 83, para. 1, are to come into force shall be determined by the Government of the Reich.

For a suitable transition period, the collection and administration of customs and excise may, at their request, be left to the States.

Art. 170
The administration of the postal and telegraphic services of Bavaria and Württemberg shall be transferred to the Reich by 1 April 1921 at the latest.

Should no agreement as to the conditions of transfer have been attained by 1 October 1920 the decision shall be given by the Supreme Court.

Up to the date of transfer the existing rights and responsibilities of Bavaria and Württemberg shall remain in force. Postal and telegraphic communications with neighbouring foreign States shall, however, be regulated exclusively by the Reich.

Art. 171

State railways, waterways and navigation marks shall be transferred to the Reich by 1 April 1921 at the latest.

Should no agreement as to the conditions of transfer have been attained by 1 October 1920 the decision shall be given by the Supreme Court.

Art. 172

Up to the date at which the law of the Reich as to the Supreme Court comes into force, its functions shall be discharged by a Senate of seven members, four of whom shall be elected by the Reichstag and three by the High Court from its own members. It shall regulate its own procedure.

Art. 173

Until the promulgation of a law of the Reich in accordance with Art. 138, the hitherto existing State liabilities to religious bodies, founded upon legislation, contract, or exceptional legal titles, shall remain in force.

Art. 174

Until the promulgation of the law of the Reich provided for in Art. 146, para. 2, the existing legal position shall be maintained. The law must give special consideration to those districts of the Reich in which a school is already legally established which is not divided according to religious creeds.

Art. 175

The provisions of Art. 109 do not apply to orders and decorations conferred for merit during the war years, 1914 to 1919.

Art. 176

All public officials and members of the armed forces must take the oath of allegiance to this Constitution. Details shall be determined by decree of the President of the Reich.

Art. 177

Where in existing laws the use of a religious formula is required in taking an oath, the person concerned may legally replace the religious formula by the declaration 'I swear'. Otherwise the substance of the oath as provided by law remains unaltered.

Art. 178

The constitution of the German Reich of 16 April 1871 and the law of 10 February 1919 as to the provisional government of the Reich are repealed.

The remaining laws and decrees of the Reich remain in force, so far as they are not in conflict with the present Constitution. The provisions of the Treaty of Peace signed at Versailles on 28 June 1919 are unaffected by the Constitution.

Regulations of authorities, issued in due legal manner upon the basis of existing laws, remain valid until they are annulled by the issue of further regulations or by legislation.

Art. 179

Where, in laws or decrees, reference is made to provisions or institutions abolished by this Constitution, they shall be replaced by the corresponding provisions or institutions of this Constitution. In particular, the National Assembly is replaced by the Reichstag, the Committee of the States by the Reichsrat, and the President of the Reich elected on the basis of the law as to the provisional government of the Reich, is replaced by the President of the Reich elected upon the basis of this Constitution.

The power of issuing decrees vested in the Committee of the States in accordance with hitherto existing regulations is transferred to the Government of the Reich; the consent of the Reichsrat shall be requisite for the issue of decrees, in accordance with the provisions of this Constitution.

Art. 180

Until the meeting of the first Reichstag, the National Assembly shall have the status of the Reichstag. Until the first President of the Reich enters upon his office, the duties of his office shall be discharged by the President of the Reich elected under the law as to the provisional government of the Reich.

Art. 181

The German people, through their National Assembly, have decreed and prescribed this Constitution. It comes into force upon the day of its promulgation.

The Basic Law of the Federal Republic of Germany

Bundesgesetzblatt

| 1 9 4 9 | Ausgegeben in Bonn am 23. Mai 1949 | Nr. 1 |

Inhalt: Grundgesetz für die Bundesrepublik Deutschland vom 23. Mai 1949 .... Seite 1

Grundgesetz
für die Bundesrepublik Deutschland
vom 23. Mai 1949.

Der Parlamentarische Rat hat am 23. Mai 1949 in Bonn am Rhein in öffentlicher Sitzung festgestellt, daß das am 8. Mai des Jahres 1949 vom Parlamentarischen Rat beschlossene G r u n d g e s e t z f ü r d i e B u n d e s r e p u b l i k D e u t s c h - l a n d in der Woche vom 16. — 22. Mai 1949 durch die Volksvertretungen von mehr als Zweidritteln der beteiligten deutschen Länder angenommen worden ist.

Auf Grund dieser Feststellung hat der Parlamentarische Rat, vertreten durch seinen Präsidenten, das Grundgesetz ausgefertigt und verkündet.

Das Grundgesetz wird hiermit gemäß Artikel 145 Absatz 3 im Bundesgesetzblatt veröffentlicht:

Präambel

Im Bewußtsein seiner Verantwortung vor Gott und den Menschen, von dem Willen beseelt, seine nationale und staatliche Einheit zu wahren und als gleichberechtigtes Glied in einem vereinten Europa dem Frieden der Welt zu dienen, hat das Deutsche Volk in den Ländern Baden, Bayern, Bremen, Hamburg, Hessen, Niedersachsen, Nordrhein-Westfalen, Rheinland-Pfalz, Schleswig-Holstein, Württemberg-Baden und Württemberg-Hohenzollern, um dem staatlichen Leben für eine Übergangszeit eine neue Ordnung zu geben, kraft seiner verfassunggebenden Gewalt dieses Grundgesetz der Bundesrepublik Deutschland beschlossen. Es hat auch für jene Deutschen gehandelt, denen mitzuwirken versagt war.

Das gesamte Deutsche Volk bleibt aufgefordert, in freier Selbstbestimmung die Einheit und Freiheit Deutschlands zu vollenden.

I. Die Grundrechte

Artikel 1

(1) Die Würde des Menschen ist unantastbar. Sie zu achten und zu schützen ist Verpflichtung aller staatlichen Gewalt.

(2) Das Deutsche Volk bekennt sich darum zu unverletzlichen und unveräußerlichen Menschenrechten als Grundlage jeder menschlichen Gemeinschaft, des Friedens und der Gerechtigkeit in der Welt.

(3) Die nachfolgenden Grundrechte binden Gesetzgebung, Verwaltung und Rechtsprechung als unmittelbar geltendes Recht.

Artikel 2

(1) Jeder hat das Recht auf die freie Entfaltung seiner Persönlichkeit, soweit er nicht die Rechte anderer verletzt und nicht gegen die verfassungsmäßige Ordnung oder das Sittengesetz verstößt.

(2) Jeder hat das Recht auf Leben und körperliche Unversehrtheit. Die Freiheit der Person ist unverletzlich. In diese Rechte darf nur auf Grund eines Gesetzes eingegriffen werden.

Artikel 3

(1) Alle Menschen sind vor dem Gesetz gleich.

(2) Männer und Frauen sind gleichberechtigt.

(3) Niemand darf wegen seines Geschlechtes, seiner Abstammung, seiner Rasse, seiner Sprache, seiner Heimat und Herkunft, seines Glaubens, seiner religiösen oder politischen Anschauungen benachteiligt oder bevorzugt werden.

Artikel 4

(1) Die Freiheit des Glaubens, des Gewissens und die Freiheit des religiösen und weltanschaulichen Bekenntnisses sind unverletzlich.

(2) Die ungestörte Religionsausübung wird gewährleistet.

(3) Niemand darf gegen sein Gewissen zum Kriegsdienst mit der Waffe gezwungen werden. Das Nähere regelt ein Bundesgesetz.

Artikel 5

(1) Jeder hat das Recht, seine Meinung in Wort, Schrift und Bild frei zu äußern und zu verbreiten und sich aus allgemein zugänglichen Quellen un-

Announcement by the Parliamentary Council

The Parliamentary Council, meeting in public session at Bonn am Rhein on 23 May 1949, confirmed the fact that the Basic Law for the Federal Republic of Germany, which was adopted by the Parliamentary Council on 8 May 1949, was ratified in the week of 16 to 22 May 1949 by the diets of more than two-thirds of the participating constituent states (Länder).

By virtue of this fact the Parliamentary Council, represented by its Presidents, has signed and promulgated the Basic Law.

The Basic Law is hereby published in the *Federal Law Gazette* pursuant to paragraph (3) of Article 145.[1]

Preamble

The German People
in the Länder of Baden, Bavaria, Bremen, Hamburg, Hesse, Lower Saxony, North-Rhine/Westphalia, Rhineland-Palatinate, Schleswig-Holstein, Württemberg-Baden and Württemberg-Hohenzollern,[2]
conscious of their responsibility before God and men,

animated by the resolve to preserve their national and political unity and to serve the peace of the world as an equal partner in a united Europe,

desiring to give a new order to political life for a transitional period,

have enacted, by virtue of their constituent power, this Basic Law for the Federal Republic of Germany.

They also have acted on behalf of those Germans to whom participation was denied.

The entire German people are called upon to achieve in free self-determination the unity and freedom of Germany.

---

1. The above notice of publication appeared in the first issue of the *Federal Law Gazette* [hereafter *FLG*] dated 23 May 1949.
2. See footnote 13 to Art. 23.

I. Basic Rights

Art. 1
(Protection of human dignity)

(1) The dignity of man shall be inviolable. To respect and protect it shall be the duty of all state authority.

(2) The German people therefore acknowledge inviolable and inalienable human rights as the basis of every community, of peace and of justice in the world.

(3)[3] The following basic rights shall bind the legislature, the executive and the judiciary as directly enforceable law.

Art. 2
(Rights of liberty)

(1) Everyone shall have the right to the free development of his personality in so far as he does not violate the rights of others or offend against the constitutional order or the moral code.

(2) Everyone shall have the right to life and to inviolability of his person. The liberty of the individual shall be inviolable. These rights may only be encroached upon pursuant to a law.

Art. 3
(Equality before the law)

(1) All persons shall be equal before the law.

(2) Men and women shall have equal rights.

(3) No one may be prejudiced or favoured because of his sex, his parentage, his race, his language, his homeland and origin, his faith, or his religious or political opinions.

Art. 4
(Freedom of faith and creed)

(1) Freedom of faith, of conscience, and freedom of creed, religious or ideological (*weltanschaulich*), shall be inviolable.

(2) The undisturbed practice of religion is guaranteed.

(3) No one may be compelled against his conscience to render war service involving the use of arms. Details shall be regulated by a federal law.

---

3. As amended by federal law of 19 March 1956 (*FLG*, I, p. 111).

Art. 5
(Freedom of expression)

(1) Everyone shall have the right freely to express and disseminate his opinion by speech, writing and pictures and freely to inform himself from generally accessible sources. Freedom of the press and freedom of reporting by means of broadcasts and films are guaranteed. There shall be no censorship.

(2) These rights are limited by the provisions of the general laws, the provisions of law for the protection of youth, and by the right to inviolability of personal honour.

(3) Art and science, research and teaching, shall be free. Freedom of teaching shall not absolve from loyalty to the constitution.

Art. 6
(Marriage; family; illegitimate children)

(1) Marriage and family shall enjoy the special protection of the state.

(2) The care and upbringing of children are a natural right of, and a duty primarily incumbent on, the parents. The national community shall watch over their endeavours in this respect.

(3) Children may not be separated from their families against the will of the persons entitled to bring them up, except pursuant to a law, if those so entitled fail or the children are otherwise threatened with neglect.

(4) Every mother shall be entitled to the protection and care of the community.

(5) Illegitimate children shall be provided by legislation with the same opportunities for their physical and spiritual development and their place in society as are enjoyed by legitimate children.

Art. 7
(Education)

(1) The entire educational system shall be under the supervision of the state.

(2) The persons entitled to bring up a child shall have the right to decide whether it shall receive religious instruction.

(3) Religious instruction shall form part of the ordinary curriculum in state and municipal schools, except in secular (*bekenntnisfrei*) schools. Without prejudice to the state's right of supervision, religious instruction shall be given in accordance with the tenets of the religious communities. No teacher may be obliged against his will to give religious instruction.

(4) The right to establish private schools is guaranteed. Private schools, as a substitute for state or municipal schools, shall require the approval of the state and shall be subject to the laws of the Länder. Such approval must be given if private schools are not inferior to the state or municipal schools in their educational aims, their facilities and the professional training of their teaching staff, and if segregation of pupils according to the means of the parents is not promoted thereby. Approval must be withheld if the economic and legal position of the teaching staff is not sufficiently assured.

(5) A private elementary school shall be permitted only if the education authority finds that it serves a special pedagogic interest, or if, on the application of persons entitled to bring up children, it is to be established as an inter-denominational or denominational or ideological school and a state or municipal elementary school of this type does not exist in the commune (*Gemeinde*).

(6) Preparatory schools (*Vorschulen*) shall remain abolished.

Art. 8
(Freedom of assembly)
(1) All Germans shall have the right to assemble peaceably and unarmed without prior notification or permission.

(2) With regard to open-air meetings this right may be restricted by or pursuant to a law.

Art. 9
(Freedom of association)
(1) All Germans shall have the right to form associations and societies.

(2) Associations, the purposes or activities of which conflict with criminal laws or which are directed against the constitutional order or the concept of international understanding, are prohibited.

(3) The right to form associations to safeguard and improve working and economic conditions is guaranteed to everyone and to all trades, occupations and professions. Agreements which restrict or seek to impair this right shall be null and void; measures directed to this end shall be illegal. Measures taken pursuant to Art. 12a, to paragraphs (2) and (3) of Art. 35, to paragraph (4) of Art. 87a, or to Art. 91, may not be directed against any industrial conflicts engaged in by associations within the meaning of the first sentence of this paragraph in order to safeguard and improve working and economic conditions.[4]

Art. 10[5]
(Privacy of posts and telecommunications)

(1) Privacy of posts and telecommunications shall be inviolable.

(2) This right may be restricted only pursuant to a law. Such law may lay down that the person affected shall not be informed of any such restriction if it serves to protect the free democratic basic order or the existence or security of the Federation or a Land, and that recourse to the courts shall be replaced by a review of the case by bodies and auxiliary bodies appointed by Parliament.

Art. 11
(Freedom of movement)

(1) All Germans shall enjoy freedom of movement throughout the federal territory.

(2)[6] This right may be restricted only by or pursuant to a law and only in cases in which an adequate basis of existence is lacking and special burdens would arise to the community as a result thereof, or in which such restriction is necessary to avert an imminent danger to the existence or the free democratic basic order of the Federation or a Land, to combat the danger of epidemics, to deal with natural disasters or particularly grave accidents, to protect young people from neglect or to prevent crime.

Art. 12[7]
(Right to choose trade, occupation or profession)

(1) All Germans shall have the right freely to choose their trade, occupation, or profession, their place of work and their place of training. The practice of trades, occupations, and professions may be regulated by or pursuant to a law.

(2) No specific occupation may be imposed on any person except within the framework of a traditional compulsory public service that applies generally and equally to all.

(3) Forced labour may be imposed only on persons deprived of their liberty by court sentence.

---

4. Last sentence inserted by federal law of 24 June 1968 (*FLG*, I, p. 709).

5. As amended by federal law of 24 June 1968 (ibid).

6. Ibid.

7. As amended by federal laws of 19 March 1956 (*FLG*, I, p. 111) and 24 June 1968 (*FLG*, p. 709).

Art. 12a[8]
(Liability to military and other service)

(1) Men who have attained the age of eighteen years may be required to serve in the Armed Forces, in the Federal Border Guard, or in a Civil Defence organization.

(2) A person who refuses, on grounds of conscience, to render war service involving the use of arms may be required to render a substitute service. The duration of such substitute service shall not exceed the duration of military service. Details shall be regulated by a law which shall not interfere with the freedom of conscience and must also provide for the possibility of a substitute service not connected with units of the Armed Forces or of the Federal Border Guard.

(3) Persons liable to military service who are not required to render service pursuant to paragraph (1) or (2) of this Article may, when a state of defence (*Verteidigungsfall*) exists, be assigned by or pursuant to a law to specific occupations involving civilian services for defence purposes, including the protection of the civilian population; it shall, however, not be permissible to assign persons to an occupation subject to public law except for the purpose of discharging police functions or such other functions of public administration as can only be discharged by persons employed under public law. Persons may be assigned to occupations — as referred to in the first sentence of this paragraph — with the Armed Forces, including the supplying and servicing of the latter, or with public administrative authorities; assignments to occupations connected with supplying and servicing the civilian population shall not be permissible except in order to meet their vital requirements or to guarantee their safety.

(4) If, while a state of defence exists, civilian service requirements in the civilian public health and medical system or in the stationary military hospital organization cannot be met on a voluntary basis, women between eighteen and fifty-five years of age may be assigned to such services by or pursuant to a law. They may on no account render service involving the use of arms.

(5) During the time prior to the existence of any such state of defence, assignments under paragraph (3) of this Article may be effected only if the requirements of paragraph (1) of Art. 80a are satisfied. It shall be admissible to require persons by or pursuant to a law to attend training courses in order to prepare them for the

8. Inserted by federal law of 24 June 1968 (*FLG*, I, p. 710).

performance of such services in accordance with paragraph (3) of this Article as presuppose special knowledge or skills. To this extent, the first sentence of this paragraph shall not apply.

(6) If, while a state of defence exists, the labour requirements for the purposes referred to in the second sentence of paragraph (3) of this Article cannot be met on a voluntary basis, the right of a German to give up the practice of his trade or occupation or profession, or his place of work, may be restricted by or pursuant to a law in order to meet these requirements. The first sentence of paragraph (5) of this Article shall apply *mutatis mutandis* prior to the existence of a state of defence.

Art. 13
(Inviolability of the home)

(1) The home shall be inviolable.

(2) Searches may be ordered only by a judge or, in the event of danger in delay, by other organs as provided by law and may be carried out only in the form prescribed by law.

(3) In all other respects, this inviolability may not be encroached upon or restricted except to avert a common danger or a mortal danger to individuals, or, pursuant to a law, to prevent imminent danger to public safety and order, especially to alleviate the housing shortage, to combat the danger of epidemics or to protect endangered juveniles.

Art. 14
(Property; right of inheritance; expropriation)

(1) Property and the right of inheritance are guaranteed. Their content and limits shall be determined by the laws.

(2) Property imposes duties. Its use should also serve the public weal.

(3) Expropriation shall be permitted only in the public weal. It may be effected only by or pursuant to a law which shall provide for the nature and extent of the compensation. Such compensation shall be determined by establishing an equitable balance between the public interest and the interests of those affected. In case of dispute regarding the amount of compensation, recourse may be had to the ordinary courts.

Art. 15
(Socialisation)

Land, natural resources and means of production may for the

purpose of socialisation be transferred to public ownership or other forms of publicly controlled economy by a law which shall provide for the nature and extent of compensation. In respect of such compensation the third and fourth sentences of paragraph (3) of Art. 14 shall apply *mutatis mutandis*.

Art. 16
(Deprivation of citizenship; extradition; right of asylum)
(1) No one may be deprived of his German citizenship. Loss of citizenship may arise only pursuant to a law, and against the will of the person affected only if such person does not thereby become stateless.

(2) No German may be extradited to a foreign country. Persons persecuted on political grounds shall enjoy the right of asylum.

Art. 17
(Right of petition)
Everyone shall have the right individually or jointly with others to address written requests or complaints to the appropriate agencies and to parliamentary bodies.

Art. 17a[9]
(Restriction of basic rights for members of the Armed Forces etc.)
(1) Laws concerning military service and substitute service may, by provisions applying to members of the Armed Forces and of substitute services during their period of military or substitute service, restrict the basic right freely to express and to disseminate opinions by speech, writing and pictures (first half-sentence of paragraph (1) of Art. 5), the basic right of assembly (Art. 8), and the right of petition (Art. 17) in so far as this right permits the submission of requests or complaints jointly with others.

(2) Laws for defence purposes including the protection of the civilian population may provide for the restriction of the basic rights of freedom of movement (Art. 11) and inviolability of the home (Art. 13).

Art. 18
(Forfeiture of basic rights)
Whoever abuses freedom of expression of opinion, in particular

9. Inserted by federal law of 19 March 1956 (*FLG*, I, p. 111).

freedom of the press (paragraph (1) of Art. 5), freedom of teaching [paragraph (3) of Art. 5], freedom of assembly (Art. 8), freedom of association (Art. 9), privacy of posts and telecommunications (Art. 10), property (Art. 14), or the right of asylum (paragraph (2) of Art 16) in order to combat the free democratic basic order, shall forfeit these basic rights. Such forfeiture and the extent thereof shall be pronounced by the Federal Constitutional Court.

Art. 19
(Restriction of basic rights)

(1) In so far as a basic right may, under this Basic Law, be restricted by or pursuant to a law, such law must apply generally and not solely to an individual case. Furthermore, such law must name the basic right, indicating the Article concerned.

(2) In no case may the essential content of a basic right be encroached upon.

(3) The basic rights shall apply also to domestic juristic persons to the extent that the nature of such rights permits.

(4) Should any person's right be violated by public authority, recourse to the court shall be open to him. If jurisdiction is not specified, recourse shall be to the ordinary courts. The second sentence of paragraph (2) of Art. 10 shall not be affected by the provisions of this paragraph.[10]

II. The Federation and the Constituent States (Länder)

Art. 20
(Basic principles of the Constitution: Right to resist)

(1) The Federal Republic of Germany is a democratic and social federal state.

(2) All state authority emanates from the people. It shall be exercised by the people by means of elections and voting and by specific legislative, executive, and judicial organs.

(3) Legislation shall be subject to the constitutional order; the executive and the judiciary shall be bound by law and justice.

10. Last sentence inserted by federal law of 24 June 1968 (*FLG*, I, p. 710).

(4) All Germans shall have the right to resist any person or persons seeking to abolish that constitutional order, should no other remedy be possible.[11]

Art. 21
(Political parties)

(1) The political parties shall participate in the forming of the political will of the people. They may be freely established. Their internal organisation must conform to democratic principles. They must publicly account for the sources and use of their funds and for their assets.

(2) Parties which, by reason of their aims or the behaviour of their adherents, seek to impair or abolish the free democratic basic order or to endanger the existence of the Federal Republic of Germany, shall be unconstitutional. The Federal Constitutional Court shall decide on the question of unconstitutionality.

(3) Details shall be regulated by federal laws.

Art. 22
(Federal flag)

The federal flag shall be black–red–gold.

Art. 23
(Jurisdiction of the Basic Law)

For the time being, this Basic Law shall apply in the territory of the Länder of Baden, Bavaria, Bremen, Greater Berlin,[12] Hamburg, Hesse, Lower Saxony, North Rhine-Westphalia, Rhineland-Palatinate, Schleswig-Holstein, Württemberg-Baden, and Württemberg-Hohenzollern.[13] In other parts of Germany it shall be put into force on their accession.[14]

---

11. Inserted by federal law of 24 June 1968 (ibid.).
12. Some restrictions were imposed by the military governors.
13. By federal law of 4 May 1951 (*FLG*, I, p. 284) the Land of Baden-Württemberg was created out of the former Länder of Baden, Württemberg-Baden and Württemberg-Hohenzollern.
14. This Basic Law became effective in the Saarland by virtue of paragraph (1) of section 1 of the federal law of 23 December 1956 (*FLG*, I, p. 1011).

Art. 24
(Entry into a collective security system)

(1) The Federation may by legislation transfer sovereign powers to inter-governmental institutions.

(2) For the maintenance of peace, the Federation may enter a system of mutual collective security; in doing so it will consent to such limitations upon its rights of sovereignty as will bring about and secure a peaceful and lasting order in Europe and among the nations of the world.

(3) For the settlement of disputes between states, the Federation will accede to agreements concerning international arbitration of a general, comprehensive and obligatory nature.

Art. 25
(International law integral part of federal law)

The general rules of public international law shall be an integral part of federal law. They shall take precedence over the laws and shall directly create rights and duties for the inhabitants of the federal territory.

Art. 26
(Ban on war of aggression)

(1) Acts tending to and undertaken with the intent to disturb the peaceful relations between nations, especially to prepare for aggressive war, shall be unconstitutional. They shall be made a punishable offence.

(2) Weapons designed for warfare may not be manufactured, transported or marketed except with the permission of the Federal Government. Details shall be regulated by a federal law.

Art. 27
(Merchant fleet)

All German merchant vessels shall form one merchant fleet.

Art. 28
(Federal guarantee of Länder constitutions)

(1) The constitutional order in the Länder must conform to the principles of republican, democratic and social government based on the rule of law, within the meaning of this Basic Law. In each of the Länder, counties (*Kreise*), and communes (*Gemeinden*), the people must be represented by a body chosen in general, direct, free, equal, and secret elections. In the communes the assembly

of the commune may take the place of an elected body.

(2) The communes must be guaranteed the right to regulate on their own responsibility all the affairs of the local community within the limits set by law. The associations of communes (*Gemeindeverbände*) shall also have the right of self-government in accordance with the law and within the limits of the functions assigned to them by law.

(3) The Federation shall ensure that the constitutional order of the Länder conforms to the basic rights and to the provisions of paragraphs (1) and (2) of this Article.

Art. 29[15]
(Reorganisation of the federal territory)

(1) The federal territory may be reorganised to ensure that the Länder by their size and capacity are able effectively to fulfil the functions incumbent upon them. Due regard shall be given to regional, historical and cultural ties, economic expediency, regional policy, and the requirements of town and country planning.

(2) Measures for the reorganisation of the federal territory shall be introduced by federal laws which shall be subject to confirmation by referendum. The Länder thus affected shall be consulted.

(3) A referendum shall be held in the Länder from whose territories or partial territories a new Land or Land with redefined boundaries is to be formed (affected Länder). The referendum shall decide whether the affected Länder shall remain in their existing state or whether the new Land or Land with redefined boundaries shall be formed. The referendum shall be in favour of the formation of a new Land or Land with redefined boundaries if in its future territory and the whole of the territories or partial territories of an affected Land whose incorporation is to be modified in the same sense a majority vote for the modification. It shall not be in favour if in the territory of one of the affected Länder a majority reject the modification; such rejection shall, however, be of no consequence if in one part of the territory whose incorporation in the affected Land is to be modified a majority of two-thirds approve of the modification, unless in the entire territory of the affected Land a majority of two-thirds reject the modification.

(4) If in an integral settlement and economic agglomeration, the parts of which lie in several Länder and which has a population of at

15. As amended by federal laws of 19 August 1969 (*FLG*, I, p. 1241) and of 23 August 1976 (*FLG*, I, p. 2381).

least one million, one-tenth of those of its population entitled to vote in Bundestag elections petition by popular initiative for the incorporation of that area in one Land, a decision shall be taken within two years by means of a federal law as to whether such reorganisation shall be carried out pursuant to paragraph (2) of this Article or to the effect that a referendum shall be held in the affected Länder.

(5) The referendum shall establish whether a modification to be proposed in the law meets with approval. The law may submit different but no more than two proposals for the referendum. If a majority approve of such a proposed modification a decision shall be taken by means of a federal law within two years as to whether the reorganisation shall take place pursuant to paragraph (2) of this Article. If a proposal which has been made the subject of a referendum meets with approval in accordance with the third and fourth sentences of paragraph (3) of this Article, a federal law providing for the formation of the proposed Land shall be enacted within two years after the referendum and shall no longer be subject to confirmation by referendum.

(6) Referendums shall be decided by the majority of votes cast if they make up at least one quarter of the population entitled to vote in Bundestag elections. Other details with regard to referendums and initiatives (*Volksentscheide, Volksbegehren, Volksbefragungen*) shall be regulated by a federal law; such federal law may also provide that initiatives may not be repeated within a period of five years.

(7) Other modifications of the territory of the Länder may be effected by state agreements between the Länder concerned or by a federal law with the approval of the Bundesrat if the territory which is to be the subject of reorganisation does not have more than 10,000 inhabitants. The details shall be regulated by a federal law requiring the approval of the Bundesrat and the majority of the members of the Bundestag. It must make provision for the affected communes and districts to be heard.

Art. 30
(Functions of the Länder)

The exercise of governmental powers and the discharge of governmental functions shall be incumbent on the Länder in so far as this Basic Law does not otherwise prescribe or permit.

Art. 31
(Priority of federal law)
Federal law shall override Land law.

Art. 32
(Foreign relations)
(1) Relations with foreign states shall be conducted by the Federation.

(2) Before the conclusion of a treaty affecting the special circumstances of a Land, that Land must be consulted in sufficient time.

(3) In so far as the Länder have power to legislate, they may, with the consent of the Federal Government, conclude treaties with foreign states.

Art. 33
(All Germans have equal political status)
(1) Every German shall have in every Land the same political (*staatsbürgerlich*) rights and duties.

(2) Every German shall be equally eligible for any public office according to his aptitude, qualifications, and professional achievements.

(3) Enjoyment of civil and political rights, eligibility for public office, and rights acquired in the public service shall be independent of religious denomination. No one may suffer any disadvantage by reason of his adherence or non-adherence to a denomination or ideology.

(4) The exercise of state authority as a permanent function shall as a rule be entrusted to members of the public service whose status, service and loyalty are governed by public law.

(5) The law of the public service shall be regulated with due regard to the traditional principles of the professional civil service.

Art. 34
(Liability in the event of malfeasance)
If any person, in the exercise of a public office entrusted to him, violates his official obligations to a third party, liability shall rest in principle on the state or the public body which employs him. In the event of wilful intent or gross negligence the right of recourse shall be reserved. In respect of the claim for compensation or the right of recourse, the jurisdiction of the ordinary courts must not be excluded.

Art. 35[16]
(Legal, administrative and police assistance)

(1) All federal and Land authorities shall render each other legal and administrative assistance.

(2) In order to maintain or to restore public security or order, a Land may, in cases of particular importance, call upon forces and facilities of the Federal Border Guard to assist its police if, without this assistance, the police could not, or only with considerable difficulty, fulfil a task. In order to deal with a natural disaster or an especially grave accident, a Land may request the assistance of the police forces of other Länder or of forces and facilities of other administrative authorities or of the Federal Border Guard or the Armed Forces.[17]

(3) If the natural disaster or the accident endangers a region larger than a Land, the Federal Government may, in so far as this is necessary effectively to deal with such danger, instruct the Land governments to place their police forces at the disposal of other Länder, and may commit units of the Federal Border Guard or the Armed Forces to support the police forces. Measures taken by the Federal Government pursuant to the first sentence of this paragraph must be revoked at any time upon the request of the Bundesrat, and in any case without delay upon removal of the danger.

Art. 36
(Personnel of the federal authorities)

(1) Civil servants employed in the highest federal authorities shall be drawn from all Länder in appropriate proportion. Persons employed in other federal authorities should, as a rule, be drawn from the Land in which they serve.

(2)[18] Military laws shall, *inter alia*, take into account both the division of the Federation into Länder and the regional ties of their populations.

Art. 37
(Federal enforcement)

(1) If a Land fails to comply with its obligations of a federal character imposed by this Basic Law or another federal law, the

---

16. As amended by federal law of 24 June 1968 (*FLG*, I, p. 710).
17. As amended by federal law of 28 July 1972 (*FLG*, I, p. 1305).
18. Inserted by federal law of 19 March 1956 (*FLG*, I, p. 111).

Federal Government may, with the consent of the Bundesrat, take the necessary measures to enforce such compliance by the Land by way of federal enforcement.

(2) To carry out such federal enforcement the Federal Government or its commissioner shall have the right to give instructions to all Länder and their authorities.

III. The Federal Parliament (Bundestag)

Art. 38
(Elections)

(1) The deputies to the German Bundestag shall be elected in general, direct, free, equal, and secret elections. They shall be representatives of the whole people, not bound by orders and instructions, and shall be subject only to their conscience.

(2)[19] Anyone who has attained the age of eighteen years shall be entitled to vote; anyone who has attained full legal age shall be eligible for election.

(3) Details shall be regulated by a federal law.

Art. 39
(Assembly and legislative term)

(1)[20] The Bundestag shall be elected for a four-year term. Its legislative term shall end with the assembly of a new Bundestag. The new election shall be held at the earliest forty-five, at the latest forty-seven, months after the beginning of the legislative term. If the Bundestag is dissolved the new election shall be held within sixty days.

(2)[21] The Bundestag shall assemble at the latest on the thirtieth day after the election.

(3) The Bundestag shall determine the termination and resumption of its meetings. The President of the Bundestag may convene it at an earlier date. He must do so if one-third of its members or the Federal President or the Federal Chancellor so demand.

---

19. Amended by federal law of 31 July 1970 (*FLG*, I, p. 1161).
20. As amended by federal law of 23 August 1976 (*FLG*, I, p. 2381).
21. Ibid.

Art. 40
(President; rules of procedure)

(1) The Bundestag shall elect its President, vice-presidents, and secretaries. It shall draw up its rules of procedure.

(2) The President shall exercise the proprietary and police powers in the Bundestag building. No search or seizure may take place in the premises of the Bundestag without his permission.

Art. 41
(Scrutiny of elections)

(1) The scrutiny of elections shall be the responsibility of the Bundestag. It shall also decide whether a deputy has lost his seat in the Bundestag.

(2) Complaints against such decisions of the Bundestag may be lodged with the Federal Constitutional Court.

(3) Details shall be regulated by a federal law.

Art. 42
(Proceedings; voting)

(1) The meetings of the Bundestag shall be public. Upon a motion of one-tenth of its members, or upon a motion of the Federal Government, the public may be excluded by a two-thirds majority. The decision on the motion shall be taken at a meeting not open to the public.

(2) Decisions of the Bundestag shall require a majority of the votes cast unless this Basic Law provides otherwise. The rules of procedure may provide exceptions for elections to be made by the Bundestag.

(3) True and accurate reports on the public meetings of the Bundestag and of its committees shall not give rise to any liability.

Art. 43
(Presence of the Federal Government)

(1) The Bundestag and its committees may demand the presence of any member of the Federal Government.

(2) The members of the Bundesrat or of the Federal Government as well as persons commissioned by them shall have access to all meetings of the Bundestag and its committees. They must be heard at any time.

Art. 44
(Committees of investigation)

(1) The Bundestag shall have the right, and upon the motion of one-fourth of its members the duty, to set up a committee of investigation which shall take the requisite evidence at public hearings. The public may be excluded.

(2) The rules of criminal procedure shall apply *mutatis mutandis* to the taking of evidence. The privacy of posts and telecommunications shall remain unaffected.

(3) Courts and administrative authorities shall be bound to render legal and administrative assistance.

(4) The decisions of committees of investigation shall not be subject to judicial consideration. The courts shall be free to evaluate and judge the facts on which the investigation is based.

Art. 45[22]
(Standing Committee)

Art. 45a[23]
(Committees on Foreign Affairs and Defence)

(1)[24] The Bundestag shall appoint a Committee on Foreign Affairs and a Committee on Defence.

(2) The Committee on Defence shall also have the rights of a committee of investigation. Upon the motion of one-fourth of its members it shall have the duty to make a specific matter the subject of investigation.

(3) Paragraph (1) of Art. 44 shall not be applied in matters of defence.

Art. 45b[25]
(Defence Commissioner of the Bundestag)

A Defence Commissioner of the Bundestag shall be appointed to safeguard the basic rights and to assist the Bundestag in exercising parliamentary control. Details shall be regulated by a federal law.

---

22. Deleted by federal law of 23 August 1976 (*FLG*, I, p. 2381).
23. Inserted by federal law of 19 March 1956 (*FLG*, I, p. 111).
24. Second sentence deleted by federal law of 23 August 1976 (*FLG*, I, p. 2381).
25. Inserted by federal law of 15 July 1975 (*FLG*, I, p. 1901).

Art. 45c[26]
(Petitions Committee)

(1) The Bundestag shall appoint a Petitions Committee to deal with requests and complaints addressed to the Bundestag pursuant to Article 17.

(2) The powers of the Committee to consider complaints shall be regulated by a federal law.

Art. 46
(Indemnity and immunity of deputies)

(1) A deputy may not at any time be prosecuted in the courts or subjected to disciplinary action or otherwise called to account outside the Bundestag for a vote cast or a statement made by him in the Bundestag or any of its committees. This shall not apply to defamatory insults.

(2) A deputy may not be called to account or arrested for a punishable offence except by permission of the Bundestag, unless he is apprehended in the commission of the offence or in the course of the following day.

(3) The permission of the Bundestag shall also be necessary for any other restriction of the personal liberty of a deputy or for the initiation of proceedings against a deputy under Art. 18.

(4) Any criminal proceedings or any proceedings under Art. 18 against a deputy, any detention or any other restriction of his personal liberty shall be suspended upon the request of the Bundestag.

Art. 47
(Right of deputies to refuse to give evidence)

Deputies may refuse to give evidence concerning persons who have confided facts to them in their capacity as deputies, or to whom they have confided facts in such capacity, as well as concerning these facts themselves. To the extent that this right to refuse to give evidence exists, no seizure of documents shall be permissible.

Art. 48
(Entitlements of deputies)

(1) Any candidate for election to the Bundestag shall be entitled to the leave necessary for his election campaign.

---

26. Ibid.

(2) No one may be prevented from accepting and exercising the office of deputy. He may not be given notice of dismissal nor dismissed from employment on this ground.

(3) Deputies shall be entitled to a remuneration adequate to ensure their independence. They shall be entitled to the free use of all state-owned means of transport. Details shall be regulated by a federal law.

Art. 49[27]
(Repealed)

IV. The Council of Constituent States
(Bundesrat)

Art. 50
(Function)

The Länder shall participate through the Bundesrat in the legislation and administration of the Federation.

Art. 51
(Composition)

(1) The Bundesrat shall consist of members of the Land governments which appoint and recall them. Other members of such governments may act as substitutes.

(2) Each Land shall have at least three votes; Länder with more than two million inhabitants shall have four, Länder with more than six million inhabitants five votes.

(3) Each Land may delegate as many members as it has votes. The votes of each Land may be cast only as a block vote and only by members present or their substitutes.

Art. 52
(President, rules of procedure)

(1) The Bundesrat shall elect its President for one year.

(2) The President shall convene the Bundesrat. He must con-

---

27. Amended by federal law of 19 March 1956 (*FLG*, I, p. 111); deleted by federal law of 23 August 1976 (*FLG*, I, p. 2381).

vene it if the members for at least two Länder or the Federal Government so demand.

(3) The Bundesrat shall take its decisions with at least the majority of its votes. It shall draw up its rules of procedure. Its meetings shall be public. The public may be excluded.

(4) Other members of, or persons commissioned by, Land governments may serve on the committees of the Bundesrat.

Art. 53
(Participation of the Federal Government)

The members of the Federal Government shall have the right, and on demand the duty, to attend the meetings of the Bundesrat and of its committees. They must be heard ˊat any time. The Bundesrat must be currently kept informed by the Federal Government of the conduct of affairs.

IVa.[28] The Joint Committee

Art. 53a

(1) Two-thirds of the members of the Joint Committee shall be deputies of the Bundestag and one-third shall be members of the Bundesrat. The Bundestag shall delegate its deputies in proportion to the sizes of its parliamentary groups; such deputies must not be members of the Federal Government. Each Land shall be represented by a Bundesrat member of its choice; these members shall not be bound by instructions. The establishment of the Joint Committee and its procedures shall be regulated by rules of procedure to be adopted by the Bundestag and requiring the consent of the Bundesrat.

(2) The Federal Government must inform the Joint Committee about its plans in respect of a state of defence. The rights of the Bundestag and its committees under paragraph (1) of Art. 43 shall not be affected by the provision of this paragraph.

---

28. Inserted by federal law of 24 June 1968 (*FLG*, I, p. 710).

V. The Federal President

Art. 54
(Election by the Federal Convention)
(1) The Federal President shall be elected, without debate, by the Federal Convention (*Bundesversammlung*). Every German shall be eligible who is entitled to vote for Bundestag candidates and has attained the age of forty years.

(2) The term of office of the Federal President shall be five years. Re-election for a consecutive term shall be permitted only once.

(3) The Federal Convention shall consist of the members of the Bundestag and an equal number of members elected by the diets of the Länder according to the principles of proportional representation.

(4) The Federal Convention shall meet not later than thirty days before the expiration of the term of office of the Federal President or, in the case of premature termination, not later than thirty days after that date. It shall be convened by the President of the Bundestag.

(5) After the expiration of a legislative term, the period specified in the first sentence of paragraph (4) of this Article shall begin with the first meeting of the Bundestag.

(6) The person receiving the votes of the majority of the members of the Federal Convention shall be elected. If such majority is not obtained by any candidate in two ballots, the candidate who receives the largest number of votes in the next ballot shall be elected.

(7) Details shall be regulated by a federal law.

Art. 55
(No secondary occupation)
(1) The Federal President may not be a member of the government nor of a legislative body of the Federation or of a Land.

(2) The Federal President may not hold any other salaried office, nor engage in a trade or occupation, nor practise a profession, nor belong to the management or the board of directors of an enterprise carried on for profit.

Art. 56
(Oath of office)

On assuming his office the Federal President shall take the following oath before the assembled members of the Bundestag and the Bundesrat: 'I swear that I will dedicate my efforts to the well-being of the German people, enhance its benefits, ward harm from it, uphold and defend the Basic Law and the laws of the Federation, fulfil my duties conscientiously, and do justice to all. So help me God'.

The oath may also be taken without religious affirmation.

Art. 57
(Representation)

If the Federal President is prevented from acting, or if his office falls prematurely vacant, his powers shall be exercised by the President of the Bundesrat.

Art. 58
(Countersignature)

Orders and decrees of the Federal President shall require for their validity the countersignature of the Federal Chancellor or the appropriate Federal Minister. This shall not apply to the appointment and dismissal of the Federal Chancellor, the dissolution of the Bundestag under Art. 63 and the request under paragraph (3) of Art. 69.

Art. 59
(Authority to represent [the] Federation in international relations)

(1) The Federal President shall represent the Federation in its international relations. He shall conclude treaties with foreign states on behalf of the Federation. He shall accredit and receive envoys.

(2) Treaties which regulate the political relations of the Federation or relate to matters of federal legislation shall require the consent or participation, in the form of a federal law, of the bodies competent in any specific case for such federal legislation. As regards administrative agreements, the provisions concerning the federal administration shall apply *mutatis mutandis*.

Art. 59a[29]
(Repealed)

Art. 60
(Appointment of federal civil servants and officers)

(1)[30] The Federal President shall appoint and dismiss the federal judges, the federal civil servants, the officers and non-commissioned officers, unless otherwise provided for by law.

(2) He shall exercise the right of pardon in individual cases on behalf of the Federation.

(3) He may delegate these powers to other authorities.

(4) Paragraphs (2) to (4) of Art. 46 shall apply *mutatis mutandis* to the Federal President.

Art. 61
(Impeachment before the Federal Constitutional Court)

(1) The Bundestag or the Bundesrat may impeach the Federal President before the Federal Constitutional Court for wilful violation of this Basic Law or any other federal law. The motion for impeachment must be brought forward by at least one-fourth of the members of the Bundestag or one-fourth of the votes of the Bundesrat. The decision to impeach shall require a majority of two-thirds of the members of the Bundestag or of two-thirds of the votes of the Bundesrat. The impeachment shall be substantiated by a person commissioned by the impeaching body.

(2) If the Federal Constitutional Court finds the Federal President guilty of a wilful violation of this Basic Law or of another federal law, it may declare him to have forfeited his office. After impeachment, it may issue an interim order preventing the Federal President from exercising his functions.

---

29. Inserted by federal law of 19 March 1956 (*FLG*, I, p. 111) and repealed by federal law of 24 June 1968 (*FLG*, I, p. 711).
30. As amended by federal law of 19 March 1956 (*FLG*, I, p. 111).

VI. The Federal Government

Art. 62
(Composition)

The Federal Government shall consist of the Federal Chancellor and the Federal Ministers.

Art. 63
(Election of the Federal Chancellor — Dissolution of the Bundestag)

(1) The Federal Chancellor shall be elected, without debate, by the Bundestag upon the proposal of the Federal President.

(2) The person obtaining the votes of the majority of the members of the Bundestag shall be elected. The person elected must be appointed by the Federal President.

(3) If the person proposed is not elected, the Bundestag may elect within fourteen days of the ballot a Federal Chancellor by more than one-half of its members.

(4) If no candidate has been elected within this period, a new ballot shall take place without delay, in which the person obtaining the largest number of votes shall be elected. If the person elected has obtained the votes of the majority of the members of the Bundestag, the Federal President must appoint him within seven days of the election. If the person elected did not obtain such a majority, the Federal President must within seven days either appoint him or dissolve the Bundestag.

Art. 64
(Appointment of Federal Ministers)

(1) The Federal Ministers shall be appointed and dismissed by the Federal President upon the proposal of the Federal Chancellor.

(2) The Federal Chancellor and the Federal Ministers, on assuming office, shall take before the Bundestag the oath provided for in Art. 56.

Art. 65
(Distribution of responsibility)

The Federal Chancellor shall determine, and be responsible for, the general policy guidelines. Within the limits set by these guidelines, each Federal Minister shall conduct the affairs of his department autonomously and on his own responsibility. The Federal Government shall decide on differences of opinion between Federal Ministers. The Federal Chancellor shall conduct the affairs of the Federal Government in accordance with rules of procedure adopted by it and approved by the Federal President.

Art. 65a[31]
(Power of command over Armed Forces)
Power of command in respect of the Armed Forces shall be vested in the Federal Minister of Defence.

Art. 66
(No secondary occupation)
The Federal Chancellor and the Federal Ministers may not hold any other salaried office, nor engage in a trade or occupation, nor practise a profession, nor belong to the management or, without the consent of the Bundestag, to the board of directors of an enterprise carried on for profit.

Art. 67
(Vote of no-confidence)
(1) The Bundestag can express its lack of confidence in the Federal Chancellor only be electing a successor with the majority of its members and by requesting the Federal President to dismiss the Federal Chancellor. The Federal President must comply with the request and appoint the person elected.

(2) Forty-eight hours must elapse between the motion and the election.

Art. 68
(Vote of confidence — Dissolution of the Bundestag)
(1) If a motion of the Federal Chancellor for a vote of confidence is not assented to by the majority of the members of the Bundestag, the Federal President may, upon the proposal of the Federal Chancellor, dissolve the Bundestag within twenty-one days. The right to dissolve shall lapse as soon as the Bundestag with the majority of its members elects another Federal Chancellor.

(2) Forty-eight hours must elapse between the motion and the vote thereon.

---

31. Inserted by federal law of 19 March 1956 (*FLG*, I, p. 111) and amended by federal law of 24 June 1968 (*FLG*, I, p. 711).

Art. 69
(Deputy of the Federal Chancellor)

(1) The Federal Chancellor shall appoint a Federal Minister as his deputy.

(2) The tenure of office of the Federal Chancellor or a Federal Minister shall end in any event on the first meeting of a new Bundestag; the tenure of office of a Federal Minister shall also end on any other termination of the tenure of office of the Federal Chancellor.

(3) At the request of the Federal President the Federal Chancellor, or at the request of the Federal Chancellor or of the Federal President a Federal Minister, shall be bound to continue to transact the affairs of his office until the appointment of a successor.

VII. Legislative Powers of the Federation

Art. 70
(Legislation of the Federation and the Länder)

(1) The Länder shall have the right to legislate in so far as this Basic Law does not confer legislative power on the Federation.

(2) The division of competence between the Federation and the Länder shall be determined by the provisions of this Basic Law concerning exclusive and concurrent legislative powers.

Art. 71
(Exclusive legislation of the Federation, definition)

In matters within the exclusive legislative power of the Federation the Länder shall have power to legislate only if, and to the extent that, a federal law explicitly so authorises them.

Art. 72
(Concurrent legislation of the Federation, definition)

(1) In matters within concurrent legislative powers the Länder shall have power to legislate as long as, and to the extent that, the Federation does not exercise its right to legislate.

(2) The Federation shall have the right to legislate in these matters to the extent that a need for regulation by federal legislation exists because:

1. a matter cannot be effectively regulated by the legislation of individual Länder, or
2. the regulation of a matter by a Land law might prejudice the interests of other Länder or of the people as a whole, or
3. the maintenance of legal or economic unity, especially the maintenance of uniformity of living conditions beyond the territory of any one Land, necessitates such regulation.

Art. 73
(Exclusive legislation, catalogue)

The Federation shall have exclusive power to legislate in the following matters:

1.[32] foreign affairs as well as defence including the protection of the civilian population;
2. citizenship in the Federation;
3. freedom of movement, passport matters, immigration, emigration, and extradition;
4. currency, money and coinage, weights and measures, as well as the determination of standards of time;
5. the unity of the customs and commercial territory, treaties on commerce and on navigation, the freedom of movement of goods, and the exchanges of goods and payments with foreign countries, including customs and other frontier protection;
6. federal railroads and air transport;
7. postal and telecommunication services;
8. the legal status of persons employed by the Federation and by federal corporate bodies under public law;
9. industrial property rights, copyrights and publishers' rights;
10.[33] co-operation of the Federation and the Länder in matters of
    (a) criminal police,
    (b) protection of the free democratic basic order, of the existence and the security of the Federation or of a Land (protection of the constitution) and
    (c) protection against efforts in the federal territory which, by the use of force or actions in preparation for the use of force, endanger the foreign interests of the Federal Republic of Germany,

---

32. As amended by federal laws of 26 March 1954 (*FLG*, I, p. 45) and 24 June 1968 (*FLG*, I, p. 711).
33. As amended by federal law of 28 July 1972 (*FLG*, I, p. 1305).

as well as the establishment of a Federal Criminal Police Office and the international control of crime;

11. statistics for federal purposes.

Art. 74
(Concurrent legislation, catalogue)

Concurrent legislative powers shall extend to the following matters:

1. civil law, criminal law and execution of sentences, the organisation and procedure of courts, the legal profession, notaries, and legal advice (*Rechtsberatung*);
2. registration of births, deaths, and marriages;
3. the law of association and assembly;
4. the law relating to residence and establishment of aliens;
4a.[34] the law relating to weapons and explosives;
5. the protection of German cultural treasures against removal abroad;
6. refugee and expellee matters;
7. public welfare;
8. citizenship in the Länder;
9. war damage and reparations;
10.[35] benefits to war-disabled persons and to dependants of those killed in the war as well as assistance to former prisoners of war;
10a.[36] war graves of soldiers, graves of other victims of war and of victims of despotism;
11. the law relating to economic matters (mining, industry, supply of power, crafts, trades, commerce, banking, stock exchanges, and private insurance);
11a.[37] the production and utilisation of nuclear energy for peaceful purposes, the construction and operation of installations serving such purposes, protection against hazards arising from the release of nuclear energy or from ionising radiation, and the disposal of radioactive substances;
12. labour law, including the legal organisation of enterprises, protection of workers, employment exchanges

34. Inserted by federal law of 28 July 1972 (*FLG*, I, p. 1305) and amended by federal law of 23 August 1976 (*FLG*, I, p. 2383).
35. As amended by federal law of 16 June 1965 (*FLG*, I, p. 513).
36. Inserted by federal law of 16 June 1965 (*FLG*, I, p. 513).
37. Inserted by federal law of 23 December 1959 (*FLG*, I, p. 813).

13.[38]   the regulation of educational and training grants and the promotion of scientific research;

14.   the law regarding expropriation, to the extent that matters enumerated in Articles 73 and 74 are concerned;

15.   transfer of land, natural resources and means of production to public ownership or other forms of publicly controlled economy;

16.   prevention of the abuse of economic power;

17.   promotion of agricultural and forest production, safeguarding of the supply of food, the importation and exportation of agricultural and forest products, deep-sea and coastal fishing, and preservation of the coasts;

18.   real estate transactions, land law and matters concerning agricultural leases, as well as housing, settlement and homestead matters;

19.   measures against human and animal diseases that are communicable or otherwise endanger public health, admission to the medical profession and to other health occupations or practices, as well as trade in medicines, curatives, narcotics, and poisons;

19a.[39]   the economic viability of hospitals and the regulation of hospitalisation fees;

20.[40]   protection regarding the marketing of food, drink and tobacco, of [the] necessities of life, fodder, agricultural and forest seeds and seedlings, and protection of plants against diseases and pests, as well as the protection of animals;

21.   ocean and coastal shipping as well as aids to navigation, inland navigation, meteorological services, sea routes, and inland waterways used for general traffic;

22.[41]   road traffic, motor transport, construction and maintenance of long-distance highways as well as the collection of charges for the use of public highways by vehicles and the allocation of revenue therefrom;

23.   non-federal railroads, except mountain railroads;

38. As amended by federal law of 12 May 1969 (*FLG*, I, p. 363).
39. Inserted by federal law of 12 May 1969 (*FLG*, I, p. 363).
40. As amended by federal law of 18 March 1971 (*FLG*, I, p. 207).
41. As amended by federal law of 12 May 1969 (*FLG*, I, p. 363).

24.[42] waste disposal, air purification, and noise abatement.

Art. 74a[43]
(Wider competence of [the] Federation for pay scales)

(1) Concurrent legislation shall further extend to the pay scales and pensions of members of the public service whose service and loyalty are governed by public law, in so far as the Federation does not have exclusive power to legislate pursuant to item 8 of Art. 73.

(2) Federal laws enacted pursuant to paragraph (1) of this Article shall require the consent of the Bundesrat.

(3) Federal laws enacted pursuant to item 8 of Art. 73 shall likewise require the consent of the Bundesrat, in so far as they prescribe for the structure and computation of pay scales and pensions, including the appraisal of posts, criteria or minimum or maximum rates other than those provided for in federal laws enacted pursuant to paragraph (1) of this Article.

(4) Paragraphs (1) and (2) of this Article shall apply *mutatis mutandis* to the pay scales and pensions for judges in the Länder. Paragraph (3) of this Article shall apply *mutatis mutandis* to laws enacted pursuant to paragraph (1) of Art. 98.

Art. 75[44]
(General provisions of the Federation, catalogue)

Subject to the conditions laid down in Art. 72, the Federation shall have the right to enact skeleton provisions concerning:

1.[45] the legal status of persons in the public service of the Länder, communes, or other corporate bodies under public law, in so far as Art. 74a does not provide otherwise;

1a.[46] the general principles governing higher education;

2. the general legal status of the press and the film industry;

3. hunting, nature conservation and landscape management;

4. land distribution, regional planning, and water regime;

5. matters relating to the registration of changes of residence or domicile (*Meldewesen*) and to identity cards.

---

42. As amended by federal law of 12 April 1972 (*FLG*, I, p. 593).
43. As inserted by federal law of 18 March 1971 (*FLG*, I, p. 206).
44. As amended by federal law of 12 May 1969 (*FLG*, I, p. 363).
45. As amended by federal law of 18 March 1971 (*FLG*, I, p. 206).
46. Inserted by federal law of 12 May 1969 (*FLG*, I, p. 363).

Art. 76
(Bills)

(1) Bills shall be introduced in the Bundestag by the Federal Government or by members of the Bundestag or by the Bundesrat.

(2)[47] Bills of the Federal Government shall be submitted first to the Bundesrat. The Bundesrat shall be entitled to state its position on such bills within six weeks. A bill exceptionally submitted to the Bundesrat as being particularly urgent by the Federal Government may be submitted by the latter to the Bundestag three weeks later, even though the Federal Government may not yet have received the statement of the Bundesrat's position; such statement shall be transmitted to the Bundestag by the Federal Government without delay upon its receipt.

(3)[48] Bills of the Bundesrat shall be submitted to the Bundestag by the Federal Government within three months. In doing so, the Federal Government must state its own view.

Art. 77
(Procedure concerning adopted bills — Objection of the Bundesrat)

(1) Bills intended to become federal laws shall require adoption by the Bundestag. Upon their adoption they shall, without delay, be transmitted to the Bundesrat by the President of the Bundestag.

(2)[49] The Bundesrat may, within three weeks of the receipt of the adopted bill, demand that a committee for joint consideration of bills, composed of members of the Bundestag and members of the Bundesrat, be convened. The composition and the procedure of this committee shall be regulated by rules of procedure to be adopted by the Bundestag and requiring the consent of the Bundesrat. The members of the Bundesrat on this committee shall not be bound by instructions. If the consent of the Bundesrat is required for a bill to become a law, the convening of this committee may also be demanded by the Bundestag or the Federal Government. Should the committee propose any amendment to the adopted bill, the Bundestag must again vote on the bill.

(3)[50] In so far as the consent of the Bundesrat is not required for a bill to become a law, the Bundesrat may, when the proceedings

---

47. As amended by federal law of 15 November 1968 (*FLG*, I, p. 1177).
48. As amended by federal law of 17 July 1969 (*FLG*, I, p. 817).
49. As amended by federal law of 15 November 1968 (*FLG*, I, p. 1177).
50. Ibid.

under paragraph (2) of this Article are completed, enter an objection within two weeks against a bill adopted by the Bundestag. This period shall begin, in the case of the last sentence of paragraph (2) of this Article, on the receipt of the bill as readopted by the Bundestag, and in all other cases on the receipt of a communication from the chairman of the committee provided for in paragraph (2) of this Article, to the effect that the committee's proceedings have been concluded.

(4) If the objection was adopted with the majority of the votes of the Bundesrat, it can be rejected by a decision of the majority of the members of the Bundestag. If the Bundesrat adopted the objection with a majority of at least two-thirds of its votes, its rejection by the Bundestag shall require a majority of two-thirds, including at least the majority of the members of the Bundestag.

Art. 78
(Conditions for passing of federal laws)

A bill adopted by the Bundestag shall become a law if the Bundesrat consents to it, or fails to make a demand pursuant to paragraph (2) of Art. 77, or fails to enter an objection within the period stipulated in paragraph (3) of Art. 77, or withdraws such objection, or if the objection is overridden by the Bundestag.

Art. 79
(Amendment of the Basic Law)

(1) This Basic Law can be amended only by laws which expressly amend or supplement the text thereof. In respect of international treaties the subject of which is a peace settlement, the preparation of a peace settlement, or the abolition of an occupation regime, or which are designed to serve the defence of the Federal Republic, it shall be sufficient, for the purpose of clarifying that the provisions of this Basic Law do not preclude the conclusion and entry into force of such treaties, to effect a supplementation of the text of this Basic Law confined to such clarification.[51]

(2) Any such law shall require the affirmative vote of two-thirds of the members of the Bundestag and two thirds of the votes of the Bundesrat.

(3) Amendments of this Basic Law affecting the division of the Federation into Länder, the participation on principle of the

---

51. Second sentence inserted by federal law of 26 March 1954 (*FLG*, I, p. 45).

Länder in legislation, or the basic principles laid down in Arts. 1 and 20, shall be inadmissible.

Art. 80
(Issue of ordinances having force of law)

(1) The Federal Government, a Federal Minister or the Land governments may be authorised by a law to issue ordinances having the force of law (*Rechtsverordnungen*). The content, purpose, and scope of the authorisation so conferred must be set forth in such law. This legal basis must be stated in the ordinance. If a law provides that such authorisation may be delegated, such delegation shall require another ordinance having the force of law.

(2) The consent of the Bundesrat shall be required, unless otherwise provided by federal legislation, for ordinances having the force of law issued by the Federal Government or a Federal Minister concerning basic rules for the use of facilities of the federal railroads and of postal and telecommunication services, or charges therefor, or concerning the construction and operation of railroads, as well as for ordinances having the force of law issued pursuant to federal laws that require the consent of the Bundesrat or that are executed by the Länder as agents of the Federation or as matters of their own concern.

Art. 80a[52]
(State of tension)

(1) Where this Basic Law or a federal law on defence, including the protection of the civilian population, stipulates that legal provisions may only be applied in accordance with this Article, their application shall, except when a state of defence exists, be admissible only after the Bundestag has determined that a state of tension (*Spannungsfall*) exists or if it has specifically approved such application. In respect of the cases mentioned in the first sentence of paragraph (5) and the second sentence of paragraph (6) of Art. 12a, such determination of a state of tension and such specific approval shall require a two-thirds majority of the votes cast.

(2) Any measures taken by virtue of legal provisions enacted under paragraph (1) of this Article shall be revoked whenever the Bundestag so requests.

(3) In derogation of paragraph (1) of this Article, the application of such legal provisions shall also be admissible by virtue of, and in

52. Inserted by federal law of 24 June 1968 (*FLG*, I, p. 711).

accordance with, a decision taken with the consent of the Federal Government by an international organ within the framework of a treaty of alliance. Any measures taken pursuant to this paragraph shall be revoked whenever the Bundestag so requests with the majority of its members.

Art. 81
(State of legislative emergency)

(1) Should, in the circumstances of Art. 68, the Bundestag not be dissolved, the Federal President may, at the request of the Federal Government and with the consent of the Bundesrat, declare a state of legislative emergency with respect to a bill, if the Bundestag rejects the bill although the Federal Government has declared it to be urgent. The same shall apply if a bill has been rejected although the Federal Chancellor had combined with it the motion under Art. 68.

(2) If, after a state of legislative emergency has been declared, the Bundestag again rejects the bill or adopts it in a version stated to be unacceptable to the Federal Government, the bill shall be deemed to have become a law to the extent that the Bundesrat consents to it. The same shall apply if the bill is not passed by the Bundestag within four weeks of its reintroduction.

(3) During the term of office of a Federal Chancellor, any other bill rejected by the Bundestag may become a law in accordance with paragraphs (1) and (2) of this Article within a period of six months after the first declaration of a state of legislative emergency. After the expiration of this period, a further declaration of a state of legislative emergency shall be inadmissible during the term of office of the same Federal Chancellor.

(4) This Basic Law may not be amended nor repealed nor suspended in whole or in part by a law enacted pursuant to paragraph (2) of this Article.

Art. 82
(Promulgation and effective date of laws)

(1) Laws enacted in accordance with the provisions of this Basic Law shall, after countersignature, be signed by the Federal President and promulgated in the *Federal Law Gazette*. Ordinances having the force of law shall be signed by the agency which issues them, and, unless otherwise provided by law, shall be promulgated in the *Federal Law Gazette*.

(2) Every law or every ordinance having the force of law should

specify its effective date. In the absence of such a provision, it shall become effective on the fourteenth day after the end of the day on which the *Federal Law Gazette* containing it was published.

VIII. The Execution of Federal Laws and the Federal Administration

Art. 83
(Execution of federal laws by the Länder)

The Länder shall execute federal laws as matters of their own concern in so far as this Basic Law does not otherwise provide or permit.

Art. 84
(Land administration and Federal Government supervision)

(1) Where the Länder execute federal laws as matters of their own concern, they shall provide for the establishment of the requisite authorities and the regulation of administrative procedures in so far as federal laws consented to by the Bundesrat do not otherwise provide.

(2) The Federal Government may, with the consent of the Bundesrat, issue pertinent general administrative rules.

(3) The Federal Government shall exercise supervision to ensure that the Länder execute the federal laws in accordance with applicable law. For this purpose the Federal Government may send commissioners to the highest Land authorities and with their consent or, if such consent is refused, with the consent of the Bundesrat, also to subordinate authorities.

(4) Should any shortcomings which the Federal Government has found to exist in the execution of federal laws in the Länder not be corrected, the Bundesrat shall decide, on the application of the Federal Government or the Land concerned, whether such Land has violated applicable law. The decision of the Bundesrat may be challenged in the Federal Constitutional Court.

(5) With a view to the execution of federal laws, the Federal Government may be authorised by a federal law requiring the consent of the Bundesrat to issue individual instructions for particular cases. They shall be addressed to the highest Land auth-

orities unless the Federal Government considers the matter urgent.

Art. 85
(Execution by Länder as agents of the Federation)

(1) Where the Länder execute federal laws as agents of the Federation, the establishment of the requisite authorities shall remain the concern of the Länder except in so far as federal laws consented to by the Bundesrat otherwise provide.

(2) The Federal Government may, with the consent of the Bundesrat, issue pertinent general administrative rules. It may regulate the uniform training of civil servants (*Beamte*) and other salaried public employees (*Angestellte*). The heads of authorities at the intermediate level shall be appointed with its agreement.

(3) The Land authorities shall be subject to the instructions of the appropriate highest federal authorities. Such instructions shall be addressed to the highest Land authorities unless the Federal Government considers the matter urgent. Execution of the instructions shall be ensured by the highest Land authorities.

(4) Federal supervision shall extend to conformity with law and appropriateness of execution. The Federal Government may, for this purpose, require the submission of reports and documents and send commissioners to all authorities.

Art. 86
(Direct federal administration)

Where the Federation executes laws by means of direct federal administration or by federal corporate bodies or institutions under public law, the Federal Government shall, in so far as the law concerned contains no special provision, issue pertinent general administrative rules. The Federal Government shall provide for the establishment of the requisite authorities in so far as the law concerned does not otherwise provide.

Art. 87[53]
(Matters of direct federal administration)

(1) The foreign service, the federal finance administration, the federal railroads, the federal postal service, and, in accordance with the provisions of Art. 89, the administration of federal waterways and of shipping shall be conducted as matters of direct federal

---

53. Inserted by federal law of 19 March 1956 (*FLG*, I, p. 111) and amended by federal law of 24 June 1968 (*FLG*, I, p. 711).

administration with their own administrative substructures. Federal Border Guard authorities, central offices for police information and communications, for the criminal police and for the compilation of data for the purposes of protection of the constitution and protection against efforts in the Federal territory which, by the use of force or actions in preparation for the use of force, endanger the foreign interests of the Federal Republic of Germany may be established by federal legislation.[54]

(2) Social insurance institutions whose sphere of competence extends beyond the territory of one Land shall be administered as federal corporate bodies under public law.

(3) In addition, autonomous federal higher authorities as well as federal corporate bodies and institutions under public law may be established by federal legislation for matters in which the Federation has the power to legislate. If new functions arise for the Federation in matters in which it has the power to legislate, federal authorities at the intermediate and lower levels may be established, in case of urgent need, with the consent of the Bundesrat and of the majority of the members of the Bundestag.

Art. 87a[55]
(Build-up, strength, use and functions of the Armed Forces)

(1) The Federation shall build up Armed Forces for defence purposes. Their numerical strength and general organisational structure shall be shown in the budget.

(2) Apart from defence, the Armed Forces may only be used to the extent explicitly permitted by this Basic Law.

(3) While a state of defence or a state of tension exists, the Armed Forces shall have the power to protect civilian property and discharge functions of traffic control in so far as this is necessary for the performance of their defence mission. Moreover, the Armed Forces may, when a state of defence or a state of tension exists, be entrusted with the protection of civilian property in support of police measures; in this event the Armed Forces shall co-operate with the competent authorities.

(4) In order to avert any imminent danger to the existence or to the free democratic basic order of the Federation or a Land, the Federal Government may, should conditions as envisaged in paragraph (2) of Art. 91 obtain and the police forces and the Federal

---

54. As amended by federal law of 28 July 1972 (*FLG*, I, p. 1305).
55. Inserted by federal law of 19 March 1956 (*FLG*, I, p. 111).

Border Guard be inadequate, use the Armed Forces to support the police and the Federal Border Guard in the protection of civilian property and in combating organised and militarily armed insurgents. Any such use of Armed Forces must be discontinued whenever the Bundestag or the Bundesrat so requests.

Art. 87b[56]
(Administration of the Armed Forces)

(1) The Federal Armed Forces Administration shall be conducted as a direct federal administration with its own administrative substructure. Its function shall be to administer personnel matters and directly to meet the material requirements of the Armed Forces. Tasks connected with benefits to injured persons or with construction work shall not be assigned to the Federal Armed Forces Administration except by federal legislation requiring the consent of the Bundesrat. Such consent shall also be required for any laws to the extent that they empower the Federal Armed Forces Administration to interfere with rights of third parties; this shall, however, not apply in the case of laws concerning personnel.

(2) Moreover, federal laws concerning defence including recruitment for military service and protection of the civilian population may, with the consent of the Bundesrat, provide that they shall be carried out, wholly or in part, either by means of direct federal administration having its own administrative substructure or by the Länder acting as agents of the Federation. If such laws are executed by the Länder acting as agents of the Federation, they may, with the consent of the Bundesrat, provide that the powers vested in the Federal Government or appropriate highest federal authorities by virtue of Art. 85 shall be transferred wholly or in part to higher federal authorities; in such an event it may be enacted that these authorities shall not require the consent of the Bundesrat in issuing general administrative rules as referred to in the first sentence of paragraph (2) of Art. 85.

Art. 87c[57]
(Production and utilization of nuclear energy)

Laws enacted under item 11a of Art. 74 may, with the consent of

---

56. Inserted by federal law of 19 March 1956 (ibid.).
57. Inserted by federal law of 23 December 1959 (*FLG*, I, p. 813).

the Bundesrat, provide that they shall be executed by the Länder acting as agents of the Federation.

Art. 87d[58]
(Aviation Administration)

(1) The Aviation Administration shall be conducted as a direct federal administration.

(2) By means of federal legislation requiring the consent of the Bundesrat, functions of the Aviation Administration may be delegated to the Länder acting as agents of the Federation.

Art. 88
(Federal Bank)

The Federation shall establish a note-issuing and currency bank as the Federal Bank.

Art. 89
(Federal waterways)

(1) The Federation shall be the owner of the former Reich waterways.

(2) The Federation shall administer the federal waterways through its own authorities. It shall exercise those governmental functions relating to inland shipping which extend beyond the territory of one Land, and those governmental functions relating to maritime shipping which are conferred on it by law. Upon request, the Federation may transfer the administration of federal waterways, in so far as they lie within the territory of one Land, to that Land as its agent. If a waterway touches the territories of several Länder, the Federation may designate one Land as its agent if so requested by the Länder concerned.

(3) In the administration, development, and new construction of waterways the needs of land improvement and of water economy shall be safeguarded in agreement with the Länder.

Art. 90
(Federal highways)

(1) The Federation shall be the owner of the former Reich motorways (*Reichsautobahnen*) and Reich highways.

(2) The Länder, or such self-governing corporate bodies as are competent under Land law, shall administer as agents of the Feder-

---

58. Inserted by federal law of 6 February 1961 (*FLG*, I, p. 65).

ation the federal motorways and other federal highways used for long-distance traffic.

(3) At the request of a Land, the Federation may take under direct federal administration federal motorways and other federal highways used for long-distance traffic, in so far as they lie within the territory of that Land.

Art. 91[59]
(Aversion of dangers to the existence of the Federation or of a Land)

(1) In order to avert any imminent danger to the existence or to the free democratic basic order of the Federation or a Land, a Land may request the services of the police forces of other Länder, or of the forces[60] and facilities of other administrative authorities and of the Federal Border Guard.

(2) If the Land where such danger is imminent is not itself willing or able to combat the danger, the Federal Government may place the police in that Land and the police forces of other Länder under its own instructions and commit units of the Federal Border Guard. The order for this shall be rescinded after the removal of the danger or else at any time upon the request of the Bundesrat. If the danger extends to a region larger than a Land, the Federal Government may, in so far as is necessary for effectively combating such danger, issue instructions to the Land governments; the first and second sentences of this paragraph shall not be affected by this provision.

VIIIa. Joint Tasks[61]

Art. 91a[62]
(Definition of joint tasks)

(1) The Federation shall participate in the discharge of the

---

59. As amended by federal law of 24 June 1968 (*FLG*, I, p. 711).
60. E.g., civil defence corps, emergency civil engineering corps, fire brigades, etc.
61. Inserted by federal law of 12 May 1969 (*FLG*, I, p. 359).
62. Ibid.

following responsibilities of the Länder, provided that such responsibilities are important to society as a whole and that federal participation is necessary for the improvement of living conditions (joint tasks):

1.[63] extension and construction of institutions of higher education including university clinics;
2. improvement of regional economic structures;
3. improvement of the agrarian structure and of coast preservation.

(2) Joint tasks shall be defined in detail by federal legislation requiring the consent of the Bundesrat. Such legislation should include general principles governing the discharge of joint tasks.

(3) Such legislation shall provide for the procedure and the institutions required for joint overall planning. The inclusion of a project in the overall planning shall require the consent of the Land in which it is to be carried out.

(4) In cases to which items 1 and 2 of paragraph (1) of this Article apply, the Federation shall meet one-half of the expenditure in each Land. In cases to which item 3 paragraph (1) of this Article applies, the Federation shall meet at least one-half of the expenditure, and such proportion shall be the same for all the Länder. Details shall be regulated by legislation. Provision of funds shall be subject to appropriation in the budgets of the Federation and the Länder.

(5) The Federal Government and the Bundesrat shall be informed about the execution of joint tasks, should they so demand.

Art. 91b[64]
(Co-operation of Federation and Länder in educational planning and in research)

The Federation and the Länder may pursuant to agreements cooperate in educational planning and in the promotion of institutions and projects of scientific research of supraregional importance. The apportionment of costs shall be regulated in the pertinent agreements.

---

63. As amended by federal law of 31 July 1970 (*FLG*, I, p. 1161).
64. Inserted by federal law of 12 May 1969 (*FLG*, I, p. 359).

IX. The Administration of Justice

Art. 92[65]
(Court organisation)

Judicial power shall be vested in the judges; it shall be exercised by the Federal Constitutional Court, by the federal courts provided for in this Basic Law, and by the courts of the Länder.

Art. 93
(Federal Constitutional Court, competency)

(1) The Federal Constitutional Court shall decide:

1. on the interpretation of this Basic Law in the event of disputes concerning the extent of the rights and duties of a highest federal organ or of other parties concerned who have been vested with rights of their own by this Basic Law or by rules of procedure of a highest federal organ;

2. in case of differences of opinion or doubts on the formal and material compatibility of federal law or Land law with this Basic Law, or on the compatibility of Land law with other federal law, at the request of the Federal Government, of a Land government, or of one-third of the Bundestag members;

3. in case of differences of opinion on the rights and duties of the Federation and the Länder, particularly in the execution of federal law by the Länder and in the exercise of federal supervision;

4. on other disputes involving public law, between the Federation and the Länder, between different Länder or within a Land, unless recourse to another court exists;

4a.[66] on complaints of unconstitutionality, which may be entered by any person who claims that one of his basic rights or one of his rights under paragraph (4) of Art. 20, under Arts. 33, 38, 101, 103, or 104 has been violated by public authority;

4b.[67] on complaints of unconstitutionality, entered by communes or associations of communes on the ground that their right to self-government under Art. 28 has been

---

65. As amended by federal law of 18 June 1968 (*FLG*, I, p. 657).
66. Inserted by federal law of 29 January 1969 (*FLG*, I, p. 97).
67. Ibid.

violated by a law other than a Land law open to complaint to the respective Land constitutional court;

5.   in the other cases provided for in this Basic Law.

(2) The Federal Constitutional Court shall also act in such other cases as are assigned to it by federal legislation.

Art. 94
(Federal Constitutional Court, composition)

(1) The Federal Constitutional Court shall consist of federal judges and other members. Half of the members of the Federal Constitutional Court shall be elected by the Bundestag and half by the Bundesrat. They may not be members of the Bundestag, the Bundesrat, the Federal Government, nor of any of the corresponding organs of a Land.

(2) The constitution and procedure of the Federal Constitutional Court shall be regulated by a federal law which shall specify in what cases its decisions shall have the force of law.[68] Such law may require that all other legal remedies must have been exhausted before any such complaint of unconstitutionality can be entered, and may make provision for a special procedure as to admissibility.

Art. 95[69]
(Highest courts of justice of the Federation — Joint Panel)

(1) For the purposes of ordinary, administrative, fiscal, labour, and social jurisdiction, the Federation shall establish as highest courts of justice the Federal Court of Justice, the Federal Administrative Court, the Federal Fiscal Court, the Federal Labour Court, and the Federal Social Court.

(2) The judges of each of these courts shall be selected jointly by the competent Federal Minister and a committee for the selection of judges consisting of the competent Land Ministers and an equal number of members elected by the Bundestag.

(3) In order to preserve uniformity of jurisdiction, a Joint Panel (*Senat*) of the courts specified in paragraph (1) of this Article shall be set up. Details shall be regulated by a federal law.

68. Ibid.
69. As amended by federal law of 18 June 1968 (*FLG*, I, 657).

Art. 96[70]
(Federal courts)

(1) The Federation may establish a Federal Court for matters concerning industrial property rights.

(2) The Federation may establish military criminal courts for the Armed Forces as federal courts. They shall exercise criminal jurisdiction while a state of defence exists, and otherwise only over members of the Armed Forces serving abroad or on board warships. Details shall be regulated by a federal law. These courts shall be within the competence of the Federal Minister of Justice. Their full-time judges must be persons qualified to exercise the functions of a judge.

(3) The highest court of justice for appeals from the courts mentioned in paragraphs (1) and (2) of this Article shall be the Federal Court of Justice.

(4)[71] The Federation may establish federal courts for disciplinary proceedings against, and for proceedings in pursuance of complaints by, persons in the federal public service.

(5)[72] In respect of criminal proceedings under paragraph (1) of Article 26 or involving the protection of the State, a federal law requiring the consent of the Bundesrat may provide that Land courts shall exercise federal jurisdiction.

Art. 96a[73]

Art. 97
(Independence of the judges)

(1) The judges shall be independent and subject only to the law.

(2) Judges appointed permanently on a full-time basis in established positions cannot against their will be dismissed or permanently or temporarily suspended from office or given a different function or retired before the expiration of their term of office except by virtue of a judicial decision and only on the grounds and in the form provided for by law. Legislation may set age limits for

70. The original Article 96 was repealed by federal law of 18 June 1968 (*FLG*, I, p. 658). The present Article 96 is the former Article 96a as inserted by federal law of 19 March 1956 (*FLG*, I, p. 111) and amended by federal laws of 6 March 1961 (*FLG*, I, p. 141), 18 June 1968 (*FLG*, I, p. 658), 12 May 1969 (*FLG*, I, p. 363), and 26 August 1969 (*FLG*, I, p. 1357).

71. As amended by federal law of 12 May 1969 (*FLG*, I, p. 363).

72. Inserted by federal law of 26 August 1969 (*FLG*, I, p. 1357).

73. See note 70, above.

the retirement of judges appointed for life. In the event of changes in the structure of courts or in districts of jurisdiction, judges may be transferred to another court or removed from office, provided they retain their full salary.

Art. 98[74]
(Legal status of judges)

(1) The legal status of the federal judges shall be regulated by a special federal law.

(2) If a federal judge, in his official capacity or unofficially, infringes the principles of this Basic Law or the constitutional order of a Land, the Federal Constitutional Court may decide by a two-thirds majority, upon the request of the Bundestag, that the judge be given a different function or retired. In a case of intentional infringement, his dismissal may be ordered.

(3)[75] The legal status of the judges in the Länder shall be regulated by special Land laws. The Federation may enact general provisions, in so far as paragraph (4) of Art. 74a does not provide otherwise.

(4) Länder may provide that the Land Minister of Justice together with a committee for the selection of judges shall decide on the appointment of judges in the Länder.

(5) The Länder may, in respect of Land judges, enact provisions corresponding to those of paragraph (2) of this Article. Existing Land constitutional law shall remain unaffected. The decision in a case of impeachment of a judge shall rest with the Federal Constitutional Court.

Art. 99[76]
(Assignment of competencies to Federal Constitutional Court and highest federal courts in matters involving Land law)

The decision on constitutional disputes within a Land may be assigned by Land legislation to the Federal Constitutional Court, and the decision of last instance in matters involving the application of Land law, to the highest courts of justice referred to in paragraph (1) of Art. 95.

---

74. As amended by federal law of 18 March 1971 (*FLG*, I, p. 206).
75. Ibid.
76. As amended by federal law of 18 June 1968 (*FLG*, I, p. 658).

Art. 100
(Compatibility of statutory law with Basic Law)

(1) If a court considers unconstitutional a law the validity of which is relevant to its decision, the proceedings shall be stayed, and a decision shall be obtained from the Land court competent for constitutional disputes if the constitution of a Land is held to be violated, or from the Federal Constitutional Court if this Basic Law is held to be violated. This shall also apply if this Basic Law is held to be violated by Land law or if a Land law is held to be incompatible with a federal law.

(2) If, in the course of litigation, doubt exists whether a rule of public international law is an integral part of federal law and whether such rule directly creates rights and duties for the individual (Art. 25), the court shall obtain a decision from the Federal Constitutional Court.

(3)[77] If the constitutional court of a Land, in interpreting this Basic Law, intends to deviate from a decision of the Federal Constitutional Court or of the constitutional court of another Land, it must obtain a decision from the Federal Constitutional Court.

Art. 101
(Ban on extraordinary courts)

(1) Extraordinary courts shall be inadmissible. No one may be removed from the jurisdiction of his lawful judge.

(2) Courts for special fields may be established only by legislation.

Art. 102
(Abolition of capital punishment)

Capital punishment shall be abolished.

Art. 103
(Basic rights in the courts)

(1) In the courts everyone shall be entitled to a hearing in accordance with the law.

(2) An act can be punished only if it was an offence against the law before the act was committed.

(3) No one may be punished for the same act more than once under general penal legislation.

---

77. Ibid.

Art. 104
(Legal guarantees in the event of deprivation of liberty)

(1) The liberty of the individual may be restricted only by virtue of a formal law and only with due regard to the forms prescribed therein. Detained persons may not be subjected to mental nor to physical ill-treatment.

(2) Only judges may decide on the admissibility or continuation of any deprivation of liberty. Where such deprivation is not based on the order of a judge, a judicial decision must be obtained without delay. The police may hold no one on their own authority in their own custody longer than the end of the day after the day of apprehension. Details shall be regulated by legislation.

(3) Any person provisionally detained on suspicion of having committed an offence must be brought before a judge not later than the day following the day of apprehension; the judge shall inform him of the reasons for the detention, examine him, and give him an opportunity to raise objections. The judge must, without delay, either issue a warrant of arrest setting forth the reasons therefor or order his release from detention.

(4) A relative or a person enjoying the confidence of the person detained must be notified without delay of any judicial decision ordering or continuing his deprivation of liberty.

X. Finance

Art. 104a[78]
(Apportionment of expenditure, financial assistance)

(1) The Federation and the Länder shall meet separately the expenditure resulting from the discharge of their respective tasks in so far as this Basic Law does not provide otherwise.

(2) Where the Länder act as agents of the Federation, the Federation shall meet the resulting expenditure.

(3) Federal laws to be executed by the Länder and involving the disbursement of funds may provide that such funds shall be contributed wholly or in part by the Federation. Where any such law provides that the Federation shall meet one-half of the expenditure

78. Inserted by federal law of 12 May 1969 (*FLG*, I, p. 359).

or more, the Länder shall execute it as agents of the Federation. Where any such law provides that the Länder shall meet one-quarter of the expenditure or more, it shall require the consent of the Bundesrat.

(4) The Federation may grant the Länder financial assistance for particularly important investments by the Länder or communes or associations of communes, provided that such investments are necessary to avert a disturbance of the overall economic equilibrium or to equalise differences of economic capacities within the federal territory or to promote economic growth. Details, especially concerning the kinds of investments to be promoted, shall be regulated by federal legislation requiring the consent of the Bundesrat, or by administrative arrangements based on the federal budget.

(5) The Federation and the Länder shall meet the administrative expenditure incurred by their respective authorities and shall be responsible to each other for ensuring proper administration. Details shall be regulated by a federal law requiring the consent of the Bundesrat.

Art. 105
(Customs duties, monopolies, taxes — Legislation)

(1) The Federation shall have exclusive power to legislate on customs matters and fiscal monopolies.

(2)[79] The Federation shall have concurrent power to legislate on all other taxes the revenue from which accrues to it wholly or in part or where the conditions provided for in paragraph (2) of Article 72 apply.

(2a)[80] The Länder shall have power to legislate on local excise taxes as long and in so far as they are not identical with taxes imposed by federal legislation.

(3) Federal laws relating to taxes the receipts from which accrue wholly or in part to the Länder or communes or associations of communes shall require the consent of the Bundesrat.

---

79. As amended by federal law of 12 May 1969 (ibid.).
80. Inserted by federal law of 12 May 1969 (ibid.).

Art. 106[81]
(Apportionment of tax revenue)

(1) The yield of fiscal monopolies and the revenue from the following taxes shall accrue to the Federation:

1. customs duties;
2. excise taxes in so far as they do not accrue to the Länder pursuant to paragraph (2) of this Article, or jointly to the Federation and the Länder in accordance with paragraph (3) of this Article, or to the communes in accordance with paragraph (6) of this Article;
3. the road freight tax;
4. the capital transfer taxes, the insurance tax and the tax on drafts and bills of exchange;
5. non-recurrent levies on property, and contributions imposed for the purpose of implementing the equalisation of burdens legislation;[82]
6. income and corporation surtaxes;
7. charges imposed within the framework of the European Communities.

(2) Revenue from the following taxes shall accrue to the Länder:

1. property (net worth) tax;
2. inheritance tax;
3. motor-vehicle tax;
4. such taxes on transactions as do not accrue to the Federation pursuant to paragraph (1) of this Article or jointly to the Federation and the Länder pursuant to paragraph (3) of this Article;
5. beer tax;
6. taxes on gambling establishments.

(3) Revenue from income taxes, corporation taxes and turnover taxes shall accrue jointly to the Federation and the Länder (joint taxes) to the extent that the revenue from income tax is not allocated to the communes pursuant to paragraph (5) of this Article. The Federation and the Länder shall share equally the revenues from income taxes and corporation taxes. The respective shares of the Federation and the Länder in the revenue from turnover tax shall be determined by federal legislation requiring

---

81. As amended by federal laws of 23 December 1955 (*FLG*, I, p. 817), of 24 December 1956 (*FLG*, I, p. 1077), and of 12 May 1969 (*FLG*, I, p. 359).

82. I.e., contributions imposed on persons having suffered no war damage and used to indemnify persons having suffered such damage.

the consent of the Bundesrat. Such determination shall be based on the following principles:

1. The Federation and the Länder shall have an equal claim to coverage from current revenues of their respective necessary expenditures. The extent of such expenditures shall be determined within a system of pluri-annual financial planning;

2. the coverage requirements of the Federation and of the Länder shall be co-ordinated in such a way that a fair balance is struck, any overburdening of taxpayers precluded, and uniformity of living standards in the federal territory ensured.

(4) The respective shares of the Federation and the Länder in the revenue from the turnover tax shall be apportioned anew whenever the relation of revenues to expenditures in the Federation develops substantially differently from that of the Länder. Where federal legislation imposes additional expenditures on, or withdraws revenue from, the Länder, the additional burden may be compensated by federal grants under federal laws requiring the consent of the Bundesrat, provided such additional burden is limited to a short period. Such laws shall lay down the principles for calculating such grants and distributing them among the Länder.

(5) A share of the revenue from income tax shall accrue to the communes, to be passed on by the Länder to their communes on the basis of income taxes paid by the inhabitants of the latter. Details shall be regulated by a federal law requiring the consent of the Bundesrat. Such law may provide that communes shall assess communal percentages of the communal share.

(6) Revenue from taxes on real property and businesses shall accrue to the communes; revenue from local excise taxes shall accrue to the communes or, as may be provided for by Land legislation, to associations of communes. Communes shall be authorised to assess the communal percentages of taxes on real property and businesses within the framework of existing laws. Where there are no communes in a Land, revenue from taxes on real property and businesses as well as from local excise taxes shall accrue to the Land. The Federation and the Länder may participate, by assessing an impost, in the revenue from the trade tax. Details regarding such impost shall be regulated by a federal law requiring the consent of the Bundesrat. Within the framework of Land legislation, taxes on real property and businesses as well as the communes' share of revenue from income tax may be taken as a basis for calculating the amount of such impost.

(7) An overall percentage, to be determined by Land legislation,

of the Land share of total revenue from joint taxes shall accrue to the communes and associations of communes. In all other respects Land legislation shall determine whether and to what extent revenue from Land taxes shall accrue to communes and associations of communes.

(8) If in individual Länder or communes or associations of communes the Federation causes special facilities to be established which directly result in an increase of expenditure or a loss of revenue (special burden) to these Länder or communes or associations of communes, the Federation shall grant the necessary compensation, if and in so far as such Länder or communes or associations of communes cannot reasonably be expected to bear such special burden. In granting such compensation, due account shall be taken of third-party indemnities and financial benefits accruing to the Länder or communes or associations of communes concerned as a result of the institution of such facilities.

(9) For the purpose of this Article, revenues and expenditures of communes and associations of communes shall be deemed to be Land revenues and expenditures.

Art. 107[83]
(Financial equalisation)

(1) Revenue from Land taxes and the Land share of revenue from income and corporation taxes shall accrue to the individual Länder to the extent that such taxes are collected by revenue authorities within their respective territories (local revenue). Federal legislation requiring the consent of the Bundesrat may provide in detail for the delimitation as well as the manner and scope of allotment of local revenue from corporation and wage taxes. Legislation may also provide for the delimitation and allotment of local revenue from other taxes. The Land share of revenue from the turnover tax shall accrue to the individual Länder on a per capita basis; federal legislation requiring the consent of the Bundesrat may provide for supplemental shares not exceeding one-quarter of a Land share to be granted to Länder whose per capita revenue from Land taxes and from the income and corporation taxes is below the average of all the Länder combined.

(2) Federal legislation shall ensure a reasonable equalisation between financially strong and financially weak Länder, due ac-

83. As amended by federal laws of 23 December 1955 (*FLG*, I, p. 817) and of 12 May 1969 (*FLG*, I, p. 359).

count being taken of the financial capacity and financial requirements of communes and associations of communes. Such legislation shall specify the conditions governing equalisation claims of Länder entitled to equalisation payments and equalisation liabilities of Länder owing equalisation payments as well as the criteria for determining the amounts of equalisation payments. Such legislation may also provide for grants to be made by the Federation from federal funds to financially weak Länder in order to complement the coverage of their general financial requirements (complemental grants).

Art. 108[84]
(Fiscal administration)

(1) Customs duties, fiscal monopolies, excise taxes subject to federal legislation, including the excise tax on imports, and charges imposed within the framework of the European Communities, shall be administered by federal revenue authorities. The organisation of these authorities shall be regulated by federal legislation. The heads of authorities at the intermediate level shall be appointed in consultation with the respective Land governments.

(2) All other taxes shall be administered by Land revenue authorities. The organisation of these authorities and the uniform training of their civil servants may be regulated by federal legislation requiring the consent of the Bundesrat. The heads of authorities at the intermediate level shall be appointed in agreement with the Federal Government.

(3) To the extent that taxes accruing wholly or in part to the Federation are administered by Land revenue authorities, those authorities shall act as agents of the Federation. Paragraphs (3) and (4) or Art. 85 shall apply, the Federal Minister of Finance being, however, substituted for the Federal Government.

(4) In respect of the administration of taxes, federal legislation requiring the consent of the Bundesrat may provide for collaboration between federal and Land revenue authorities, or in the case of taxes under paragraph (1) of this Article for their administration by Land revenue authorities, or in the case of other taxes for their administration by federal revenue authorities, if and to the extent that the execution of tax laws is substantially improved or facilitated thereby. As regards taxes the revenue from which accrues exclusively to communes or associations of communes, their administra-

---

84. As amended by federal law of 12 May 1969 (*FLG*, I, p. 359).

tion may wholly or in part be transferred by Länder from the appropriate Land revenue authorities to communes or associations of communes.

(5) The procedure to be applied by federal revenue authorities shall be laid down by federal legislation. The procedure to be applied by Land revenue authorities or, as envisaged in the second sentence of paragraph (4) of this Article, by communes or associations of communes, may be laid down by federal legislation requiring the consent of the Bundesrat.

(6) The jurisdiction of fiscal courts shall be uniformly regulated by federal legislation.

(7) The Federal Government may issue pertinent general administrative rules which, to the extent that administration is incumbent upon Land revenue authorities or communes or associations of communes, shall require the consent of the Bundesrat.

Art. 109[85]
(Separate budgets for Federation and Länder)

(1) The Federation and the Länder shall be autonomous and independent of each other in their fiscal administration.

(2) The Federation and the Länder shall take due account in their fiscal administration of the requirements of overall economic equilibrium.

(3)[86] By means of federal legislation requiring the consent of the Bundesrat, principles applicable to both the Federation and the Länder may be established governing budgetary law, responsiveness of the fiscal administration to economic trends, and financial planning to cover several years ahead.

(4) With a view to averting disturbances of the overall economic equilibrium, federal legislation requiring the consent of the Bundesrat may be enacted providing for:

1. maximum amounts, terms and timing of loans to be raised by public administrative entities, whether territorial (*Gebietskoerperschaften*) or functional (*Zweckverbaende*), and

2. an obligation on the part of the Federation and the Länder to maintain interest-free deposits in the German Federal Bank (reserves for counterbalancing economic trends).

Authorisations to enact pertinent ordinances having the force of

---

85. As amended by federal law of 8 June 1967 (*FLG*, I, p. 581).
86. As amended by federal law of 12 May 1969 (*FLG*, I, p. 357).

law may be issued only to the Federal Government. Such ordinances shall require the consent of the Bundesrat. They shall be repealed in so far as the Bundestag may demand; details shall be regulated by federal legislation.

Art. 110[87]
(Budget of the Federation)

(1) All revenues and expenditures of the Federation shall be included in the budget; in respect of federal enterprises and special funds, only allocations to or remittances from them need be included. The budget must be balanced as regards revenue and expenditure.

(2) The budget shall be established by means of a law covering one year or several fiscal years separately before the beginning of the first of those fiscal years. Provision may be made for parts of the budget to apply to periods of different duration, but divided into fiscal years.

(3) Bills within the meaning of the first sentence of paragraph (2) of this Article as well as bills to amend the budget law and the budget shall be submitted simultaneously to the Bundesrat and to the Bundestag; the Bundesrat shall be entitled to state its position on such bills within six weeks or, in the case of amending bills, within three weeks.

(4) The budget law may contain only such provisions as apply to revenues and expenditures of the Federation and to the period for which the budget law is being enacted. The budget law may stipulate that certain provisions shall cease to apply only upon the promulgation of the next budget law or, in the event of an authorisation pursuant to Art. 115, at a later date.

Art. 111
(Payments before approval of the budget)

(1) If, by the end of a fiscal year, the budget for the following year has not been established by law, the Federal Government may, until such law comes into force, make all payments which are necessary:

(a) to maintain institutions existing by law and to carry out measures authorised by law;

(b) to meet the Federation's statutory, contractual, and treaty obligations;

87. Ibid.

(c) to continue building projects, procurements, and other services, or to continue to grant subsidies for these purposes, provided that pertinent amounts have already been appropriated in the budget of a previous year.

(2) To the extent that revenues provided by specific legislation and derived from taxes or duties or any other charges or sources, or the working capital reserves, do not cover the expenditures referred to in paragraph (1) of this Article, the Federal Government may borrow the funds necessary for the conduct of current operations up to a maximum of one-quarter of the total amount of the previous budget.

Art. 112[88]
(Expenditure in excess of budgetary estimates)

Expenditures in excess of budgetary appropriations and extra-budgetary expenditures shall require the consent of the Federal Minister of Finance. Such consent may be given only in the case of an unforeseen and compelling necessity. Details may be regulated by federal legislation.

Art. 113[89]
(Increases in expenditure)

(1) Laws increasing the budget expenditures proposed by the Federal Government or involving, or likely in future to cause, new expenditures shall require the consent of the Federal Government. This shall also apply to laws involving, or likely in future to cause, decreases in revenue. The Federal Government may require the Bundestag to postpone its vote on such bills. In this case the Federal Government shall state its position to the Bundestag within six weeks.

(2) Within four weeks after the Bundestag has adopted such a bill, the Federal Government may require it to vote on that bill again.

(3) If the bill has become a law pursuant to Art. 78, the Federal Government may withhold its consent only within six weeks and only after having initiated the procedure provided for in the third and fourth sentences of paragraph (1) or in paragraph (2) of the present Article. Upon the expiry of this period such consent shall be deemed to have been given.

88. Ibid.
89. Ibid.

Art. 114[90]
(Rendering of accounts, Audit Office)

(1) The Federal Minister of Finance shall, on behalf of the Federal Government, submit annually to the Bundestag and to the Bundesrat for their approval an account, covering the preceding fiscal year, of all revenues and expenditures as well as of property and debt.

(2) The Federal Audit Office, the members of which shall enjoy judicial independence, shall audit the account and examine the management of the budget and the conduct of business as to economy and correctness. The Federal Audit Office shall submit an annual report directly to the Federal Government as well as to the Bundestag and to the Bundesrat. In all other respects the powers of the Federal Audit Office shall be regulated by federal legislation.

Art. 115[91]
(Procurement of credit)

(1) The borrowing of funds and the assumption of pledges, guarantees or other commitments, as a result of which expenditure may be incurred in future fiscal years, shall require federal legislative authorisation indicating, or permitting computation of, the maximum amounts involved. Revenue obtained by borrowing shall not exceed the total of expenditures for investments provided for in the budget; exceptions shall be permissible only to avert a disturbance of the overall economic equilibrium. Details shall be regulated by federal legislation.

(2) In respect of special funds of the Federation, exceptions from the provisions of paragraph (1) of this Article may be authorised by federal legislation.

---

90. Ibid.
91. Ibid.

Xa.[92] State of Defence

Art. 115a
(Determination of a state of defence)

(1) The determination that the federal territory is being attacked by armed force or that such an attack is directly imminent (state of defence) shall be made by the Bundestag with the consent of the Bundesrat. Such determination shall be made at the request of the Federal Government and shall require a two-thirds majority of the votes cast, which shall include at least the majority of the members of the Bundestag.

(2) If the situation imperatively calls for immediate action and if insurmountable obstacles prevent the timely meeting of the Bundestag, or if there is no quorum in the Bundestag, the Joint Committee shall make this determination with a two-thirds majority of the votes cast, which shall include at least the majority of its members.

(3) The determination shall be promulgated in the Federal Law Gazette by the Federal President pursuant to Art. 82. If this cannot be done in time, the promulgation shall be effected in another manner; it shall subsequently be printed in the *Federal Law Gazette* as soon as circumstances permit.

(4) If the Federal territory is being attacked by armed force and if the competent organs of the Federation are not in a position at once to make the determination provided for in the first sentence of paragraph (1) of this Article, such determination shall be deemed to have been made and promulgated at the time the attack began. The Federal President shall announce such time as soon as circumstances permit.

(5) When the determination of the existence of a state of defence has been promulgated and if the federal territory is being attacked by armed force, the Federal President may, with the consent of the Bundestag, issue internationally valid declarations regarding the existence of such state of defence. Subject to the conditions mentioned in paragraph (2) of this Article, the Joint Committee shall thereupon deputise for the Bundestag.

---

92. Entire section Xa inserted by federal law of 24 June 1968 (*FLG*, I, p. 711).

Art. 115b
(Power of command during state of defence)

Upon the promulgation of a state of defence, the power of command over the Armed Forces shall pass to the Federal Chancellor.

Art. 115c
(Legislative competence of the Federation during state of defence)

(1) The Federation shall have the right to exercise concurrent legislation even in matters belonging to the legislative competence of the Länder by enacting laws to be applicable upon the occurrence of a state of defence. Such laws shall require the consent of the Bundesrat.

(2) Federal legislation to be applicable upon the occurrence of a state of defence to the extent required by conditions obtaining while such state of defence exists, may make provision for:

1. preliminary compensation to be made in the event of expropriations, thus diverging from the second sentence of paragraph (3) of Art. 14;
2. deprivations of liberty for a period not exceeding four days, if no judge has been able to act within the period applying in normal times, thus diverging from the third sentence of paragraph (2) and the first sentence of paragraph (3) of Art. 104.

(3)[93] Federal legislation to be applicable upon the occurrence of a state of defence to the extent required for averting an existing or directly imminent attack may, subject to the consent of the Bundesrat, regulate the administration and the fiscal system of the Federation and the Länder in divergence from Sections VIII, VIIIa and X, provided that the viability of the Länder, communes and associations of communes is safeguarded, particularly in fiscal matters.

(4) Federal laws enacted pursuant to paragraph (1) or subparagraph (1) of paragraph (2) of this Article may, for the purpose of preparing for their execution, be applied even prior to the occurrence of a state of defence.

---

93. As amended by federal law of 12 May 1969 (*FLG*, I, p. 359).

Art. 115d
(Shortened procedure in the case of urgent bills during state of defence)

(1) While a state of defence exists, the provisions of paragraphs (2) and (3) of this Article shall apply in respect of federal legislation, notwithstanding the provisions of paragraph (2) of Art. 76, the second sentence of paragraph (1) and paragraphs (2) to (4) of Art. 77, Art. 78, and paragraph (1) of Art. 82.

(2) Bills submitted as urgent by the Federal Government shall be forwarded to the Bundesrat at the same time as they are submitted to the Bundestag. The Bundestag and the Bundesrat shall debate such bills in common without delay. In so far as the consent of the Bundesrat is necessary, the majority of its votes shall be required for any such bill to become a law. Details shall be regulated by rules of procedure adopted by the Bundestag and requiring the consent of the Bundesrat.

(3) The second sentence of paragraph (3) of Art. 115a shall apply *mutatis mutandis* in respect of the promulgation of such laws.

Art. 115e
(Status and functions of the Joint Committee)

(1) If, while a state of defence exists, the Joint Committee determines with a two-thirds majority of the votes cast, which shall include at least the majority of its members, that insurmountable obstacles prevent the timely meeting of the Bundestag, or that there is no quorum in the Bundestag, the Joint Committee shall have the status of both the Bundestag and the Bundesrat and shall exercise their rights as one body.

(2) The Joint Committee may not enact any law to amend this Basic Law or to deprive it of effect or application either in whole or in part. The Joint Committee shall not be authorised to enact laws pursuant to paragraph (1) of Art. 24 or to Art. 29.

Art. 115f
(Extraordinary powers of the Federation during state of defence)

(1) While a state of defence exists, the Federal Government may to the extent necessitated by circumstances:

1. commit the Federal Border Guard throughout the federal territory;
2. issue instructions not only to federal administrative authorities but also to Land governments and, if it deems the

matter urgent, to Land authorities, and may delegate this power to members of Land governments to be designated by it.

(2) The Bundestag, the Bundesrat, and the Joint Committee, shall be informed without delay of the measures taken in accordance with paragraph (1) of this Article.

Art. 115g
(Status and functions of the Federal Constitutional Court during state of defence)

The constitutional status and the exercise of the constitutional functions of the Federal Constitutional Court and its judges must not be impaired. The Law on the Federal Constitutional Court may not be amended by a law enacted by the Joint Committee except in so far as such amendment is required, also in the opinion of the Federal Constitutional Court, to maintain the capability of the Court to function. Pending the enactment of such a law, the Federal Constitutional Court may take such measures as are necessary to maintain the capability of the Court to carry out its work. Any decisions by the Federal Constitutional Court in pursuance of the second and third sentences of this Article shall require a two-thirds majority of the judges present.

Art. 115h
(Legislative terms and terms of office during state of defence)

(1) Any legislative terms of the Bundestag or of Land diets due to expire while a state of defence exists shall end six months after the termination of such state of defence. A term of office of the Federal President due to expire while a state of defence exists, and the exercise of his functions by the President of the Bundesrat in case of the premature vacancy of the Federal President's office, shall end nine months after the termination of such state of defence. The term of office of a member of the Federal Constitutional Court due to expire while a state of defence exists shall end six months after the termination of such state of defence.

(2) Should the necessity arise for the Joint Committee to elect a new Federal Chancellor, the Committee shall do so with the majority of its members; the Federal President shall propose a candidate to the Joint Committee. The Joint Committee can express its lack of confidence in the Federal Chancellor only by electing a successor with a two-thirds majority of its members.

(3) The Bundestag shall not be dissolved while a state of defence exists.

Art. 115i
(Extraordinary power of the Land governments)

(1) If the competent federal organs are incapable of taking the measures necessary to avert the danger, and if the situation imperatively calls for immediate independent action in individual parts of the federal territory, the Land governments or the authorities or commissioners designated by them shall be authorised to take, within their respective spheres of competence, the measures provided for in paragraph (1) of Art. 115f.

(2) Any measures taken in accordance with paragraph (1) of the present Article may be revoked at any time by the Federal Government, or in the case of Land authorities and subordinate federal authorities, by Land Prime Ministers.

Art. 115k
(Grade and duration of validity of extraordinary laws and ordinances having the force of law)

(1) Laws enacted in accordance with Articles 115c, 115e, and 115g, as well as ordinances having the force of law issued by virtue of such laws, shall, for the duration of their applicability, suspend legislation contrary to such laws or ordinances. This shall not apply to earlier legislation enacted by virtue of Arts. 115c, 115e, or 115g.

(2) Laws adopted by the Joint Committee, and ordinances having the force of law issued by virtue of such laws, shall cease to have effect not later than six months after the termination of a state of defence.

(3)[94] Laws containing provisions that diverge from Arts. 91a, 91b, 104a, 106 and 107, shall apply no longer than the end of the second fiscal year following upon the termination of the state of defence. After such termination they may, with the consent of the Bundesrat, be amended by federal legislation so as to lead up to the settlement provided for in Sections VIIIa and X.

Art. 115l
(Repealing of extraordinary laws, termination of state of defence, conclusion of peace)

(1)The Bundestag, with the consent of the Bundesrat, may at any time repeal laws enacted by the Joint Committee. The Bundesrat may request the Bundestag to make a decision in any such matter. Any measures taken by the Joint Committee or the Federal

94. Ibid.

Government to avert a danger shall be revoked if the Bundestag and the Bundesrat so decide.

(2) The Bundestag, with the consent of the Bundesrat, may at any time declare the state of defence terminated by a decision to be promulgated by the Federal President. The Bundesrat may request the Bundestag to make a decision in any such matter. The state of defence must be declared terminated without delay when the prerequisites for the determination thereof no longer exist.

(3) The conclusion of peace shall be the subject of a federal law.

XI. Transitional and Concluding Provisions

Art. 116
(Definition of 'German', regranting of citizenship)

(1) Unless otherwise provided by law, a German within the meaning of this Basic Law is a person who possesses German citizenship or who has been admitted to the territory of the German Reich within the frontiers of 31 December 1937 as a refugee or expellee of German stock (*Volkszugehörigkeit*) or as the spouse or descendant of such person.

(2) Former German citizens who, between 30 January 1933 and 8 May 1945, were deprived of their citizenship on political, racial, or religious grounds, and their descendants, shall be regranted German citizenship on application. They shall be considered as not having been deprived of their German citizenship if they have established their domicile (*Wohnsitz*) in Germany after 8 May 1945 and have not expressed a contrary intention.

Art. 117
(Temporary ruling for Art. 3 and Art. 11)

(1) Law which conflicts with paragraph (2) of Art. 3 shall remain in force until adapted to that provision of this Basic Law, but not beyond 31 March 1953.

(2) Laws which restrict the right of freedom of movement in view of the present housing shortage shall remain in force until repealed by federal legislation.

Art. 118
(Reorganisation of the Länder of Baden, Württemberg-Baden and Württemberg-Hohenzollern)

The reorganisation of the territory comprising the Länder of Baden, Württemberg-Baden, and Württemberg-Hohenzollern may be effected, notwithstanding the provisions of Art. 29, by agreement between the Länder concerned. If no agreement is reached, the reorganisation shall be effected by federal legislation which must provide for a referendum.[95]

Art. 119
(Refugees and expellees)

In matters relating to refugees and expellees, in particular as regards their distribution among the Länder, the Federal Government may, with the consent of the Bundesrat, issue regulations having the force of law, pending the settlement of the matter by federal legislation. The Federal Government may in this matter be authorised to issue individual instructions for particular cases. Except where there is danger in delay, such instructions shall be addressed to the highest Land authorities.

Art. 120[96]
(Occupation costs and burdens as consequence of the war)

(1)[97] The Federation shall meet the expenditure for occupation costs and the other internal and external burdens caused as a consequence of the war, as provided for in detail by federal legislation. To the extent that these costs and other burdens have been provided for by federal legislation on or before 1 October 1969, the Federation and the Länder shall meet such expenditure between them in accordance with such federal legislation. In so far as expenditures for such of these costs and burdens as neither have been nor will be provided for by federal legislation have been met on or before 1 October 1965 by Länder, communes, associations of communes or other entities performing functions of Länder or communes, the Federation shall not be obliged to meet expenditure of that nature even if arising after that date. The Federation shall pay the subsidies towards the burdens of social insurance institutions, including unemployment insurance and public assist-

95. See footnote 13 to Article 23.
96. As amended by federal laws of 30 July 1965 (*FLG*, I, p. 649) and of 28 July 1969 (*FLG*, I, p. 985).
97. As amended by federal law of 28 July 1969 (ibid.).

ance to the unemployed. The distribution between the Federation and the Länder of costs and other burdens caused as a consequence of the war, as provided for in this paragraph, shall not affect any legislative settlement of claims for indemnification in respect of consequences of the war.

(2) The corresponding revenue shall pass to the Federation at the same time as the latter assumes responsibility for the expenditure referred to in this Article.

Art. 120a[98]
(Implementation of equalisation of burdens legislation)

(1) Laws concerning the implementation of the equalisation of burdens legislation may, with the consent of the Bundesrat, stipulate that they shall be executed, as regards equalisation benefits, partly by the Federation and partly by the Länder acting as agents of the Federation, and that the relevant powers vested in the Federal Government and the competent highest federal authorities by virtue of Art. 85, shall be wholly or partly delegated to the Federal Equalisation Office. In exercising these powers, the Federal Equalisation Office shall not require the consent of the Bundesrat; with the exception of urgent cases, its instructions shall be given to the highest Land authorities (Land Equalisation Offices).

(2) The provisions of the second sentence of paragraph (3) of Article 87 shall not be affected hereby.

Art. 121
(Definition of 'majority')

Within the meaning of this Basic Law, a majority of the members of the Bundestag and a majority of the members of the Federal Convention (*Bundesversammlung*) shall be the majority of the respective statutory number of their members.

Art. 122
(Legislative competencies hitherto existing)

(1) From the date of the first meeting of the Bundestag, laws shall be enacted exclusively by the legislative organs recognised in this Basic Law.

(2) Legislative bodies and bodies participating in legislation in an advisory capacity, whose competence ends by virtue of paragraph

---

98. Inserted by federal law of 14 August 1952 (*FLG*, I, p. 445).

(1) of this Article, are herewith dissolved with effect from that date.

Art. 123
(Continued validity of old law and old treaties)

(1) Law in force before the first meeting of the Bundestag shall remain in force in so far as it does not conflict with this Basic Law.

(2) Subject to all rights and objections of the interested parties, the treaties concluded by the German Reich concerning matters which, under this Basic Law, shall be within the competence of Land legislation, shall remain in force, if they are and continue to be valid in accordance with general principles of law, until new treaties are concluded by the agencies competent under this Basic Law, or until they are in any other way terminated pursuant to their provisions.

Art. 124
(Old law affecting matters subject to exclusive legislation)

Law, wherever applicable[99] affecting matters subject to the exclus-ve legislative power of the Federation, shall become federal law.

Art. 125
(Old law affecting matters subject to concurrent legislation)

Law, wherever applicable[100] affecting matters subject to the concurrent legislative power of the Federation, shall become federal law:

1. in so far as it applies uniformly within one or more zones of occupation;
2. in so far as it is law by which former Reich law has been amended after 8 May 1945.

Art. 126
(Disputes regarding continued validity of old law)

Disputes regarding the continuance of law as federal law shall be cecided by the Federal Constitutional Court.

Art. 127
(Legislation of the Bizonal Economic Administration)

Within one year of the promulgation of this Basic Law the Federal Government may, with the consent of the governments of the

99. I.e., Land or zonal law.
100. Ibid.

Länder concerned, extend to the Länder of Baden, Greater Berlin, Rhineland-Palatinate and Württemberg-Hohenzollern any _egislation of the Bizonal Economic Administration, in so far as it continues to be in force as federal law under Arts. 124 or 125.

Art. 128
(Continuance of powers to give instructions)
In so far as law continuing in force provides for powers to give instructions within the meaning of paragraph (5) of Art. 84, these powers shall remain in existence until otherwise provided by law.

Art. 129
(Continued validity of authorisations)
(1) In so far as legal provisions which continue in force as federal law contain authorisations to issue ordinances having the force of law or to issue general administrative rules or to perform administrative acts, such authorisations shall pass to the agencies henceforth competent in the matter. In case of doubt, the Federal Government shall decide in agreement with the Bundesrat; such decisions must be published.

(2) In so far as legal provisions which continue in force as Land law contain such authorisations, they shall be exercised by the agencies competent under Land law.

(3) In so far as legal provisions within the meaning of paragraphs (1) and (2) of this Article authorise their amendment or supplementation or the issue of legal provisions instead of laws, such authorisations have expired.

(4) The provisions of paragraphs (1) and (2) of this Article shall apply *mutatis mutandis* where legal provisions refer to regulations no longer valid or to institutions no longer in existence.

Art. 130
(Corporate bodies under public law)
(1) Administrative agencies and other institutions which serve the public administration or the administration of justice and are not based on Land law or treaties between Länder, as well as the Association of Management of South-west German Railroads and the Administrative Council for the Postal Services and Telecommunications of the French Zone of Occupation, shall be placed under the Federal Government. The Federal Government shall provide, with the consent of the Bundesrat, for their transfer, dissolution, or liquidation.

(2) The highest disciplinary superior of the personnel of these administrations and institutions shall be appropriate Federal Minister.

(3) Corporate bodies and institutions under public law not directly under a Land nor based on treaties between Länder shall be under the supervision of the appropriate highest federal authority.

Art. 131
(Persons formerly employed in the public service)

Federal legislation shall regulate the legal position of persons, including refugees and expellees, who, on 8 May 1945, were employed in the public service, have left the service for reasons other than those arising from civil service regulations or collective agreement rules, and have not until now been reinstated or are employed in a position not corresponding to their former one. The same shall apply *mutatis mutandis* to persons, including refugees and expellees, who, on 8 May 1945, were entitled to a pension and who no longer receive any such pension or'any commensurate pension for reasons other than those arising from civil service regulations or collective agreement rules. Until the pertinent federal law comes into force, no legal claims can be made, unless otherwise provided by Land legislation.

Art. 132
(Temporary revocation of rights of civil servants)

(1) Civil servants and judges who, when this Basic Law comes into force, are appointed for life, may, within six months after the first meeting of the Bundestag, be placed on the retired list or waiting list or be given a different function with lower remuneration if they lack the personal or professional aptitude for their present function. This provision shall apply *mutatis mutandis* also to salaried public employees, other than civil servants or judges, whose service cannot be terminated by notice. If, however, such service can be terminated by notice, periods of notice in excess of the periods fixed by collective agreement rules may be cancelled within the six months referred to above.

(2) The preceding provision shall not apply to members of the public service who are not affected by the provisions regarding the Liberation from National Socialism and Militarism or who are recognized victims of National Socialism, except on important grounds in respect of their personality.

(3) Those affected may have recourse to the courts in accord-

ance with paragraph (4) of Art. 19.

(4) Details shall be specified by a regulation of the Federal Government requiring the consent of the Bundesrat.

Art. 133
(Bizonal Economic Administration, succession to rights)

The Federation shall succeed to the rights and obligations of the Bizonal Economic Administration.

Art. 134
(Reich property to become federal property)

(1) Reich property shall on principle become federal property.

(2) In so far as such property was originally intended to be used predominantly for administrative tasks which, under this Basic Law, are not administrative tasks of the Federation, it shall be transferred without compensation to the agencies now charged with such tasks, and to the Länder in so far as it is being used at present, and not merely temporarily, for administrative tasks which under this Basic Law are now within the administrative competence of the Länder. The Federation may also transfer other property to the Länder.

(3) Property which was placed at the disposal of the Reich by Länder or communes or associations of communes without compensation, shall again become the property of such Länder or communes or associations of communes, in so far as it is not required by the Federation for its own administrative tasks.

(4) Details shall be regulated by a federal law requiring the consent of the Bundesrat.

Art. 135
(Property in the event of territorial changes)

(1) If after 8 May 1945 and before the coming into force of this Basic Law an area has passed from one Land to another, the Land to which the area now belongs shall be entitled to the property located therein of the Land to which it belonged.

(2) Property of Länder or corporate bodies or institutions under public law which no longer exist shall pass, in so far as it was originally intended to be used predominantly for administrative tasks or is being used at present, and not merely temporarily, predominantly for administrative tasks, to the Land or the corporate body or institution under public law which now discharges these tasks.

(3) Real estate of Länder which no longer exist, including appurtenances, shall pass to the Land within which it is located, in so far as it is not included among property within the meaning of paragraph (1) of this Article.

(4) If an overriding interest of the Federation or the particular interest of an area so requires, a settlement in divergence from paragraphs (1) to (3) of this Article may be effected by federal legislation.

(5) In all other respects, the succession in title and the settlement of the property, in so far as it has not been effected before 1 January 1952 by agreement between the Länder or corporate bodies or institutions under public law concerned, shall be regulated by federal legislation requiring the consent of the Bundesrat.

(6) Interests of the former Land of Prussia in enterprises under private law shall pass to the Federation. A federal law, which may also be in divergence from this provision, shall regulate details.

(7) In so far as property which on the coming into force of this Basic Law would devolve upon a Land or a corporate body or institution under public law pursuant to paragraphs (1) to (3) of this Article, has been disposed of through or by virtue of a Land law or in any other manner by the party thus entitled, the transfer of the property shall be deemed to have taken place before such disposition.

Art. 135a[101]
(Discharging, wholly or partially, of certain liabilities of, inter alia, the Reich and the former Land of Prussia)

The legislation reserved to the Federation in paragraph (4) of Article 134 and in paragraph (5) of Article 135 may also stipulate that the following liabilities shall not be discharged, or not to their full extent:

1. liabilities of the Reich or liabilities of the former Land of Prussia or liabilities of such corporate bodies and institutions under public law as no longer exist;
2. such liabilities of the Federation or corporate bodies and institutions under public law as are connected with the transfer of properties pursuant to Arts. 89, 90, 134 or 135, and such liabilities of these entities as arise from measures taken by the entities mentioned under item 1;
3. such liabilities of Länder or communes or associations of

101. Inserted by federal law of 22 October 1957 (*FLG*, I, p. 1745).

communes as have arisen from measures taken by these entities before 1 August 1945 within the framework of administrative functions incumbent upon, or delegated by, the Reich to comply with regulations of occupying Powers or to remove a state of emergency due to the war.

Art. 136
(First assembly of the Bundesrat)

(1) The Bundesrat shall assemble for the first time on the day of the first meeting of the Bundestag.

(2) Until the election of the first Federal President his powers shall be exercised by the President of the Bundesrat. He shall not have the right to dissolve the Bundestag.

Art. 137
(Right of civil servants to stand for election)

(1)[102] The right of civil servants, of other salaried public employees, of professional soldiers, of temporary volunteer soldiers, or of judges, to stand for election in the Federation, in the Länder, or in the communes, may be restricted by legislation.

(2) The electoral law to be adopted by the Parliamentary Council shall apply to the election of the/first Bundestag, of the first Federal Convention, and of the first Federal President of the Federal Republic.

(3) The function of the Federal Constitutional Court pursuant to paragraph (2) of Art. 41 shall, pending its establishment, be exercised by the German High Court for the Combined Economic Area, which shall decide in accordance with its rules of procedure.

Art. 138
(Notaries)

Changes in the rules relating to notaries as they now exist in the Länder of Baden, Bavaria, Württemberg-Baden, and Württemberg-Hohenzollern[103] shall require the consent of the governments of these Länder.

---

102. As amended by federal law of 19 March 1956 (*FLG*, I, p. 111).
103. See footnote 13 to Article 23.

Art. 139
(Liberation Law)

The legislation enacted for the Liberation of the German People from National Socialism and Militarism shall not be affected by the provisions of this Basic Law.

Art. 140
(Validity of Articles of the Weimar Constitution)

The provisions of Arts. 136, 137, 138, 139, and 141 of the German Constitution of 11 August 1919 shall be an integral part of this Basic Law.[104]

Art. 141
('Bremen Clause')

The first sentence of paragraph (3) of Art. 7 shall not be applied in any Land in which different provisions of Land law were in force on 1 January 1949.

Art. 142
(Basic rights in Land constitutions)

Notwithstanding the provision of Art. 31, such provisions of Land constitutions shall also remain in force as guarantee basic rights in conformity with Arts. 1 to 18 of this Basic Law.

Art. 142a[105]
(Repealed)

Art. 143[106]
(Repealed)

Art. 144
(Ratification of the Basic Law: Berlin representatives in the Bundestag and Bundesrat)

(1) This Basic Law shall require ratification by the representative assemblies of two-thirds of the German Länder in which it is for the time being to apply.

---

104. Printed as an Appendix to the Basic Law. Here, see pp. 181–2 above.
105. Inserted by federal law of 26 March 1954 (*FLG*, I, p. 45) and repealed by federal law of 24 June 1968 (*FLG*, I, p. 714).
106. Amended by federal law of 19 March 1956 (*FLG*, I, p. 111) and repealed by federal law of 24 June 1968 (*FLG*, I, p. 714).

(2) In so far as the application of this Basic Law is subject to restrictions in any Land listed in Art. 23 or in any part thereof, such Land or part thereof shall have the right to send representatives to the Bundestag in accordance with Art. 38 and to the Bundesrat in accordance with Art. 50.

Art. 145
(Promulgation of the Basic Law)

(1) The Parliamentary Council shall confirm in public session, with the participation of the deputies of Greater Berlin, the fact of ratification of this Basic Law and shall sign and promulgate it.

(2) This Basic Law shall come into force at the end of the day of promulgation.

(3) It shall be published in the *Federal Law Gazette*.

Art. 146
(Duration of validity of the Basic Law)

This Basic Law shall cease to be in force on the day on which a constitution adopted by a free decision of the German people comes into force.